Milk Street is changing how we cook by searching
the world for bold, simple recipes. Adapted
and tested for home cooks everywhere, this is what
we call the *new* home cooking.

CHRISTOPHER KIMBALL'S

MILK STREET

CHRISTOPHER KIMBALL'S

MILK STREET

THE NEW HOME COOKING

with Matthew Card, J.M. Hirsch,
Michelle Locke and Jennifer Baldino Cox

LITTLE, BROWN AND COMPANY

NEW YORK BOSTON LONDON

Little, Brown and Company
Hachette Book Group
1290 Avenue of the Americas, New York, NY 10104
littlebrown.com

First Edition: September 2017

Little, Brown and Company is a division of Hachette Book Group, Inc. The Little, Brown name and logo are trademarks of Hachette Book Group, Inc.

The publisher is not responsible for websites (or their content) that are not owned by the publisher.

The Hachette Speakers Bureau provides a wide range of authors for speaking events. To find out more, go to hachettespeakersbureau.com or call (866) 376-6591.

Photography credits: Connie Miller of CB Creatives. Other photography by page: Channing Johnson, pages V, VI-VII, VIII; Shannon Frandsen, pages XIII, XIV, XVI-XVII, XXV; Sylvain Cherkaoui, pages XVIII-XIX; Noam Moskowitz, pages XX-XXI; Marco Simola, pages XXII-XXIII; Kristin Teig, pages 22, 24-25, 116, 145; Heidi Murphy of White Loft Studios, page 61; Michael Piazza, pages 44, 76, 147, 211, 230; Joyelle West, pages II, 85, 102-103, 141. Index photography: Channing Johnson and CB Creatives. Styling credits: Christine Tobin except as noted—Catrine Kelty, pages 22, 24-25, 26, 44, 52-53, 54-55, 61, 67, 71, 76, 79, 98, 107, 116, 145, 147, 148, 153, 166, 209, 211, 220-221, 223, 224, 227, 229, 230, 232, 234, 251, 253; Molly Shuster, pages 29, 64, 68, 111, 119, 124, 157, 241, 263; Catherine Smart, pages 95, 108, 112, 126, 158-159, 206; Monica Mariano, pages 62, 74-75, 164, 236; Sally Staub, page 202.

ISBN 978-0-316-43728-8

LCCN 2017937767

10 9 8 7 6 5 4 3 2 1

IM

Print book interior design by Gary Tooth / Empire Design Studio
Printed in China

This book is dedicated to the
notion that cooking is the universal language
of the human spirit.

Contents

THE NEW HOME COOKING

I recently dined at La Grenouille in New York—the last of the old-world French restaurants. It provided a timely reminder that classic American cooking is based largely on the cuisines of northern Europe. Traditional French cooking, in particular, is poorly suited to the home kitchen. It depends on a marriage of top-notch ingredients and advanced culinary technique to coax flavors, often slowly, into perfect harmony. Poached sea bass with a mélange of tiny vegetables surrounded by a delicate nage is a case in point. One false step and triumph turns into an overcooked disaster. After 40 years of cooking, I've learned to leave that approach to the professionals.

The rest of the world thinks differently about cooking. While so much of northern European cuisine relies on heat and time to build flavor—long simmers and roasts fueled by fire—elsewhere, flavors are built by layering bold, simple ingredients. The Ottoman Empire had access to 88 spices. Northern Europe was happy with salt, pepper and a bit of caraway kneaded into rye bread. Herbs are limited to a spare sprig or two. Yet from Lima to Sichuan, they are used by the handful, to say nothing of Middle Eastern tabbouleh, for which herbs are the main ingredient. Chilies, fermented sauces, flavored oils and condiments, ginger, turmeric, scallions and lemon grass. They abound.

And so the world offers us the opportunity to simplify and improve our cooking. Hot oil flash-cooks Chinese greens topped with ginger and scallions. Water instead of stock produces cleaner flavors. Fish sauce, soy sauce, miso, rice vinegar and other pantry staples give the home cook a head start toward culinary success. Instead of apple pie spice and a few dried herbs, what about za'atar, dukkah, ras el hanout, togarashi, garam masala and baharat? And when it comes to pepper, there are myriad choices, from aleppo and urfa to Sichuan peppercorns and the spicy white pepper popular in Asian cooking.

For the most part, the cooking itself is quicker or, at the very least, easier. A whole chicken is simmered effortlessly in water for the classic Chinese dish, white-cooked chicken. Thai fried rice takes just minutes, as does an herb and pistachio couscous or spicy red lentil soup. Start with the right ingredients and the cooking almost takes care of itself. The beauty of this approach is that you get both bolder and simpler food.

Milk Street offers the proposition that America, and the rest of the world, is experiencing a watershed moment. Like music and fashion, cooking is becoming a mashup of ingredients and techniques. It's an opportunity to learn, rather than appropriate. Ethnic cooking is dead. We are all simply making dinner. A couple in Mexico City doesn't cook "Mexican food." They cook. And they might well prepare a Ligurian pesto or a quick stir-fry instead of a mole negro from Oaxaca. Why should we aspire to authentically reproduce what is natural and necessary in another culture? Food is imbued with cultural intimacy, defined by the unique nature of local ingredients, and experienced by different societies in a thousand unique ways.

Attempting to reproduce that elsewhere ignores its import. Sharing a dish of thieboudienne (a rice and seafood platter) in Senegal is about being seated in a circle on a stone terrace, scooping portions with bare hands, and obeying rules of sharing food borne out of the overwhelming hospitality of the Senegalese. Make that recipe in an apartment on the Upper East Side of New York City and much is lost in translation. Yet, there are enduring kitchen values that travel easily from Saigon to Kiev to Jerusalem to Quito to London to New York.

We strive to learn, hoping to find bits and pieces of things we can bring home as the basis for a new repertoire. We might stick to the original, if it makes sense—a classic such as Chinese stir-fried eggs with tomatoes, for example—or we might borrow a flavor profile from Turkish cooking and marry it with a method from Morocco. A simple variation can be a quick pasta dish with Asian flavors—soy sauce, toasted sesame oil and scallions—instead of pesto. This approach has history on its side. In late 19th century Japan, American dishes were adapted to Japanese tastes in a style of cooking referred to as "yoshoku." The Japanese potato salad in this book is a good example. And don't forget that Spam, the ultimate American export, is a hugely popular ingredient in South Korea. Culinary mashup is nothing new.

If this is old news, what then does Milk Street have to offer? We put our culinary experience at your disposal—whether on location, where a practiced eye is necessary to spot the techniques and flavors that will travel best back to America, or here in our kitchen, where we apply years of hard-won recipe development experience to produce well-tested recipes. That process, from inspiration to reliable recipe, is arduous and filled with dead ends, but this is our vocation. It's what we love to do.

But reliability is insufficient. We travel for inspiration and understanding. In the suburbs of Tel Aviv, we line up at 7 a.m. with workers waiting for their breakfast—warm, whipped hummus—then eat with them, standing by the side of the road. In the townships of Cape Town, we not only taste peri peri chicken, we spend most of a Sunday waiting for a bucket of raw meat, delivering it to a cook who works 12 hours a day before wood-fired grills. Outside, you eat, standing, no utensils needed. It is a raucous celebration of cooked meat, singing and dancing, a form of culinary revival. These moments infuse our words and cooking.

Naomi Duguid, author of "The Taste of Persia," once said that it is time for the cooks of the world to sit at the same table. We share a common language and passion, not just for cooking, but for what it represents. Whether it is a perfectly sliced apple and a cup of tea in a modest home in Azerbaijan or a noisy celebration of grilled meat in Cape Town, it is no longer a world of our food and their food. Cooking and sharing food is central to the human condition. The fire. The pot. The knife. The table.

Welcome to Milk Street.

Christopher Kimball
Founder, Christopher Kimball's Milk Street

INTRODUCTION

Ten years ago, I was driving into Hanoi from the airport. We overtook a sea of motorbikes, some with crates of piglets on back, one with a middle-aged man balancing lumber on his shoulder, and more than one family of five perched on the long pillion facing every which way. It was a foreign shore.

Then I ate the food. Lemon grass with clams. Pho. A breakfast banh mi. Roadside stalls selling grilled foods—eggs in the shell and sweet potato. Mango and papaya. And the salads. Hot, sweet, salty and bitter. Broth and noodles. Coffee with condensed milk and raw egg.

The realization dawned. Slowly. There is no "ethnic" cooking. It's a myth. It's just dinner or lunch served somewhere else in the world.

A week later in Saigon, I was picked up outside our hotel on a motor-bike. Though I had driven a taxi in New York City, the 20-minute journey was heart-in-mouth. Intersections were vehicular Russian roulette. A game of chicken at every corner.

We made it to a ground floor apartment. I was introduced to a local cooking teacher who was patient. She taught me to make a variety of dumplings in a kitchen that was mostly table with no oven and two small propane burners. During the afternoon, a woman with a large wooden cart came through the alley, calling for odds bits and pieces—collecting junk for a living.

Slowly, I started to feel at home. The slicing, the shaping of the dumplings, the shared effort. I was the novice and a cook halfway around the world was the expert.

Many years later in Chiang Mai, the largest city in northern Thailand, I learned that it takes two hours to cook chicken feet and dried chicken blood is sold in bricks. Cold ash is poured over live coals to moderate the temperature when grilling chicken. Pork intestines are chopped and added to the minced pork dish "larb." And be sure to say "mai wan," or "not too sweet," when ordering a cocktail. Bartenders tend to overdo the sugar.

Chiang Mai is a city of over 1 million. They shop in large indoor markets such as Sanpakoy, love to have their wedding photos taken at the main gate to the city, Thapae. They enjoy variations in texture, including gnarly bits of chicken. They sell eggs in bright colors, including pink. And, if you do something fast and sneaky, one says that you are "stealing the chicken."

Everything has variations. There are three types of soy sauce—white, black and sweet. There are over a dozen types of durian, some of them delicacies, though I still think it tastes the way a septic tank smells. Thais greet each other with hands in prayer formation (the "wai"), chin held high, with a gentle nod of the head. Minor variations telegraph a range of sentiments. Higher hands and deeper bows confer more respect. Tourists are told not to initiate the "wai," but it is an insult not to return it.

Even a short trip to Thailand offers a suggestion of another world beneath the surface. The frenetic undercurrent of modern life, even in the noise and traffic of a big city, seems just a step away from a quiet temple or a seat at Jok Sompet, where one enjoys a bowl of rice porridge with pork balls, fried garlic, cilantro and white pepper. Or from a flash-steamed mess of greens at The Hot Basil Restaurant for People Who Like Spicy Food served with

garlic and red chilies with soy, fish and oyster sauces to finish. Restaurants have their own structure, their own ecosphere, from the silent empress dowager who sits behind the cash register at "Hot Basil" to Mame Tu at Jok Sompet, the reigning doyenne of porridge. Charming, energetic and joyfully in charge.

I left Thailand with soft, enduring memories. Twilight over rice fields. The scent of lemon grass. The deep shade of tamarind trees. The taste of red chilies, cilantro roots and fresh turmeric. A house cat sitting on a roof, alert for an offering of food. Slices of speckled dragon fruit and oblong tubes of papaya at breakfast.

When I arrived at Chiang Mai airport I was met by Nok, the charming, soft-spoken local fixer who greeted me in the wai fashion. I didn't know how to return the gesture. Three days later, as we were

saying our goodbyes, I bowed and prayed to Nam Tan (a nickname for "sugar"), one of the local crew, in my best imitation of wai. I had learned something, just a gesture, but enough to remind me that I was bringing back something precious from Thailand, something old and something new.

And so one asks, "What's a recipe?" We can start by saying what it is not. It's not just what's on the plate. It starts in collective memory. It has roots. And it's not an exercise in food science or a laboratory formula. Scientists may discover the secret to life, but even if it turns out to be nothing more than ones and zeros—and evolving digital movie if you will—it will also have to be about consciousness, sentient beings who put a name to it. And it's a lot more than simply turning raw ingredients into more efficient providers of nutrients.

And now we can say what recipe is. Like music, great recipes speak to the soul, not just the palate. They are reductionist; without trimmings. And they are alive; the ingredients going into the pot are a far cry from what comes out. There is some measure of alchemy in good cooking; life starts without expectations. And recipes like company—great food is only great when shared.

As a friend of mine once said, "I love to cook because every time I step into the kitchen I am a beginner." Exactly right. If you teach long enough, you eventually realize that you were the student all along. And that, perhaps, is the definition of a recipe. It is moment of learning. As the ingredients are being brought to life in the pot, we arise as well. Something stirs our soul. We cook with our hearts. Food, much like science, also stirs the soul.

Pantry

1

PANTRY

The Milk Street pantry focuses on easy ways to add lots of flavor and draws on a broad mix of bold ingredients from around the world. Many will be familiar. Most can be found in the international aisle of larger grocers, but all are available online.

FATS

Butter

Breaking with convention, we use salted butter for everything. Our motivation? It simply tastes better. Not to mention it's simpler to keep just one variety of butter on hand for all uses, whether for toast or cooking. Our recipes are written with the extra salt of salted butter in mind (roughly ¼ teaspoon per 4-ounce stick). To use salted butter in recipes that assume unsalted, scale back slightly on other salt added during cooking. If using unsalted butter in Milk Street recipes, add a pinch more salt than specified. Butter readily absorbs surrounding flavors, so store it tightly wrapped in the refrigerator. For longer storage, it also can be frozen.

Coconut Oil

Coconut oil is a fat we use sparingly, generally when cooking with other coconut ingredients. Its flavor is particularly good in Indian and Southeast Asian dishes, but be mindful of its low smoke point; it's inappropriate for anything beyond a light saute. It also is excellent on popcorn.

Cooking Spray

We use nonstick cooking spray judiciously. It's undeniably convenient and works well (the lecithin in the spray ensures even the stickiest foods release). Baking spray, which contains flour, is ideal for coating baking pans, especially the deep grooves of Bundt pans.

Grapeseed Oil

We like the neutral flavor, light mouthfeel and high smoke point of grapeseed oil. It's our go-to choice for a neutral cooking oil.

Lard

Though it's a four-letter word for many, we think lard has a place in modern cooking. It tastes awfully good stirred into a pot of beans or used to add flakiness to savory baked goods, such as our piadine (p. 191). Most stores sell Armour brand lard, which is hydrogenated (in some markets, it will be easier to find Armour labeled in Spanish as "manteca"). Lately, it has become easier to find high-quality lard; look for it in jars. If you can find it, "leaf" lard has the lightest flavor. Lard stores indefinitely in the refrigerator or freezer, but will absorb other flavors; wrap it well.

Olive Oil

Arguably, we use olive oil more than any other oil. In most cases, we favor full-flavored extra-virgin olive oil. Buying extra-virgin olive oil is a gamble; expense doesn't always guarantee quality and there are few safeguards against adulterated oils. While there are, in fact, wonderful imported oils, we think California oils are generally fresher and a better bet. California Olive Ranch extra-virgin olive oil, for example, is a terrific product that can be found in most any supermarket. Regular olive oil—not extra-virgin—is made from subsequent pressings and thus lacks the more robust flavor of extra-virgin. Its mild flavor and higher smoke point make it better for sauteing and in baked goods.

Peanut Oil

The light, nutty flavor and high smoke point of peanut oil make it particularly good for deep-frying, as with our Japanese fried chicken (p. 150). Toasted peanut oil has a more pronounced nutty flavor.

Sesame Oil

Sesame oil is pressed from either raw or toasted seeds; we prefer the richer flavor of the latter, which we drizzle over many Asian dishes. As with most seed and nut oils, sesame oil is volatile and can go rancid. We recommend buying small bottles that can be used within a couple months. Sesame oil has a low smoke point and is not suitable for sauteing.

Tahini

Tahini is a paste made from ground sesame seeds. Good tahini is pleasantly bitter. As with sesame oil, it can be made from raw or toasted sesame seeds. We often prefer the stronger flavor of the latter and, when possible, stone-ground varieties (the label should indicate). Tahini is fine for a month or less at room temperature, though we recommend refrigeration beyond that to maintain freshness. From hummus (p. 140) and roasted cauliflower (p. 280) to tahini-swirl brownies (p. 207), we use tahini liberally. Also try stirring it into your morning yogurt with a little jam, smearing it on toast with honey or drizzling over roasted chicken or vegetables.

ACIDS

Cider Vinegar

The mildly acidic, lightly fruity flavor of cider vinegar is neutral enough to work in numerous dishes, making it a vinegar we turn to often. Flavor varies by brand; we prefer the mild, balanced flavor of Bragg Organic Raw Unfiltered Apple Cider Vinegar.

Citrus

The zest and juice of lemons, limes and oranges show up repeatedly in our cooking. They are excellent for balancing the flavors of other ingredients, especially anything heavy or fatty. A spritz of lemon or lime juice before serving also can brighten most any finished dish. When shopping for lemons and limes, look for round, plump fruit that feel heavy for their size. They also should give when squeezed; hard fruit won't produce much juice. Citrus should be stored in the crisper drawer of your refrigerator to maintain freshness. Use a wand-style grater for zesting citrus. It produces a light, feathery zest that blends easily into dishes. Make sure to avoid the white pith beneath the zest, which can be bitter. If you need the zest, but not the juice of citrus, be sure to wrap the fruit in plastic or a bag, otherwise it will dry out quickly. There are countless ways to juice citrus fruits (juicer, reamer, fork, tong tips), though we do recommend squeezing it over a small mesh strainer to catch seeds. For recipes calling for both zest and juice, be sure to zest before juicing.

Pomegranate Molasses

Intensely sweet and sour, pomegranate molasses is used throughout the Middle East in sweet and savory dishes. It's essentially boiled-down pomegranate juice that is rounded out with a bit of sugar and acid. We like it drizzled over grilled or roasted meats or vegetables just before serving, mixed with Greek-style yogurt for a simple dip, or added to vinaigrettes. It pairs particularly well with Aleppo pepper. Refrigerated, an open bottle will last indefinitely, though it may need to be warmed in hot water or the microwave before it will flow freely.

Sherry Vinegar

Used liberally in Spanish and French cooking, sherry vinegar has a complex, slightly spicy flavor. The best sherry vinegars have a little age on them, which softens the harsh edges. Look for labels indicating the vinegar is at least 3 years old. It will cost a little more than unaged vinegar, but the difference in flavor is worth it.

White Balsamic Vinegar

Admittedly, white balsamic is something of an ersatz ingredient having little to do with the dark, sweet, long-aged stuff most people are familiar with. But its light, neutral flavor and mild sweetness make it an ideal acid we use often. White balsamic is perfect for when we want a clean flavor that highlights, but doesn't compete with, other flavors.

Unseasoned Rice Vinegar

Rice vinegar is a staple of Japanese cooking and packs a mild, neutral acidity well suited to vegetables, seafood and poultry. It can also add kick to citrus juice. Be sure to purchase unseasoned rice vinegar; seasoned rice vinegar is used for making sushi rice and already contains salt and sugar, which can make it difficult to balance in dressings.

Verjus

Verjus is the cooking wine substitute you've been searching for. While fruit juices or vinegar can work, verjus—made from the juice of unripe wine grapes—adds a gentle mineral tang and a wine-like body. Verjus can be hard to find and may require looking online. Refrigerate after opening to prevent spoilage. It will last two to three months.

FRESH HERBS

We use fresh herbs with reckless abandon to add bold, bright flavor to many of our recipes. Instead of scant tablespoons, think in terms of handfuls.

It's important to wash and dry herbs well. Any moisture clinging to them can turn them mushy during chopping and dilute the flavors of the dish to which they are added. Salad spinners work best. Herbs also can be dried by rolling them in a towel and gently squeezing.

With a little care, most fresh herbs can be refrigerated in the crisper drawer for a week or more. Wrap loosely in paper towels, then place in a plastic bag.

Some fresh herbs, such as cilantro, have edible stems. We like to use them to flavor stocks, soups and stews.

As for dried herbs, we rarely use them. They lack much of the nuance of fresh and generally require long, steady cooking to coax out their flavors. Exceptions to that rule include oregano, both Mexican and Turkish varieties (which offer different flavors), and mint, which packs a deeper, earthier flavor than fresh.

SPICES

Despite their seeming durability, dried spices are volatile and perishable. For best flavor, we recommend buying whole spices in small volumes. It's quick work to grind them as needed in a spice mill (a cheap blade-style coffee grinder works well) or a mortar and pestle. If purchasing ground spices, choose amounts you can consume within six months. Older, flat-tasting spices can be perked up with a quick toast in a hot skillet.

Aleppo Pepper

Fruity and only moderately spicy, coarsely ground Aleppo pepper is used throughout Middle Eastern cooking. We use it frequently and consider it a valuable flavoring for all manner of dishes that benefit from a little spark of heat. Its closest substitute is dried ancho chili. Aleppo pepper can be found at most Middle Eastern shops and spice dealers.

It's typically processed with a little salt and safflower oil. Turkish Maras (or Marash) chili is another substitute, but packs a bit more heat.

Allspice

With a flavor tasting subtly of clove, cinnamon, nutmeg and black pepper, allspice works in both sweet and savory dishes. Its contribution is crucial to our rye-on-rye sticky toffee pudding (p. 237) and rounds out our Lebanese tabbouleh (p. 57). We typically buy whole allspice berries and grind it fresh for the best flavor. We also use whole allspice berries when pickling, though the berries should be removed before serving.

Bay Leaves

We think of bay leaves as we do of vanilla—it's a flavor noticed mostly by omission. Bay leaves lend a certain aroma and savory note to soups, stews and pickles. They're also great tossed with roasted vegetables. We even use them in sweet dishes, such as the syrup for our tangerine-almond cake (p. 242). Turkish bay leaves have the best flavor (California bay leaves actually are a variety of laurel and don't taste the same). Buy in bulk for economy's sake and store in the freezer to maintain flavor and aroma.

Black Pepper

Black pepper adds depth and a nominal amount of spice to dishes. We use it to give a mild kick and not always hand-in-hand with salt. For best flavor, buy whole peppercorns and grind as needed (find a good-quality, adjustable pepper mill). Preground pepper lacks the aroma and much of the flavor of freshly ground. Consider tasting different varieties of black pepper to see which you prefer, as some are more aggressive than others.

Cardamom (whole and ground)

Cardamom might be Milk Street's favorite spice. We use it widely in both sweet and savory recipes. It is sold whole in pods (white, black and green—each with a slightly different flavor), corticated (removed from the papery husk), and ground. More often than not, we use ground, as it can be difficult to grind finely. We also like to make Arabic coffee by grinding the whole pods into our coffee

beans, then brewing as normal. Use 1 tablespoon of cardamom pods per 1 cup of whole coffee beans.

Coriander

Coriander is the seed of the cilantro plant. It has a bright, citrusy flavor with a hint of mint. The seeds are tender enough to use whole—as we do in our cracked potatoes (p. 77), though it typically is used ground. We prefer to buy it whole and grind as needed.

Cumin

One of our more liberally used spices, cumin packs an earthy flavor and pungency that lends backbone to all manner of Latin, Middle Eastern and even Chinese dishes. Buy whole and grind fresh, if possible.

Dried Chilies

Dried chilies are used in many cuisines to add complexity and heat. Latin varieties tend to be the easiest to find. New Mexico chilies are perhaps the most common and very neutral tasting; we use them in our harissa (p. 250). Ancho chilies, which have a deep, almost prune-like flavor and mild spiciness, are virtually interchangeable with pasilla. Tangy, very fruity guajillo chilies are hot and bright tasting; they pair well with tomatoes and can be substituted for New Mexico chilies. Morita chilies are smoked jalapeno peppers, otherwise known as chipotle chilies They also have better flavor than canned chipotles in adobo sauce, especially if you prepare them as chipotles in adobo (p. 261). Pointy little árbol chilies can be quite hot and are great to simmer whole in a dish and pull out, as we recommend in our spicy stir-fried cumin beef (p. 128). Look for glossy, pliant-looking chilies in the Latin section of the grocer. We recommend pulling the stem off and shaking them out before using; the seeds can be bitter and overly spicy. Depending on the recipe, the chilies should be toasted or fried to deepen the flavor.

Fennel Seeds

We use both whole and ground fennel seed to add a licorice-like flavor to vegetables, meats and sauces. It pairs well with coriander and chili flakes.

Mustard Seeds

We pickle them or stir them into curries and the occasional bean dish for a pop of flavor. We prefer brown, though yellow mustard seeds are fine, too. Mustard seeds can be found in the spice section of most markets, either packaged or in bulk bins.

Nutmeg

The warm, sharp and defining flavor of ground nutmeg is used in sweet and savory dishes, both on its own and blended with other warm spices. It's especially important in cream sauces and often paired with lemon. The flavor is particularly volatile, so it is best to buy whole nutmeg and grind fresh as needed. A wand-style grater works well for this.

Paprika

Paprika adds deep, sweet and smoky flavor to countless dishes. It also has a bit of a thickening property when used in soups, stews and sauces. Paprika comes in two styles: plain and smoked. Plain paprika is produced in Hungary and Spain and is a vibrant red. Smoked paprika, also known as pimentón de La Vera, is produced only in the La Vera region of Spain, where the peppers are smoked before being ground. Both varieties are available in sweet and hot versions. We typically use the former, choosing to add a few red pepper flakes or cayenne to ratchet up the heat if the dish needs it.

Red Pepper Flakes

We use the sharp chili bite of red pepper flakes to punctuate many dishes. We don't aim for spicy food per se, just balanced dishes with a compelling range of flavors to keep things interesting start to finish. Red pepper flakes are produced from various dried peppers and intensity can vary from brand to brand. Age affects heat level as well; the older the flakes, the less intense they will be.

Salt

We use kosher salt exclusively in our cooking and baking because its larger grain makes it easier to measure and season with. The two most common brands are Diamond Crystal Kosher Salt and Morton Coarse Kosher Salt. The size of their grains varies slightly and they aren't equally saline by volume. Diamond Crystal has a slightly larger grain size than Morton, so the same amount of Diamond will taste less salty than Morton. Keep that in mind if you switch back and forth. Flaky finishing salts, such as Maldon Sea Salt Flakes, add a delicious crunch and salty pop, but should be used only at the table, not during cooking.

Shichimi Togarashi

Japanese cooks rely on a variety of seasoning blends to add fast, easy flavor to noodles and rice. One of our favorites is shichimi togarashi, a blend of sesame seeds, crushed chili pepper, citrus peel and sometimes black peppercorns, poppy seeds and hemp seeds. We use the mix to enliven Japanese rice and noodle dishes, like our soba noodles with miso butter and asparagus (p. 120) and our Japanese fried chicken (p. 150). It's also great as a seasoning for scrambled or fried eggs, broiled fish or chicken, or even roasted vegetables. Furikake is a coarse, sweeter version that includes bonito flakes and a higher ratio of seaweed. Look for them in the international foods section of your grocer or an Asian specialty market.

Sumac

Deep red and bursting with tangy zest, sumac has been an essential flavoring of Middle Eastern cooking—and closer to home, Native American cooking—for centuries. It's made from the berries of the sumac bush and usually is sold ground. You can find it online, at Middle Eastern markets and at some larger grocers. (Though they're related, this is not the poison sumac you've been warned to stay away from in the wild.) Sumac has a sour, lemony flavor and is a good way to add a tart note of citrus, without the liquid of lemon juice, as well as a bright pop of color. It works well as a condiment and can be dusted over just about anything—hummus and baba ghanoush are traditional, but it also makes a good popcorn topper. In cooking, it works well in dry rubs for chicken and fish.

Sichuan Peppercorns

Not technically pepper, Sichuan peppercorns have a high, sharp flavor and unique ability to "numb" the mouth. They are used broadly in Sichuan cooking in tandem with whole chilies in a combination known as "ma la". We use them sparingly, though do consider the flavor essential in dishes like our Sichuan chicken salad (p. 134). Make sure to sort well and remove the black seeds, which can contribute a gritty texture.

White Pepper

While we use white pepper less than black, its unique flavor and pungent aroma make it an important pantry staple for some Asian and Scandinavian dishes. It comes from the same berry (pepper nigrum) as black, but is processed differently. Like black pepper, white is best when freshly ground. For a complex flavor, consider using a blend of black and white peppercorns in your pepper mill. While you're at it, you can go old-school French and add a few allspice berries for an even more complex flavor.

WINE AND SPIRITS

The basic rule for selecting a cooking wine—don't spend a fortune, but do make sure it's drinkable. When choosing red and white wines to cook with, look for neutral, dry varietals and blends. For whites—sauvignon blanc, pinot gris, Côtes du Rhône and Spanish Rueda wines. Avoid anything oaky, such as chardonnay, or overly aromatic, like riesling and gewürztraminer. For reds, we like Côtes du Rhônes again and southern French blends, like grenache and syrah. If you have leftover drinking wine that won't be consumed within a few days, consider simmering it down to reduce by half, then freeze as ice cubes. It's a quick way to add big flavor to soups, stews, stocks and pan sauces.

Dry Sherry

Dry sherry is frequently used in Chinese cooking as a good substitute for hard-to-find Shaoxing cooking wine. We use it to flavor a poaching liquid for our white-cooked chicken (p. 144). It adds a sweet-sharp flavor that rounds out the herbs and ginger in the broth and works wonders on the flavor of the chicken. It's not necessary to spend much on a bottle. Palo cortado is a good varietal (a good bit cheaper than manzanilla or fino) and the Lustau brand is a reliable choice.

Mirin

Mirin is Japanese sweet rice wine. Aji-mirin varieties are sweetened with added sugar and sometimes seasoned with salt; hon-mirin varieties have no added sugar (and are more expensive). As with many things, the more you spend, the better the quality. Lower quality varieties are made largely from corn syrup and flavorings. We prefer the hon-mirin when available.

Rye Whiskey

The spicy flavors of rye are particularly well suited to flavoring spiced baked goods, such as our rye-on-rye sticky toffee pudding (p. 237). Among good brands for cooking, Rittenhouse Rye packs a lot of spice and doesn't cost a fortune (and it makes a great Manhattan).

Rum

We use the spicy, earthy flavor of dark rum in some baking because it does a terrific job of accenting spices, vanilla and brown sugar. Myers's Rum Original Dark and Gosling's Black Seal Bermuda Black Rum are excellent choices for cooking.

Vermouth

Vermouth is wine fortified with additional alcohol and flavored with a variety of botanicals. The herbal notes of vermouth make it particularly well suited for pairing with vegetables, poultry and seafood. An opened bottle of vermouth stores well for up to a month in the refrigerator. For cooking, be sure to use dry vermouth; sweet vermouth is best in a Manhattan or negroni.

SEASONINGS

Anchovies

Few ingredients are as polarizing as anchovies. We love them and use them often. The best come jarred, though canned will suffice. Skip those rolled around a caper. And forget about anchovy paste—it may be convenient, but the poor, salty flavor isn't worth it. Buy a jar of anchovies and keep it in the back of the refrigerator to add to sauces, soups and vegetables. Once heated and dissolved into a dish, you'll never notice them, but they will add tremendous savory flavor.

Chili Sauces

We use a variety of hot sauces in our cooking; you should taste different varieties and figure out which suits your heat threshold. We like Dynasty Thai Chili Garlic Paste. For a general Southeast Asian-style sauce, there are a variety of Sriracha sauces ranging in potency; Shark brand Thai Sriracha Chili Sauce is milder, sweeter and sharper than most.

Dried Mushrooms

Umami-rich dried mushrooms pack a flavor punch well above their weight. For the most part, we use dried shiitake mushrooms, which add deep savory flavor. To use them, dust them off, then soak them in water to soften before slicing. In some cases, we add them whole to stocks and soups. They also can be processed to a powder in a spice grinder, then added to soups, stews and sautes to give you umami flavor without the mushroom texture.

Fish Sauce

Fish sauce is just that: the fermented broth of salted-and-aged fish. The heady, amber-colored liquid is used throughout Southeast Asia as a seasoning, as well as for the base of countless sauces. We use it beyond Asian cuisines to add deep flavor to sauces and, in one instance, to baste a turkey. Brands vary widely in flavor. After tasting our way through a host of options, we found Red Boat Fish Sauce is the best. It costs more than other brands, but the clean, rich flavor makes it well worth it. And a little goes a long way.

Kimchi

Kimchi—a spicy, garlicky mix of fermented cabbage and other vegetables—has been an essential part of Korean cooking for more than 2,000 years. It began as a way to preserve food without refrigeration. The red and relatively fiery version has become more common in the U.S. as interest in Korean food has risen. You'll often find jars of it in the refrigerated section. But kimchi also can be quite mild and even white; there are more than 100 varieties. Almost all start with napa cabbage and generally include garlic, scallions, ginger, radish, cucumber and chili peppers. There's often a seafood element, such as fish sauce for flavoring. Served on the side with just about every Korean meal, kimchi can be a stand-alone snack or an easy complement to leftover rice (the combination produces a fantastic fried rice). It also serves as the basis for the classic Korean dish of kimchi-jjigae (p. 40), a stew that gets quick but deep flavor from the fermented vegetables. Brands of kimchi tend to be regional. It stores well in the refrigerator.

Miso

Miso is fermented soybean paste, and there are many varieties, from white and smooth to dark and chunky. Two versions commonly found in the U.S. are shiro (white), which has a mild, sweet-and-salty flavor, and shinshu (yellow), which is fermented a little longer than shiro but still has a delicate flavor and light golden color. The classic use of miso is in soup, though it can add a shot of umami to many dishes. Try white or yellow miso in sauces and dressings. One of our favorite ways to use miso is blended with an equal amount of softened butter and, if you like, grated fresh ginger. This mixture is terrific over pasta for a carbonara-like dish (see soba noodles with miso butter and asparagus, p. 120), or used to dress roasted or grilled vegetables. Red miso, fermented longer than shiro or shinshu, is saltier and works best where a heartier flavor is desired.

Peppadew Peppers

A little sweet, a little tart, a little spicy, Peppadews are bright red, pleasantly spicy peppers that are about the size of a cherry tomato. They are a trademarked brand that originated in South Africa. The peppers now are widely available at grocers, usually jarred, but sometimes sold loose at the olive bar. Use the peppers to add mild piquancy to a salad, as we do in our skirt steak salad (p. 110), as part of an antipasto spread, as a pizza topping or as a companion to cheese. Peppadews are sold in mild, hot and golden varieties; we most often use mild.

Soy Sauce and Shoyu

Called soy sauce in China and shoyu in Japan, the inky dark sauce is made from fermented, salted soybeans and typically some portion of wheat. It has a deep, umami-rich flavor; we use it frequently in both Asian and Western cooking. Both soy sauce and shoyu come in a variety of styles. For the most part, we use regular soy sauce. "Light" soy sauce is a lighter color from the first pressing. It's light only in color; the flavor is salty and strong. Tamari is a thick Japanese variety that is often wheat free (check the label). If sodium is an issue, choose a reduced-sodium version. "White" soy sauce or shoyu is a high-end variety that should be used only as a dipping sauce. Sweet soy sauce, otherwise known as kecap manis, is soy sauce sweetened with molasses or palm sugar. It's not an appropriate substitute.

Tamarind

Tamarind is an intensely tart fruit used to add sour flavors in the cooking of Latin America, the Indian subcontinent and Southeast Asia. While some supermarkets sell fresh tamarind pods—which look like long brown, leathery seedpods—it's most often found as a jarred concentrate or a semi-dried block of pulp. We prefer the latter for its clearer, stronger flavor. To use, cut off a chunk of the sticky dark pulp and soak in hot water to soften, about 10 minutes. Use your fingers to loosen and discard the large seeds, then force the pulp through a fine mesh strainer. We use the tangy, earthy-tasting juice in a dipping sauce for our Chaing Mai chicken (p. 180), but it also is great for adding a pleasant tartness to a variety of sauces, dressings, even cocktails. Try adding a splash to a gin and tonic, or do as Portland, Oregon's Pok Pok restaurant does and use in a whiskey sour.

Za'atar

Za'atar can refer to two things—a dried herb and an herb blend that contains it. Both are used widely in Middle Eastern cooking. The plant is reminiscent of wild thyme and oregano. The herb blend comes in many varieties, differing by region and cook. Most contain the za'atar herb, as well as sesame seeds and other spices, such as sumac. The blend often is used as a substitute for lemon or vinegar in dishes where a liquid won't work. Za'atar can be found in Middle Eastern markets, better-stocked grocers or online. It can be mixed into olive oil and spread onto flatbread as one would butter, or swirled into labneh (yogurt cheese) with vinegar and oil. It also can be baked into bread, sprinkled on salads, pizza or hummus, or rubbed into meat and vegetables.

SWEETENERS

When possible, we try to use sweeteners that contribute flavor beyond sweetness.

Agave

A honey-like syrup made from several varieties of the agave plant, agave has a clean, simple flavor and blends easily into other liquids, making it ideal for vinaigrettes and sauces. It can be purchased in a variety of grades, from light to dark. The lighter varieties are a good substitute for simple syrup in cocktails.

Brown Sugar

We like brown sugar because it adds earthy, caramel flavors that contribute so much more than basic sweetness. It may look like "raw" sugar, but it is really just white sugar blended with molasses. Light brown sugar has less molasses; dark brown has more (and consequently is more acidic).

Honey

We use honey in both sweet and savory dishes. In addition to its flavor, we also like its hygroscopic properties, meaning it holds on to moisture. This helps keep baked goods tender and prevents our charred Brussels sprouts (p. 70) from drying out. As a rule, we favor mild-flavored honeys, such as clover, which combine well with other flavors. Honey with assertive flavors can compete with the other ingredients in a recipe.

Palm Sugar

Produced from the sap of coconut palm trees, palm sugar has a creamy mouthfeel and earthy taste slightly reminiscent of maple sugar. It's used as a sweetener throughout Asia and is easily found at Asian markets. Light brown sugar is a good substitute.

STARCHES

All-Purpose Flour

We prefer unbleached flour with a lower protein level to ensure tender cookies and crisp pie dough. Brands we like include Gold Medal, Bob's Red Mill and King Arthur.

Bread Flour

High-protein flour is the best choice for chewy flatbreads and moist loaves and boules. Don't substitute it for all-purpose, as your pancakes will be chewy and your cookies tough.

Graham Flour

Graham flour is coarse-ground whole-wheat flour. We like using it in cookies and breads because it can contribute a strong, wheaty flavor without the gumminess of finer whole-wheat flour. Look for it wherever Bob's Red Mill products are sold or in bulk bins at a co-op. It is perishable and should be stored in the refrigerator or freezer. To intensify the flavor of graham flour, it can be toasted in a dry skillet until it darkens.

Potato Starch

Potato starch is essential for the crisp texture of our Korean pancakes (p. 35) and worth keeping around to use as a dusting for a variety of fried foods, such as chicken and fish. Look for potato starch under the Bob's Red Mill label or at Asian markets. Note: potato flour is different and can't be substituted.

Rye Flour

Rye flour packs a slightly spicy, earthy flavor that we use to add complexity and a pleasant bitterness to baked goods, such as our rye-on-rye sticky toffee pudding (p. 237) and rye chocolate chip cookies (p. 218). Beyond our recipes, try substituting it for a small amount of the all-purpose flour in pizza dough and pancakes for more complex flavor (no more than a 20 percent swap; otherwise the texture will be affected). Rye flour is more perishable than wheat flour and should be stored in the refrigerator or freezer.

Semolina Flour

Semolina is a protein-rich, coarse flour produced from hard durum wheat. It's most commonly used to make dried pasta, though it also is used in Italy and the Middle East (along with farina, its soft-wheat cousin and the grain behind Cream of Wheat) for cookies and sweets where a bit of texture is desired.

GRAINS AND PASTAS

Asian Noodles

There are dozens of varieties of Asian noodles made from an array of starches. Most Asian wheat noodles are made from a lower-protein wheat than is used for Italian pasta, so they tend to be softer and chewier. In our experience, udon noodles are the most widely available of this style. If you can't find any Asian wheat noodles, substitute dried Italian linguine or fettuccine.

Bulgur

Chewy and firm with a nutty flavor, bulgur is an ancient ingredient that fits well with the modern appetite for whole grains. Though often confused with plain cracked wheat, which is uncooked, bulgur is a cooked and dried cracked wheat. It is made by boiling wheat berries, usually durum (a hard, protein-rich wheat), until they are about to crack open, then allowing them to dry. The outer bran layers are rubbed off and the grains are ground in grades ranging from fine to coarse. Preparation can be as simple as a cold soak (for fine) to a gentle simmer (for coarse). As with many grains, it can be toasted to intensify its flavor. Fine-grain bulgur is essential for our Lebanese tabbouleh (p. 57). If you can't find it, coarse bulgur can be ground in a spice grinder. Process in short pulses until fine, light and fluffy, 6 to 10 pulses.

Italian Pasta

We always keep on hand a package of long, thin noodles—such as spaghetti or linguine—to use with creamy or thin sauces, as well as a pack of short or round stocky noodles—such as penne, gemelli or orecchiette—for thicker sauces. Most of our pasta recipes are designed to use 12 ounces (3 ounces per serving—Italian style), 4 ounces less than the average box of pasta. Either cook the extra pasta and save for the next day (terrific fried crisp in olive oil and topped with grated Parmesan and a fried egg), or save the surplus for a future batch. We like using tongs for stirring pasta; it makes it easy to separate any pieces stuck together. We like to slightly undercook our pasta in the water, then finish it in the sauce; it allows the pasta to better absorb the other flavors.

Rice

For basic pilafs and day-to-day eating, we like long-grain white rice. For Southeast Asian dishes, perfumed long-grain jasmine rice is ideal (note that U.S.-grown jasmine lacks the aroma and flavor of Asian-grown rice). For Indian dishes, long, thin grains of basmati are best. Rice is easy to make (see p. 95 for our basic long-grain cooking method), though it does take a bit of time. For convenience, we often make a batch or two of rice ahead and freeze it in zip-close bags. It thaws in just minutes in the microwave.

Eggs

2

A SLICKER SCRAMBLE

We were won over the first time we tried cooking scrambled eggs in oil. They were almost instantly cooked in rolling, variegated waves and came out fresh and light, not greasy or heavy.

Why? Oil gets hotter faster than butter. That's because butter is 20 percent water and can exceed 212°F only once the water has evaporated. Further, the proteins in eggs are folded. Heat unfolds (denatures) them, creating a network that traps the steam given off as the eggs cook. Extra-virgin olive oil is unique among vegetable oils since it contains surfactants (surface-area agents) that make it easier for that network to form. All of that means you have oil getting hotter more quickly and making more steam faster along with a protein network that traps that steam better. Result: Quicker, bigger puffs and more impressive scrambled eggs.

Fluffy Olive Oil **Scrambled Eggs**

Start to finish: **10 minutes** / Servings: 4

We'd never questioned the French rule that butter is best for cooking eggs. But then we noticed that chefs at hotel breakfast stations use oil to make omelets in carbon-steel pans. Likewise, the Chinese cook their well-seasoned, well-browned omelets in oil, as do the Japanese. But scrambled eggs? As a test, we heated olive oil until just smoking and poured in whisked eggs. Whoosh! In a quick puff of steam, we had light, fluffy eggs. The oil needed a full 3 minutes at medium heat to get hot enough. Higher temperatures cooked the eggs too fast, toughening them. Two tablespoons of oil was enough to coat the bottom of the skillet and flavor the eggs without making them greasy. We like our scrambled eggs particularly wet and not entirely cooked through, which takes just 30 seconds. Leave them a little longer for drier eggs. Either way, take them off the heat before they are fully cooked and let them rest on a warm plate for 30 seconds. They finish cooking off the heat. Mixing the salt into the eggs before cooking was the best way to season them.

Don't warm your plates too much. It sounds minor, but hot plates will continue to cook the eggs, making them tough and dry. Cold plates will cool the eggs too fast. The plates should be warm to the touch, but not so hot that you can't comfortably hold them.

FLUFFY OLIVE OIL SCRAMBLED EGGS

2 tablespoons extra-virgin olive oil

8 large eggs

Kosher salt and ground black pepper

1. In a 12-inch nonstick or seasoned carbon-steel skillet over medium, heat the oil until just starting to smoke, about 3 minutes. While the oil heats, in a bowl, use a fork to whisk the eggs and ¾ teaspoon salt until blended and foamy. Pour the eggs into the center of the pan.

2. Using a rubber spatula, continuously stir the eggs, pushing them toward the middle as they set at the edges and folding the cooked egg over on itself. Cook until just set, 60 to 90 seconds. The curds should be shiny, wet and soft, but not translucent or runny. Immediately transfer to warmed plates. Season with salt and pepper.

SUNNY-SIDE UP FRIED EGGS

Start to finish: **8 minutes**
Makes 4 eggs

Hot oil gave us the best scrambled eggs, but fried eggs turned out to be a different game. Here, butter truly was better; oil produced tough, greasy fried eggs. Every stovetop has a different low setting, and skillets vary in thickness and heat conductivity. It may take a few attempts to determine the best timing for your equipment. For us, 3 minutes was perfect for completely set whites and thick but runny yolks. If you like very loose yolks, shave off a minute; for lightly browned whites and firm yolks, add a minute. To make 2 eggs, use an 8-inch skillet and 2 teaspoons of butter.

Don't break the yolks when cracking the eggs into the bowl. If you're not confident in your egg-cracking skills, break the eggs one at a time into a small bowl before combining them.

4 large eggs

1 tablespoon salted butter

Kosher salt and ground black pepper

1. Heat a 10-inch nonstick skillet over low for 3 minutes. Crack the eggs into a bowl. Add the butter to the hot pan and swirl until melted. When the butter stops foaming, slowly pour the eggs into the skillet. If necessary, gently nudge the yolks with a wooden spoon to space them evenly in the pan.

2. Working quickly, season the eggs with salt and pepper, then cover the skillet and cook until the whites are completely set and the yolks are bright yellow, about 3 minutes. Slide out of the pan and onto plates.

TOSS YOUR NONSTICK SKILLET

Chefs love carbon-steel pans, and for good reason. These pans are inexpensive, rugged, heat evenly and retain heat well. Best yet, they can develop a natural nonstick coating without the worrying chemicals of typical nonstick surfaces. Turns out, they're handy for home cooks, too.

First, you need to master the (simple) art of seasoning the pans, a process that coats them with oil and heats the oil to high temperatures. This causes the oil to polymerize, or form long chains of molecules that bond to the metal. That bonding means there are fewer iron molecules available to bond with the food. And no bonding means no sticking.

Most methods call for seasoning skillets just after buying them. We do this, but got even better results by adding a trick cooks at Chinese restaurants use to keep woks (often made of carbon steel) slick. Every time they cook, they ladle oil into the hot pan to coat it, then dump it out before adding fresh oil for cooking. This fills any divots in the coating caused by daily wear.

We didn't find huge differences in brands of carbon-steel pans. It was the seasoning that made the difference. Most 10-inch pans—a practical size for home cooking—can be purchased for less than $25.

INITIAL SEASONING: Scrub the pan with hot soapy water, then dry and set over medium heat. Use a paper towel held with tongs to spread 1 tablespoon vegetable oil evenly over the pan. Leave on the heat until it smokes, then hold it at that stage for 1 minute. Use a paper towel held with tongs to wipe the pan clean. Repeat the process until the pan develops a golden-brown patina, three to five repetitions. The pan may look blotchy, but will even out with use.

DAILY USE: Set the pan over medium heat and add 1 teaspoon of vegetable oil. Use a paper towel held with tongs to wipe the oil evenly over the pan. When the oil smokes, hold it at that stage for 1 minute, then wipe clean with another paper towel held with tongs. Allow the pan to cool for 3 to 5 minutes, then add the oil or butter for cooking. Don't skip the cooling step or the pan will be too hot and burn the cooking fat.

DAILY CARE: Treat your seasoned pan well. Never plunge a hot carbon-steel pan into cold water; the thermal shock can crack the pan. And avoid soap; it will dissolve the seasoning. After cooking, clean the pan with a wet sponge (and a little coarse salt mixed with oil if needed to scrub away stubborn bits), dry it well and wipe lightly with oil before storing.

Baked Persian Herb Omelet
(*Kuku Sabzi*)

Start to finish: **1 hour (20 minutes active)** / Servings: **6**

5 tablespoons extra-virgin olive oil, divided

2 cups lightly packed fresh flat-leaf parsley leaves

2 cups lightly packed fresh cilantro leaves and tender stems

1 cup coarsely chopped fresh dill

6 scallions, trimmed and coarsely chopped

1½ teaspoons baking powder

1 teaspoon kosher salt

¾ teaspoon ground cardamom

¾ teaspoon ground cinnamon

½ teaspoon ground cumin

¼ teaspoon ground black pepper

6 large eggs

½ cup walnuts, toasted and chopped (optional)

⅓ cup dried cranberries, coarsely chopped (optional)

Whole-milk Greek-style yogurt, to serve (optional)

As France claims the omelet, Italy the frittata and Spain the tortilla, Iran has kuku, a baked egg dish. The kuku sabzi variation, gets its flavor—and a deep green color—from tons of fresh herbs. We love this approach to fresh herbs. Using heaps of them delivers big flavor effortlessly, and keeps heavy dishes feeling light and fresh. Kuku sabzi—which is served at Persian New Year's feasts—remains light despite six eggs and a handful of walnuts (for texture and richness) thanks to five cups of parsley, cilantro and dill. Also helping is baking powder, which forms tiny air bubbles that catch the steam released as the eggs cook, causing the dish to rise. While some recipes for kuku sabzi opt for stovetop cooking (with copious oil), we preferred the ease of baking. Pulsing the herbs and scallions in the food processor was easier and faster than hand chopping, and the texture was better. Dried cranberries were a good stand-in for traditional Persian barberries—lending a sweet-and-savory balance—but the recipe works without them.

Don't use less than 2 tablespoons of oil to grease the pan; the oil should pool at the bottom and generously coat the sides. This crisps the edges and boosts the omelet's flavor.

1. Heat the oven to 375°F with a rack in the upper-middle position. Trace the bottom of an 8-inch square or 9-inch round cake pan on kitchen parchment, then cut inside the line to create a piece to fit inside the pan. Coat the bottom and sides of the pan with 2 tablespoons of the oil, turning the parchment to coat both sides.

2. In a food processor, combine the parsley, cilantro, dill, scallions and the remaining 3 tablespoons of oil. Process until finely ground. In a large bowl, whisk together the baking powder, salt, cardamom, cinnamon, cumin and pepper. Add 2 of the eggs and whisk until blended. Add the remaining 4 eggs and whisk until just combined. Fold in the herb-scallion mixture and the walnuts and cranberries, if using. Pour into the prepared pan and smooth the top. Bake until the center is firm, 20 to 25 minutes.

3. Let the kuku cool in the pan on a rack for 10 minutes. Run a knife around the edges, then invert onto a plate and remove the parchment. Reinvert onto a cutting board or serving platter. Cut into wedges and serve warm, cold or room temperature with a dollop of yogurt, if desired. The kuku can be refrigerated for up to 3 days, tightly wrapped.

Curry Braised Eggs

Start to finish: 1 hour 15 minutes (50 minutes active) / Servings: 4

---

3 tablespoons grapeseed or other neutral oil

1 large yellow onion, halved and thinly sliced lengthwise

Kosher salt

2 tablespoons finely grated fresh ginger

4 teaspoons garam masala

1 teaspoon ground turmeric

¼ teaspoon cayenne pepper

Three 14½-ounce cans diced tomatoes, drained

14-ounce can coconut milk

1 tablespoon packed brown sugar

Ground black pepper

1 tablespoon lime juice, plus lime wedges to serve

8 large eggs

⅓ cup chopped fresh cilantro

Steamed basmati rice, nan or boiled potatoes, to serve (optional)

Eggs are bit players in Western dinners. We eat them for breakfast and brunch, but come evening they rarely appear except as accessories for the put-an-egg-on-it crowd. The rest of the world knows better. Portugal, for example, has ervilhas com ovos, braised eggs cooked with spicy or sweet Portuguese chourico sausage and/or bacon and peas. In India, there is muttai kuzhambu, a type of egg curry. Both dishes are built on layers of seasoning that balance the richness of the eggs. We liked the way garam masala—a warmly flavored Indian seasoning blend—added complex flavor with just one ingredient. For our vegetables, we started with onions and found that sliced worked better than diced, adding texture and helping the sauce hold its shape. We let the sauce cool a bit in the dish before adding the eggs to ensure even cooking. While we like runny yolks, feel free to leave the dish in the oven a bit longer for firm yolks.

Don't forget that every oven is different, not to mention every egg. Cooking times will depend on oven temperature, as well as the size and temperature of the eggs.

1. Heat the oven to 375°F with a rack in the lower-middle position. In a 6- to 8-quart Dutch oven over medium, heat the oil. Add the onion and ½ teaspoon salt. Cook, stirring, until browned, 7 to 9 minutes. Add the ginger, garam masala, turmeric and cayenne. Cook for 30 seconds, stirring constantly. Add the tomatoes, coconut milk, sugar, ¾ teaspoon salt and ½ teaspoon pepper. Bring to a boil, scraping up any browned bits. Reduce heat to medium and simmer, stirring and scraping the pan, until thickened, 20 to 25 minutes.

2. Remove the pan from the heat and let sit for 10 minutes, stirring occasionally. Stir in the lime juice, then taste and season with salt and pepper. Use the back of a spoon to make 8 evenly spaced wells in the sauce. Crack 1 egg into each well, then season the eggs with salt and pepper.

3. Bake until the sauce is bubbling and the egg whites are opaque but still jiggle slightly, 13 to 18 minutes, rotating the pot halfway through. Remove from the oven and let sit for 5 minutes. Sprinkle with cilantro and serve with lime wedges and rice, nan or potatoes, if desired.

Spanish-Style Eggs with Garlicky Crumbs and Chorizo (*Migas*)

Start to finish: **30 minutes** / Servings: 4

8 large eggs

Kosher salt

3 ounces cured chorizo, halved lengthwise and thinly sliced crosswise

3 tablespoons extra-virgin olive oil, divided

2½ cups ½-inch bread cubes

1 medium red onion, diced (about 1 cup)

2 garlic cloves, thinly sliced

¼ teaspoon sweet paprika

¼ teaspoon cayenne pepper (optional)

4 cups lightly packed coarsely chopped lacinato kale (about 3 ounces)

Ground black pepper

Migas evolved as a Spanish-Portuguese dish intended to use up stale bread. In fact, the word is Spanish for crumbs. Traditionally, the bread is torn into cubes, sprinkled with water and left overnight. Since most Americans don't have stale bread sitting around, we used ½-inch cubes of rustic, bread. The best way to flavor them was to toss them in garlicky oil before toasting them in a skillet. We used Spanish-style chorizo, which is cured, and added a diced red onion along with chopped fresh kale. Both curly and lacinato (dinosaur) kale gave the dish heft, color and flavor. Be sure to stem the kale before measuring or weighing it, or substitute baby kale, which requires no stemming. For a variation, reduce or omit the kale and add 1 cup of chopped roasted red peppers or frozen peas (thawed). We found the bread cubes worked best when stirred in at the end of cooking, which gave them a chance to reheat and just begin to soften at the edges without losing their crunch. Their salty, garlicky flavor came through beautifully.

Don't walk away while browning the chorizo. Chorizo brands vary widely in fat content—not to mention flavor—and can go from golden brown to burnt in seconds.

1. In a medium bowl, whisk the eggs and ½ teaspoon salt. In a 12-inch non-stick skillet over medium, cook the chorizo, stirring frequently, until browned and crisp, 2 to 5 minutes. Use a slotted spoon to transfer the chorizo to a medium bowl, leaving any fat in the pan.

2. Add 2 tablespoons of the olive oil to the skillet and return to medium-high. Add the bread and a pinch of salt, then cook, stirring and tossing frequently, until browned and crisp, 3 to 5 minutes. Transfer to the bowl with the chorizo.

3. Return the skillet to medium heat and add the remaining 1 tablespoon of oil, the onion, garlic, paprika, cayenne, if using, and ¼ teaspoon salt. Cook,

stirring frequently, until the onion and garlic are softened and lightly browned, 3 to 5 minutes. If the garlic darkens too fast, reduce the heat. Add the kale and cook until wilted but still bright green, 1 to 2 minutes.

4. Whisk the eggs to recombine, then pour into the skillet and immediately reduce the heat to low. Cook, stirring and scraping the edges of the pan constantly until barely set, about 1 minute. Stir in the bread and chorizo. Cook to desired consistency, 30 to 90 seconds. Transfer to a platter and season with salt and pepper.

Chinese Stir-Fried Eggs with Tomatoes

Start to finish: **15 minutes** / Servings: 4

3 plum tomatoes (about 12 ounces), halved, cored and seeded

4 tablespoons unseasoned rice vinegar, divided

Ground white pepper

¼ cup water

1 tablespoon ketchup

2 teaspoons finely grated fresh ginger

1 garlic clove, finely grated

½ teaspoon red pepper flakes

1 teaspoon toasted sesame oil

3 teaspoons soy sauce, divided

8 large eggs

3 tablespoons vegetable oil, divided

Kosher salt

Stir-fried eggs with tomatoes is quick Chinese comfort food, and there are endless variations. Our version has more flavor than most since we season the ingredients from the start, rather than relying on condiments. We began by giving our tomatoes a toss in vinegar and white pepper. We didn't add sugar (a classic ingredient), but did add a dollop of sweet tomato flavor via a tablespoon of ketchup. We found the best method was to cook the eggs and tomatoes separately, starting with the eggs. We then added tomatoes to the empty skillet, cooked them until just beginning to blister, then arranged them on the eggs. Finally, our sauce went into the skillet to heat and thicken. This recipe comes together quickly, so have all ingredients assembled and prepared before you begin cooking. We liked the eggs with thinly sliced scallions, toasted sesame seeds and a drizzle of chili oil. Serve it over rice and you have a quick dinner.

Don't forget to seed the tomatoes. The pulp made the dish watery.

1. Cut each tomato half into thirds. In a medium bowl, toss the tomatoes with 1 tablespoon of the vinegar and ½ teaspoon white pepper. In a small bowl, combine the remaining 3 tablespoons of vinegar, the water, ketchup, ginger, garlic, pepper flakes, sesame oil, 2 teaspoons of the soy sauce and ½ teaspoon white pepper. Set aside. In a second medium bowl, whisk the eggs, the remaining 1 teaspoon of soy sauce and ½ teaspoon white pepper.

2. Drain the tomatoes and set aside. In a 12-inch nonstick skillet over medium-high, heat 2 tablespoons of the vegetable oil until just smoking. Pour the eggs into the center of the pan, letting the eggs puff up along the edges. Use a spatula to stir the eggs, pushing them toward the middle as they begin to set at the edges and folding the cooked egg onto itself. Cook until just set, 45 to 60 seconds. Transfer to a plate.

3. In the empty skillet, heat the remaining 1 tablespoon of oil over medium-high until beginning to smoke. Add the drained tomatoes and cook undisturbed until just beginning to blister, 30 to 60 seconds. Arrange the tomatoes on top of the eggs.

4. Return the skillet to high heat and pour the sauce mixture into the skillet. Cook, stirring constantly, until thickened, about 30 seconds. Taste and season with salt and white pepper. Pour over the tomatoes.

Korean Scallion Pancakes (*Pajeon*)

Start to finish: **30 minutes** / Servings: 4

½ cup all-purpose flour

½ cup potato starch

1 teaspoon red pepper flakes

1 teaspoon kosher salt

1 cup ice water

1 large egg, beaten

6 scallions, trimmed and
cut into 1-inch pieces

¼ cup shredded carrot
(about ½ medium carrot)

¼ cup soy sauce

3 tablespoons unseasoned
rice vinegar

½ teaspoon toasted sesame oil

¼ teaspoon ground black pepper

2 tablespoons grapeseed or
other neutral oil, divided

Quick to make and with a crisp exterior but chewy center, pajeon take pancakes from breakfast to dinner. We tried several flour combinations in our search for just the right texture. We found that a combination of all-purpose flour and potato starch gave these pancakes their signature chewy texture. Using ice water in our batter encouraged the pancakes to puff while cooking, producing slightly crisped edges. Some recipes use as few as two scallions but we preferred more, settling on six. We started our pancake at a medium-high heat, but needed to reduce it after flipping to prevent the scallions from burning. If you can find gochugaru, sometimes sold as Korean chili powder, use it in place of the red pepper flakes for a sweeter, smokier flavor. Looking to switch up the flavors? We've included kimchi and seafood variations.

Don't use potato flour, which has a strong potato flavor and reacts differently with water. Bob's Red Mill makes potato starch, which is usually available in the baking aisle or natural foods section of your grocer.

1. In a medium bowl, whisk together the flour, potato starch, pepper flakes and salt. Add the water and egg and whisk until smooth. Fold in the scallions and carrots. Set aside. In a small bowl, combine the soy sauce, vinegar, sesame oil and pepper; set aside.

2. In a 10-inch nonstick skillet, heat 1 tablespoon of the grapeseed oil over medium-high until shimmering. Stir the batter to recombine, then add half (1 scant cup) to the skillet, spreading it and the vegetables evenly to the edges of the pan. Cook until the top is set and the edges begin to brown, 3 to 4 minutes.

3. Reduce heat to medium-low, then use a spatula to flip the pancake. Cook until golden brown on the second side, being careful not to burn the scallions, 1 to 2 minutes. Flip again and cook until the pancake is charred in spots and

crisp around the edges, 2 to 4 minutes. Transfer to a plate. Increase the heat to medium-high and repeat with the remaining 1 tablespoon grapeseed oil and the remaining batter. Cut the pancakes into wedges and serve with the sauce.

VARIATIONS:

For kimchi pancakes: Substitute ⅔ cup sliced napa cabbage kimchi for the scallions and carrots. Squeeze the kimchi gently before adding to remove excess liquid.

For seafood pancakes: Eliminate the carrot and add ½ cup chopped raw shrimp (peeled and deveined) to the batter with the scallions.

Soups

3

Miso-Shiitake Soup with Napa Cabbage

Start to finish: **30 minutes** / Servings: **6**

7 cups water

½ pound carrots (2 to 3 medium), peeled, halved lengthwise and cut crosswise into ½-inch pieces

2 tablespoons dried wakame seaweed

8 ounces soft tofu, drained and cut into ½-inch cubes

5 ounces fresh shiitake mushrooms, stems discarded, caps thinly sliced

4 cups chopped napa cabbage (½ small head)

6 tablespoons (3½ ounces) white miso paste

1-inch chunk fresh ginger, grated

3 teaspoons soy sauce, plus more to serve

2 teaspoons toasted sesame oil, plus more to serve

4 ounces (about 4 cups) baby spinach

6 scallions, trimmed and cut into 1-inch lengths

Hot chili oil, to serve (optional)

In Japan, where soup has evolved into high art, nabe (NAH-beh) is shorthand for nabemono, a broad category of broth-based soups that may be more recognizable by its Westernized name—hot pot. One such soup, yosenabe, loosely translates to "anything goes hot pot" and relies on layering flavors, adding them to the pot one at a time. Dense or long-cooking items go in first; more delicate ingredients follow. For our yosenabe, we leaned heavily on vegetables. Most Japanese soups begin with dashi, a broth made from kombu seaweed and bonito, or shaved shreds of smoked tuna. We used more common but equally flavorful fresh shiitake mushrooms and wakame seaweed. (Wakame comes shredded and tastes slightly sweet and oceanic; look for it in the Asian foods aisle.) Timing was simple: Each ingredient cooked through in the time it took for the pot to return to a simmer. Yosenabe is typically flavored with a blend of soy sauce, sesame oil or scallions. We added all of them.

Don't use firm or extra-firm tofu in this recipe. Soft tofu had the best texture. Silken and medium tofu were decent substitutes.

1. In a medium Dutch oven over medium, combine the water, carrots and wakame. Bring to a simmer and cook for 5 minutes. Add the tofu and mushrooms, then return to a simmer. Add the cabbage, then return to a simmer.

2. Place the miso in a 2-cup liquid measuring cup. Ladle out a bit of the cooking water and add to the miso, stirring until smooth. Pour the miso mixture back into the soup, then stir well.

3. As the soup returns to a simmer, stir in the ginger, soy sauce and sesame oil. Once the soup reaches a simmer, remove it from the heat and stir in the spinach and scallions. When the spinach is wilted, ladle the soup into serving bowls. Serve with soy sauce, sesame oil and chili oil, if using.

Korean Pork and Kimchi Stew (*Jjigae*)

Start to finish: 1 hour 15 minutes (25 minutes active) / Servings: 6

1 cup boiling water,
plus 5 cups cold water

½ ounce dried shiitake mushrooms,
brushed clean

6 scallions, white parts finely
chopped, green parts thinly sliced
on a bias, reserved separately

3 garlic cloves, smashed

1 tablespoon toasted sesame oil

1 tablespoon soy sauce

16-ounce container napa cabbage
kimchi, drained (¼ cup liquid
reserved) and coarsely chopped

4 teaspoons gochujang

1 pound baby back ribs, separated
into individual ribs

12 ounces medium-firm or firm tofu,
drained and cut into ¾-inch cubes

2 teaspoons white sugar

Looking for a stew with big flavor and easy prep, we were delighted to encounter Korean pork and kimchi stew. The assertively seasoned dish uses purchased kimchi—the pungent fermented cabbage that is a staple of Korean cooking—to easily add both vegetables and flavor. We built on our kimchi base with bone-in, baby back ribs for meaty flavor, cutting them into individual ribs so they tenderized quickly in the simmering broth. The bones and connective tissue of the ribs also add body to the broth. We layered the heat by combining another Korean favorite, gochujang chili paste, as well as the juice from the drained kimchi. For another time-saver, look for pre-sliced dried shiitake mushrooms. Serve with bowls of steamed white rice for a complete meal.

Don't use extra-firm or soft tofu. Soft or silken tofu was too fragile, and extra-firm added too much chew. Textures vary by brand, but we preferred medium-firm and firm.

1. **In a small bowl,** combine the boiling water and mushrooms. Let sit for 30 minutes.

2. **Drain the mushrooms,** reserving the soaking liquid. Discard the stems and thinly slice the caps. In a large Dutch oven over medium-high, combine the scallion whites, garlic, sesame oil and soy sauce. Cook, stirring occasionally, until softened, 3 to 4 minutes. Stir in half of the kimchi, sliced mushrooms and the gochujang. Add the cold water, the mushrooms' soaking liquid, the ribs and ¼ cup kimchi liquid and bring to a boil. Cover, leaving the lid slightly ajar, reduce the heat to medium-low and cook until rib meat is easily pierced with a knife, about 50 minutes, adjusting the heat to maintain a lively simmer.

3. **Remove the pot** from the heat. Using tongs, transfer the ribs to a plate and let rest until cool enough to handle, about 15 minutes.

4. **Shred the meat** into bite-size pieces, discarding the bones and cartilage. Add the meat to the stew along with the tofu, scallion greens, sugar and remaining kimchi. Bring to a simmer over medium and cook for 5 minutes.

Cinnamon, Beef and **Noodle Soup**

Start to finish: 3½ hours (30 minutes active) / Servings: 6

Six 3-inch cinnamon sticks

2 teaspoons anise seed

8 cups water

½ cup soy sauce

½ cup rice wine

8 scallions, trimmed, halved crosswise into white and green parts

1 bunch fresh cilantro

4-inch chunk fresh ginger (3 ounces), cut into pieces and smashed

3 pounds beef shank, trimmed

8 ounces dried udon noodles

5 ounces baby spinach

1 teaspoon chili-garlic sauce, plus more to serve

Ground white pepper

Though European cuisines rely on browning foods to develop flavor, across Asia flavor is built in layers using simple, potent ingredients. That's what drew us to Nina Simonds' recipe for Chinese cinnamon barley soup in her book, "A Spoonful of Ginger." It skips the fussy Western-style browning and instead relies on garlic, ginger, scallions, cinnamon and anise seeds. In our version, we also reached for soy sauce, with its rich umami taste, then added beef shank, a cut of meat that delivers the bonus of taste- and texture-enhancing gelatin that melts out of the meat's connective tissue. Barley was delicious, but we were after a clearer, lighter soup and settled on chewy udon noodles, cooked separately, then added to the bowls for serving. (Any Asian-style noodle will work, even fresh linguine or fettuccine in a pinch.) To make things even easier, the broth and meat can be prepared up to three days ahead and refrigerated until needed; discard the fat from the broth's surface when you're ready to proceed.

Don't substitute star anise for the anise seed. Though they are similar, the flavors are different. If you can't find anise seed, the broth is still delicious without it. And don't worry about chopping the cilantro. Add the bunch whole; it gets strained out at the end.

1. In a 7-quart Dutch oven over medium, toast the cinnamon sticks and anise until fragrant, 3 to 5 minutes. Add the water, soy sauce, rice wine, scallion whites, cilantro and ginger. Bring to a simmer. Add the beef, cover and simmer on low until the beef is tender and falling off the bone, 2½ to 3 hours.

2. Using a slotted spoon, transfer the beef to a large plate and cool. Pour the broth through a mesh strainer into a large bowl. Discard the solids and return the broth to the pot. When cool enough to handle, shred the meat, discarding fat and bones, then return the meat to the broth.

3. Bring a large pot of salted water to a boil. Add the noodles, cook until al dente, then drain. Meanwhile, return the broth to a simmer. Add the spinach and cook until wilted, about 1 minute. Off heat, stir in the chili-garlic sauce and season with white pepper. Divide the noodles between serving bowls and ladle soup over, seasoning with chili-garlic sauce, if desired. Top with scallion greens.

GOOD TO THE BONE

We prefer our soups and stews to taste
light and fresh, even those with meat.
Which is why we ease up on the amount
of meat we add. As with many cuisines,
we try to treat meat as a seasoning
rather than the main event. But we still
pick our cuts with care to ensure they
have the maximum impact on the dish.
Bony cuts are ideal because the marbled
meat is packed with flavor and the
connective tissue thickens and flavors
the broth during simmering. For
example, for Korean pork and kimchi
stew (p. 40), we use a few meaty baby
back ribs to create the soup's rich flavor
base. Once tender, the meat is pulled
from the bones and returned to the pot.
In our Turkish white beans with pickled
tomatoes (p. 131), a single beef or
lamb shank offers the dish deep flavor
that enhances rather than dominates
the beans.

Georgian Chicken Soup (*Chikhirtma*)

Start to finish: **1 hour 45 minutes (45 minutes active)** / Servings: 6

For the broth and chicken:

1 bunch fresh cilantro

1 bunch fresh dill

1 garlic head

2½ to 3 pounds bone-in skin-on chicken legs

10 cups water

1 large yellow onion, quartered

2 teaspoons kosher salt

1 teaspoon black peppercorns

½ teaspoon coriander seeds

½ teaspoon red pepper flakes (optional)

3-inch cinnamon stick

2 bay leaves

For the soup:

1 pound carrots (about 5 medium), peeled, halved lengthwise and cut crosswise into ½-inch pieces

1 large yellow onion, coarsely chopped (about 1½ cups)

3 tablespoons salted butter

½ teaspoon kosher salt

½ cup dry vermouth

1 tablespoon all-purpose flour

6 large egg yolks

¼ cup lemon juice (1 to 2 lemons)

Ground black pepper

It's easy to overcomplicate chicken soup. Too often, the broths are watery and flavorless, so we compensate by piling on the ingredients. But that only leads to a muddle of flavors and textures. We wanted a chicken soup that tastes fresh and light, yet also robust and satisfying. We wanted just the right vegetables—and in the right volumes—balanced by a gentle acidity and spice. We found our answer in chikhirtma, a traditional soup from Georgia, the Eurasian country that bridges Turkey and Russia. Georgian cuisine often marries Western techniques with Eastern flavors. We used a recipe from Darra Goldstein, author of "The Georgian Feast," as our starting point. Her chikhirtma calls for a whole chicken, but that much meat made the soup feel heavy, so we used just chicken legs. We built flavor with bunches of dill and cilantro stems and a head of garlic, as well as coriander, cinnamon and bay leaves.

Don't simmer the soup after adding the eggs. Heat it gently just until warm, otherwise the eggs will curdle.

1. To make the broth, tie the stems of the cilantro and dill into bundles, then trim off the leaves, reserving ¼ cup of each for garnish. Cut off and discard the top third of the garlic head, leaving the head intact. In a large pot, combine both sets of stems, the garlic, the chicken and the remaining broth ingredients. Bring to a boil, then reduce heat to medium-low. Simmer until chicken is tender, about 45 minutes. Remove and set aside the garlic head. Transfer the chicken to a plate and cool until easily handled. Shred the chicken into bite-size pieces, discarding the skin, bones and cartilage. Set aside.

2. To make the soup, strain the broth into another pot or bowl, discarding the solids. Using tongs, squeeze the garlic head into the broth; the tender cloves should easily pop out of their skins. Whisk into the broth. Wipe out the empty pot, then add the carrots, onion, butter and salt. Set over medium-high and cook, stirring occasionally, until the onion is browned, 10 to 12 minutes. Add the vermouth, scraping up any browned bits, and cook until evaporated, 1 to 2 minutes. Add the flour and cook, stirring constantly, for 1 minute. Add 2 cups of the broth and stir until smooth, then add the remaining broth and bring to a simmer.

3. In a medium bowl, whisk the yolks. Continue whisking while slowly adding 1 cup of hot broth from the pot. Whisk in the lemon juice, then return the mixture to the pot and whisk to combine. Add the chicken and any accumulated juices and cook until just heated through (do not simmer). Taste and season with salt and pepper. Serve with the reserved chopped cilantro and dill leaves.

Spicy Red Lentil Stew with Coconut Milk and Spinach

Start to finish: **1 hour (10 minutes active)** / Servings: 4 to 6

1 medium yellow onion, diced (about 1 cup)

2 tablespoons coconut or peanut oil

4 garlic cloves, smashed

Kosher salt

3 teaspoons finely grated fresh ginger, divided

2 teaspoons mustard seeds

2 teaspoons ground turmeric

1 teaspoon ground coriander

1 teaspoon ground fennel seeds

¾ teaspoon red pepper flakes

3½ cups water

14-ounce can coconut milk

1 cup split red lentils, rinsed

6 ounces (about 6 cups) baby spinach, roughly chopped

2 tablespoons lime juice

Unsweetened coconut flakes and chopped tomato, to garnish (optional)

Located on the southwestern coast of India, Goa is known for its use of chilies, spices, coconut and bright acid (an influence from Portuguese colonization). Our spicy red lentil soup is a simplified take on a Goan staple that delivers a complete vegetarian meal in about an hour. Split red lentils, the foundation of the dish, cook in minutes. Blending turmeric, coriander and fennel created complex flavor without requiring the cook to pull out half the spice cabinet. Fresh ginger added welcome brightness, and adding a portion of it at the end kept the flavor vibrant. Both virgin and refined coconut oil worked, but virgin had a slightly stronger flavor. Yellow and brown mustard seeds both added a peppery pop to the dish.

Don't substitute brown or green lentils for the split red lentils. Red lentils break down as they cook, thickening the cooking liquid and providing the ideal texture for the soup. Other lentil varieties remain intact even when fully cooked.

1. In a large saucepan over medium-high, combine the onion, oil, garlic and 1½ teaspoons of salt. Cook, stirring occasionally, until the onions have softened and are just beginning to color, 7 to 9 minutes. Stir in 2 teaspoons of ginger, the mustard seeds, turmeric, coriander, fennel and pepper flakes. Cook, stirring frequently, until fragrant, about 1 minute. Add the water, coconut milk and lentils, then bring to a boil.

Reduce heat to low, cover and cook until the lentils have broken down, 30 to 40 minutes.

2. Stir in the spinach and return to a simmer. Off the heat, add the remaining 1 teaspoon of ginger and the lime juice. Season with salt. Serve, garnished with coconut flakes and tomato, if using.

Mexican Chicken Soup
with Tomatillos and Hominy

Start to finish: **2 hours (1 hour active)** / Servings: **6**

10 cups water

2 large white onions,
1 quartered and 1 chopped

1 bunch fresh cilantro, stems
and leaves separated

2 whole dried ancho or pasilla
chilies, stemmed, seeded and
torn into rough pieces

2 tablespoons coriander seeds,
toasted, plus 1 tablespoon ground
coriander

2 tablespoons cumin seeds,
toasted, plus 1 tablespoon
ground cumin

Kosher salt

1 garlic head

2½ to 3 pounds bone-in
skin-on chicken legs

2 fresh poblano chilies

2 fresh jalapeno chilies

1 pound fresh tomatillos,
husked and quartered

2 tablespoons grapeseed
or other neutral oil

2 teaspoons dried oregano,
preferably Mexican

15-ounce can hominy, drained

Toasted pepitas, lime wedges and
sour cream or Mexican crema
(optional), to serve

For a fresh take on chicken soup we looked to Mexico for inspiration and came up with one that builds layer upon layer of flavor—spice, chilies and herbs. We used charred fresh jalapeno and poblano peppers, a flavor-boosting technique common to Mexican and Latin American cooking. For our dried spices we added depth with relatively little effort by using toasted whole as well as ground coriander and cumin. Bone-in, skin-on chicken legs gave us broth-thickening collagen. For more spice, use serranos instead of jalapenos, or include the chilies' seeds. If you can't find fresh tomatillos, substitute canned tomatillos, drained. The broth and chicken can be made a day ahead and refrigerated separately before proceeding. However, shred the chicken while it's still warm. We liked garnishing the soup with chopped avocado, sliced jalapenos, crumbled queso fresco and fried tortilla strips.

Don't leave out the tomatillos. They give the soup acidity and texture.

1. In a large pot, combine the water, the quartered onion, cilantro stems, dried chilies, coriander seeds, cumin seeds and 1 teaspoon salt. Cut off and discard the top third of the garlic head, leaving the head intact, and add to the pot. Cover and bring to a boil, then simmer for 10 minutes. Add the chicken and return to a boil. Reduce heat to medium-low and cook partially covered for 30 minutes, maintaining a gentle simmer.

2. Meanwhile, heat the broiler to high with an oven rack 6 inches from the element. Arrange the poblanos and jalapenos on a rimmed baking sheet and broil, turning frequently, until evenly blackened and blistered, 10 to 12 minutes. Transfer to a bowl, cover tightly and set aside. Chop the cilantro leaves and set aside.

3. Peel, stem and seed the charred chilies, then roughly chop and add to a food processor along with the tomatillos. Pulse until coarsely chopped, 6 to 8 pulses.

4. Transfer the chicken and garlic head to a plate and let cool. Strain the broth, discarding the solids. Wipe out the pot. Add the oil, chopped onion and ½ teaspoon salt. Cook over medium-high, stirring occasionally, until softened and beginning to brown, 7 to 9 minutes. Add the ground coriander, ground cumin and oregano and cook, stirring constantly, for 1 minute. Add the tomatillo-chili mixture and cook, stirring frequently and scraping up any browned bits, until most of the moisture has evaporated, about 5 minutes. Add the broth and bring to a boil.

5. Shred the chicken into bite-size pieces, discarding the skin, bones and cartilage. Using tongs, squeeze the garlic head into the soup. The tender cloves should easily pop out of their skins. Add the chicken and hominy. Return to a simmer and cook until heated through, about 5 minutes. Stir in ½ cup of the chopped cilantro, then taste and season with salt. Top the soup with toasted pepitas, lime juice, more chopped cilantro and sour cream, if desired.

Spanish Garlic Soup

Start to finish: **45 minutes** / Servings: 4

6 scallions, trimmed and thinly sliced, whites and greens divided

6 garlic cloves, thinly sliced

6 tablespoons extra-virgin olive oil, divided, plus extra

4 teaspoons sweet paprika

1½ teaspoons smoked paprika

6 ounces sourdough or other rustic bread, cut into ½-inch cubes (about 4 cups), divided

6 cups water

2 tablespoons chicken bouillon (such as Knorr chicken base)

Kosher salt and ground black pepper

4 large egg yolks

Sherry vinegar, to taste

José Andrés taught us this "end of month" recipe—the sort of meal to make quickly with whatever is on hand and when money is tight. His approach: garlic cooked in copious amounts of olive oil with handfuls of thinly sliced stale bread and several tablespoons of smoked paprika. Add some water and simmer, then off heat stir in four or five whisked eggs. Supper is served. For our version, we realized the leftover bread, garlic and smoked paprika we had in our cupboards weren't up to Andrés' standards. So we needed to tweak. We boosted flavor by using chicken bouillon (an easy pantry flavor enhancer) instead of plain water, and we sautéed both sweet and smoked paprika with garlic and scallions. We actually didn't have stale bread, so we turned a loaf of rustic sourdough (a baguette or any crusty loaf will do) into delicious croutons, and added a bit of bread directly to the broth to thicken it. To serve, the soup and croutons are married in the serving bowls, allowing each person to adjust the ratio of soup to bread, as well as how long they soak.

Don't skip tempering the egg yolks with some of the hot broth before adding to the soup. This prevents them from curdling in the hot broth.

1. In a medium saucepan over medium-low, combine the scallion whites, garlic and 3 tablespoons of the oil. Cook, stirring occasionally, until beginning to color, 8 to 10 minutes. Add both paprikas and cook, stirring, until fragrant and darkened, 30 seconds.

2. Add 1 cup of the bread cubes and stir well. Whisk in the water and bouillon, increase heat to medium-high and bring to a simmer. Reduce heat to medium-low and simmer, whisking occasionally, for 15 minutes. Whisk vigorously to ensure bread is thoroughly broken up.

3. Meanwhile, in a 12-inch skillet over medium, combine the remaining 3 tablespoons of oil, the remaining 3 cups of bread, the scallion greens and ½ teaspoon each salt and pepper. Cook, stirring occasionally, until browned and crisp, 8 to 10 minutes.

4. In a medium bowl, whisk the egg yolks. Slowly whisk in 1 cup of the hot broth. Remove the soup from the heat. Off heat, vigorously whisk the egg yolks into the soup, then whisk in the vinegar. Taste and season with salt and pepper. To serve, fill individual bowls with the crouton mixture, then ladle the soup over them. Drizzle with additional oil, if desired.

Vegetables

Avocado Salad with Pickled Mustard Seeds and Marjoram Vinaigrette

Start to finish: **1 hour** / Servings: 6

For the pickled mustard seeds:

¼ cup yellow mustard seeds

½ cup cider vinegar

¼ cup white sugar

¼ cup water

1½ teaspoons black peppercorns

½ teaspoon coriander seeds

3 allspice berries

1 bay leaf

⅛ teaspoon red pepper flakes

For the dressing:

2 tablespoons pickled mustard seeds and brine

1 tablespoon minced shallot

2 teaspoons whole-grain mustard

1 teaspoon honey

¼ teaspoon kosher salt

¼ teaspoon ground black pepper

¼ cup chopped fresh marjoram

3 tablespoons canola oil

3 tablespoons extra-virgin olive oil

For the salad:

3 firm but ripe avocados

Kosher salt

6 teaspoons lemon juice

Thinly sliced ricotta salata cheese

Fresh marjoram leaves

It was the simplicity that we loved. Half an avocado, sliced and fanned across a plate. Over it, marjoram vinaigrette studded with tender spheres of pickled mustard seeds. One thing was quite clear: A handful of simple ingredients can take a stunning turn when the right flavors tie them together. In this case, that is the role of the whole mustard seeds, an ingredient Americans rarely encounter outside pickle brine. We discovered this at Stephen Oxaal's Branch Line restaurant in Watertown, Massachusetts, where the seeds take an avocado salad from simple to stunning. The pickling process takes just a few minutes and the result adds a tang and crunch that balance the lushness of the other ingredients. Conventional vinaigrettes—blends of fat and acid—tended to slide off the avocados. Instead, we eliminated the lemon juice from the dressing and drizzled it directly over the avocado slices, where it mingled with the dressing. We liked ricotta salata best, but Parmesan was a fine substitute.

1. To make the pickled mustard seeds, in a small saucepan over high, combine the mustard seeds and enough water to cover by 2 inches. Bring to a boil, then reduce heat to medium-low and simmer until the seeds are tender, about 8 minutes. Strain the seeds through a mesh strainer and transfer to a bowl. Wipe out and reserve the pan.

2. To the pan, add the remaining pickling ingredients. Place over high heat. Bring to a boil, then reduce to medium-low and simmer until fragrant and the sugar has dissolved, 3 to 5 minutes. Strain over the mustard seeds, discarding the solids. Let the mixture cool to room temperature. Use immediately or cover and refrigerate for up to 4 weeks.

3. To make the dressing, in a small bowl, mix together 2 tablespoons of the pickled mustard seeds and brine, the shallot, mustard, honey, salt and pepper. Let sit for 10 minutes. Add the marjoram and both oils and whisk until emulsified.

4. To assemble and serve, halve the avocados lengthwise, remove the pits and peel away the skins. Cut each half into slices (see sidebar), leaving the halves intact, and fan onto serving plates, cut sides down. Sprinkle a pinch of salt and 1 teaspoon of lemon juice over each half. Spoon the dressing over the avocados and garnish with ricotta salata and marjoram.

HOW TO FAN AN AVOCADO

1. Halve each avocado lengthwise and remove the pit. Peel the skin from each half.

2. Place the avocado halves cut side down. Starting at the larger end of each half, cut each into 6 lengthwise slices, leaving the top 1 inch intact.

3. Set each half on a plate, cut side down. Gently press the large end to fan the slices.

Lebanese-Style **Tabbouleh**

Start to finish: **15 minutes** / Servings: 4

½ cup boiling water

⅓ cup fine-grain bulgur

1 teaspoon ground sumac (optional)

½ teaspoon ground allspice

Kosher salt and ground black pepper

3 tablespoons lemon juice
(1 to 2 lemons)

1 small shallot, minced
(about 2 tablespoons)

¼ teaspoon white sugar

¼ cup extra-virgin olive oil

2 to 3 small vine-ripened tomatoes,
diced (about 8 ounces)

4 cups lightly packed flat-leaf parsley
leaves, well dried then minced

1 cup lightly packed mint leaves,
well dried then minced

Israeli-born British chef Yotam Ottolenghi is clear about tabbouleh. It should be "all about the parsley." But in the U.S., the Middle Eastern salad often goes heavy on the bulgur, a wheat that has been cooked, dried and cracked. The result is a salad that is mealy, bland and stubbornly soggy. That's because the bulgur sponges up all the juices from the tomatoes. Our solution was to barely cook the bulgur—essentially underhydrating it— allowing it to soak up those juices without becoming waterlogged. We added generous helpings of herbs, livening up the parsley with some mint. Wet herbs will dilute the dressing and make the bulgur gummy. Be sure to dry them thoroughly with a spinner and paper towels before mincing. Some type of onion is traditional; we used shallots, preferring their gentler bite, and soaked them in lemon juice to soften their flavor and texture. While the sumac is optional, we loved its fruity complexity and light acidity.

Don't use coarse-grain bulgur; it won't hydrate evenly. If you can't find fine-grain bulgur, process medium- or coarse-grain in short pulses until fine, light and fluffy, five to 10 pulses.

1. In a medium bowl, combine the water, bulgur, sumac, if using, allspice and ½ teaspoon of salt. Cover with plastic wrap and let sit for 10 minutes. In a large bowl, stir together the lemon juice, shallot, sugar and ¾ teaspoon of salt; let sit for 10 minutes.

2. Whisk the oil into the lemon juice mixture. Fluff the bulgur with a fork and add to the dressing along with the tomatoes; mix well. Fold the parsley and mint into the tabbouleh, then taste and season with salt, pepper and additional sumac, if needed. Can be refrigerated for up to 24 hours.

PARCH YOUR STARCH

Under hydrating starchy ingredients— such as pasta and bulgur—is a quick and easy way to boost the flavor of a dish. Under hydrated grains and pastas are able to absorb flavors from spices and sauces better, resulting in a more vibrant and appetizing dish.

We used this technique in our Lebanese-style tabbouleh, cutting back on the amount of water we normally would use to soak the bulgur, allowing it to better soak up the dressing and tomato juices without becoming watery.

Apple, Celery Root and Fennel Salad with Hazelnuts

Start to finish: **20 minutes** / Servings: 6

1 small shallot, grated

1½ tablespoons cider vinegar

3 tablespoons lightly packed grated fresh horseradish

3 tablespoons extra-virgin olive oil

1 teaspoon honey

Kosher salt and ground black pepper

1 Granny Smith apple, cored and cut into matchsticks

½ small celery root (about 8 ounces), peeled and cut into matchsticks

1 medium fennel bulb, trimmed and thinly sliced

½ cup chopped fresh parsley leaves

¼ cup chopped fresh mint leaves

½ cup hazelnuts, toasted and coarsely chopped

A winter salad needs to stand up to hearty stews and roasts, and that calls for bold, bright flavors. We started with tart apples and thin slices of fennel bulb, the latter adding a pleasant anis flavor. Celery root added a fresh crispness while grated fresh horseradish gave the dish kick. Grating the horseradish triggers a chemical reaction that enhances the root's bite. Tossing it with vinegar and salt helps preserve that heat, which otherwise dissipates quickly. Make sure you grate horseradish in an open and well-ventilated space.

In a large bowl, combine the shallot and vinegar. Let sit for 10 minutes. Whisk in the horseradish, oil, honey, 1 teaspoon salt and ½ teaspoon pepper. Add the apple, celery root and fennel, then toss. Stir in the parsley and mint, then sprinkle with hazelnuts.

Thai-style Napa Coleslaw with Mint and Cilantro

Start to finish: **25 minutes** / Servings: **6**

3 tablespoons lime juice
(1 to 2 limes)

4 teaspoons white sugar

1 tablespoon fish sauce

1 medium serrano chili,
seeded and minced

5 tablespoons coconut milk

1 pound napa cabbage
(1 small head), thinly sliced
crosswise (about 8 cups)

6 radishes, trimmed, halved
and thinly sliced

4 ounces sugar snap peas,
strings removed, thinly
sliced on a bias

½ cup coarsely chopped
fresh cilantro

½ cup coarsely chopped
fresh mint

½ cup roasted, salted cashews,
coarsely chopped

In rethinking the classic American coleslaw we took our inspiration from San Antonio chef Quealy Watson, whose slaw world changed when he traveled to Asia. Watson, the former chef at San Antonio's funky Tex-Asian barbecue joint Hot Joy, created a slaw inspired by traditional Burmese lahpet, a style of pickled tea leaves that are eaten. For our slaw, we used tender napa cabbage with red radishes and snap peas for crunch, with fresh mint and cilantro to tie it all together. Coconut milk—instead of mayonnaise—had the right balance of richness and fresh flavor. For heat, we used a fresh chili "cooked" in lime juice, which mellowed the bite and helped disperse the heat evenly. Fish sauce added a savory pungency.

Don't use "light" coconut milk or sweetened "cream of coconut" for this recipe. The former is too thin, and the latter is too sweet (think pina coladas). And don't forget to vigorously shake the can before opening to ensure the fat and liquid are fully emulsified.

In a liquid measuring cup, mix together the lime juice, sugar, fish sauce and chili. Let sit for 10 minutes. Whisk in the coconut milk until combined, then adjust seasoning with additional fish sauce, if desired. In a large bowl, combine the cabbage, radishes, peas, cilantro and mint. Add the dressing and toss until evenly coated. Stir in the cashews and serve.

Kale Salad with Smoked Almonds and Picada Crumbs

Start to finish: **15 minutes** / Servings: 6

2 shallots, thinly sliced

5 tablespoons sherry vinegar

Kosher salt

2 tablespoons honey

8 tablespoons extra-virgin olive oil, divided

Ground black pepper

1 cup smoked almonds

4 ounces chewy white bread, cut into 1-inch cubes

2 teaspoons fresh thyme leaves

1 tablespoon sweet paprika

2 bunches lacinato kale, stemmed, washed, spun dry and thinly sliced crosswise (10 cups)

1 cup lightly packed fresh mint leaves, chopped

Kale can make a flavorful and seasonal winter salad, but to be eaten raw it needs to be treated right. Otherwise, the greens can be unpleasantly tough. We started with lacinato kale, also known as dinosaur or Tuscan kale. Its long blue-green leaves are sweeter and more tender than curly kale. Slicing the greens thinly was the first step to making them more salad-friendly. Then, to soften them further, we borrowed a Japanese technique used on raw cabbage—massaging the leaves. In this case, we do it with ground smoked almonds, which help tenderize the kale and add crunch and flavor to the finished salad. An acidic shallot-sherry vinaigrette also helped soften and brighten the kale (look for a sherry vinegar aged at least 3 years). Intensely flavorful paprika breadcrumbs, inspired by the Catalan sauce picada, tied everything together.

Don't slice the kale until you're ready to make the salad; it will wilt. You can, however, stem, wash and dry it ahead of time.

1. In a small bowl, whisk together the shallots, vinegar and ½ teaspoon salt. Let sit for 10 minutes. Whisk in the honey, 5 tablespoons of the oil and ½ teaspoon pepper; set aside.

2. In a food processor, process the almonds until coarsely chopped, about 8 pulses; transfer to a large bowl. Add the bread to the processor and process to rough crumbs, about 20 seconds. Add the thyme, the remaining 3 table-spoons oil, the paprika, ½ teaspoon salt and ½ teaspoon pepper. Process until incorporated, about 10 seconds.

3. Transfer the crumb mixture to a large skillet over medium and cook, stirring frequently, until crisp and browned, 8 to 10 minutes. Transfer to a plate to cool.

4. Add the kale and mint to the bowl with the almonds and massage the greens until the kale softens and darkens, 10 to 20 seconds. Add the dressing and crumbs and toss to combine. Taste, then season with salt and pepper.

Smashed **Cucumber Salad**

Start to finish: **40 minutes (15 minutes active)** / Servings: **6**

2 pounds English cucumbers
(about 2 large)

4 teaspoons white sugar

1 tablespoon kosher salt

4 teaspoons unseasoned
rice vinegar

1 garlic clove, peeled
and smashed

2 tablespoons grapeseed or other
neutral oil

½ teaspoon red pepper flakes

1½ tablespoons soy sauce

1 tablespoon toasted sesame oil

1 tablespoon grated fresh ginger

Cilantro leaves, sliced scallions
and toasted sesame seeds, to
serve (optional)

SALT YOUR WAY
TO CRISPER VEGETABLES

A toss with salt and sugar—followed
by a brief rest and draining—helps
remove excess water from vegetables. The science at work is osmosis,
the movement of water across a cell
membrane. In our smashed cucumber salad, the ruptured cells release
water. When we add sugar and salt,
they dissolve and make a concentrated solution outside the cucumber
cells. The solution acts like a magnet
to draw out water, thus helping to dry
the cucumbers.

Slick, watery vegetables such as sliced cucumbers can be hard to season;
dressings tend to slide right off. Yet across Asia there is an whole class
of boldly flavored salads made entirely of cucumber. What do they know
that we don't? Our answer came from China's pai huang gua, or smashed
cucumber salad. In this case, it's the prep work—not the dressing—that
sets the dish apart. The cucumbers are smashed, banged and whacked.
This works for two reasons. First, it ruptures more cell walls than slicing
and dicing, making it easier to remove the seeds, the main culprit in
watery cucumbers. Second, it creates craggy, porous surfaces that absorb
more dressing. The easiest way to smash cucumbers is to place a rolling
pin or the flat side of a chef's knife over them and smack it sharply with
your hand. To draw out even more moisture from the cucumbers, we
borrowed another Asian technique, salting and sugaring. In China, dressings vary by region. We blurred regional lines, combining garlic, soy sauce,
fresh ginger and chili oil.

Don't substitute American cucumbers for English. *The ratio of seeds to flesh is
higher and the skins are too tough.*

1. Trim the ends off the cucumbers,
then halve lengthwise. Place each half
cut side down, then press a rolling pin or
the flat side of a broad knife against the
cucumber and hit firmly with the heel
of your hand. Repeat along the length of
the cucumbers until they crack. Pull the
sections apart, scraping and discarding
the seeds. Cut into rough ¾-inch pieces
and set in a large bowl.

2. In a small bowl, combine the sugar
and salt; toss the cucumbers with 5 teaspoons of the mixture. Transfer to a
colander set over a bowl. Refrigerate
for 30 to 60 minutes, tossing occasionally.
Meanwhile, stir the vinegar and garlic
into the remaining sugar-salt mixture.
Set aside.

3. In a small skillet over medium-low,
combine the grapeseed oil and pepper
flakes. Cook, stirring, until sizzling and
the pepper flakes begin to darken, 2 to
4 minutes. Strain the oil, discarding the
solids.

4. Remove and discard the garlic from
the vinegar mixture. Stir in the soy
sauce, sesame oil and ginger. Transfer
the drained cucumbers to a kitchen
towel and pat dry. In a bowl, stir together the cucumbers and dressing, then stir
in half of the chili oil. Serve drizzled with
more chili oil and sprinkled with cilantro,
scallions and sesame seeds, if desired.

French Carrot Salad

Start to finish: **20 minutes** / Servings: 6

2 tablespoons white balsamic vinegar

2 tablespoons chopped fresh tarragon

1 tablespoon minced shallot

1 teaspoon honey

⅛ teaspoon cayenne pepper

Kosher salt

¼ cup extra-virgin olive oil

1¼ pounds carrots, peeled and shredded

1 cup chopped fresh parsley

Carrots tend to be a woody afterthought on U.S. salad bars. Here, we transform them into a lively side dish by taking a tip from France, where grated carrots stand alone as an iconic side dish—salade de carottes râpées. Grating fresh carrots releases their sugars and aromas, creating an earthy sweetness that just needs a bit of acid for balance. Using relatively mild white balsamic vinegar allowed us to up the vinegar-to-oil ratio (1:2) for a punchy but not overwhelming flavor. White balsamic also paired well with a touch of honey, which heightened the carrots' natural sweetness. The French have long favored handheld rotary graters to make this salad, but we found the food processor was the fastest and easiest way to shred carrots. We also liked the meatier shreds it produces, though a box grater works fine, too. No tarragon? Use 1½ teaspoons chopped fresh thyme instead.

Don't use old bagged carrots. This salad is all about the earthy, sweet carrot flavor. Large carrots can be woody, dry and bitter; small baby carrots are too juicy. Look for bunches of medium carrots with the greens still attached.

In a large bowl, whisk together the vinegar, tarragon, shallot, honey, cayenne and 1 teaspoon of salt. Let sit for 10 minutes. Whisk in the oil until emulsified, then add the carrots and parsley. Stir until evenly coated. Season with salt. Serve or refrigerate for up to 24 hours.

THE GRATEFUL SHRED

Grating root vegetables such as carrots makes them taste sweeter and fresher than chopping or slicing. That's because when the vegetable is cut, its cells rupture and release sugars and volatile hydrocarbons, the sources of the vegetable's sweetness and aroma. The more cells you rupture, the better the taste. And grating ruptures more cells than just about any other prep technique.

Grating also changes how the vegetables interact with dressing. The process creates a more porous surface on the pieces of vegetable and exposes more of that surface. Therefore, more dressing comes into contact with more vegetable. This allows the dressing to have an outsized effect on the finished dish.

Japanese Potato Salad

Start to finish: **1 hour (15 minutes active)** / Servings: **4**

1 Persian cucumber, halved lengthwise and thinly sliced crosswise

1 medium carrot, peeled and shredded

¼ cup minced red onion

Kosher salt and ground black pepper

1½ pounds Yukon Gold potatoes, peeled and cut into ¾-inch pieces

3 tablespoons unseasoned rice vinegar

½ cup mayonnaise

2 ounces thick-cut smoked deli ham, diced (about ⅓ cup)

1 hard-cooked egg plus 1 hard-cooked egg yolk, diced

1 teaspoon white sugar

2 scallions, finely sliced

Getting potato salad right is no picnic. Too often the salad lacks the acidity or piquancy needed to cut through the richness of the mayonnaise. Our search for a better option led us to Japan, where potato salads are partially mashed to create a creamier texture. And they balance that texture with crumbled hard-boiled egg and the crisp bite of vegetables, such as cucumber and carrots. Tying everything together is Kewpie, a Japanese mayonnaise made with rice vinegar and egg yolks. It is smoother and richer than American mayonnaise. We started by looking for the right potatoes, which turned out to be Yukon Gold. Salting the cooking water ensured even seasoning, as did sprinkling them with vinegar and black pepper as they cooled. Waiting until the potatoes were at room temperature before adding mayonnaise was important to avoid oiliness. We used American mayonnaise but approximated the Kewpie flavor by increasing the vinegar and adding an extra hard-cooked egg yolk and 1 teaspoon of sugar. For a savory touch, we added diced ham and finished with scallions.

Don't substitute starchy russet or waxy new potatoes. The smooth texture of partly mashed Yukon Golds gave us the creamy consistency we wanted.

1. In a medium bowl, combine the cucumber, carrot, onion and 2 teaspoons of salt. Set aside. In a large saucepan over medium-high, combine the potatoes with enough water to cover by 1 inch. Add 1 teaspoon of salt and bring to a boil. Reduce heat to medium-high and simmer until tender, 12 to 15 minutes.

2. Drain the potatoes, then transfer to a large bowl. Using a fork, coarsely mash half of them. Sprinkle with the vinegar and ¾ teaspoon pepper. Stir to combine, then spread in an even layer along the bottom and sides of the bowl. Let cool for at least 20 minutes.

3. Transfer the vegetable mixture to a fine mesh strainer and rinse well. Working in batches, use your hands to squeeze the vegetables, removing as much liquid as possible, then add to the potatoes. Add the mayonnaise, ham, diced egg and yolk and sugar. Fold until thoroughly combined. Taste and season with salt and pepper, if necessary. Sprinkle with scallions, then serve chilled or at room temperature.

Skillet-Charred Brussels Sprouts
with Garlic, Anchovy and Chili

Start to finish: **25 minutes** / Servings: 4

1 pound small to medium Brussels sprouts, trimmed and halved

4 tablespoons extra-virgin olive oil, divided

4 teaspoons honey, divided

Kosher salt

4 garlic cloves, minced

4 anchovy fillets, minced

Red pepper flakes

2 teaspoons lemon juice

We loved the Brussels sprouts at Gjelina, a Los Angeles restaurant. Chef Travis Lett serves them with chili-lime vinaigrette, and they are both wonderfully charred and tender. We assumed they'd been roasted in a very hot oven. In fact, Lett had used a cast-iron skillet, a quicker and more efficient way to transfer heat. We tried it and loved the way the searing-hot skillet gave the sprouts a delicious char we'd never achieved in the oven. For the sauce, we were inspired by bagna càuda, the warm garlic- and anchovy-infused dip from Northern Italy, with red pepper flakes and a splash of lemon juice. A drizzle of honey in the dressing added a note of sweetness.

Don't use a stainless steel skillet. A well-seasoned cast-iron pan was key to this recipe. Stainless steel didn't hold the heat well enough to properly char. To comfortably accommodate the recipe, the pan needed to be at least 12 inches. And stick to small or medium sprouts; large ones didn't taste as good, containing a higher concentration of the compounds that lead to bitterness. Even smaller sprouts were best when cut in half, creating more surface area and contact with the skillet and therefore more charring.

1. In a large bowl, toss the sprouts with 1 tablespoon of the oil, 2 teaspoons of the honey and ½ teaspoon of salt. Set aside.

2. In a 12- to 14-inch cast-iron skillet over high, combine the remaining 3 tablespoons of oil, the garlic, anchovies and ¼ teaspoon pepper flakes. Cook, stirring, until the garlic begins to color, 3 to 4 minutes. Scrape the mixture, including the oil, into a bowl and set aside.

3. Return the skillet to high heat. Add the sprouts (reserve the bowl) and use tongs to arrange them cut side down in a single layer. Cook, without moving, until deeply browned and blackened in spots, 3 to 7 minutes, depending on your skillet. Use the tongs to flip the sprouts cut-side up and cook until charred and just tender, another 3 to 5 minutes.

4. As they finish, return the sprouts to the bowl and toss with the garlic mixture, the remaining 2 teaspoons of honey and the lemon juice. Season with salt and additional pepper flakes.

Hot Oil–Flashed Chard with
Ginger, Scallions and Chili

Start to finish: **20 minutes** / Servings: **4**

¼ cup water

¼ teaspoon kosher salt

2 large bunches Swiss chard
(1½ to 2 pounds), stems removed,
leaves sliced crosswise into
3-inch pieces

2 scallions, thinly sliced on a bias

1 tablespoon finely grated
fresh ginger

1 serrano chili, thinly sliced

2 tablespoons grapeseed oil

1 tablespoon toasted sesame oil

1 tablespoon unseasoned
rice vinegar

1 tablespoon soy sauce

2 teaspoons toasted
sesame seeds (optional)

Most hearty greens are naturally tough and bitter, requiring extended cooking. So we tamed and tenderized Swiss chard with sizzling oil, a technique we learned from cookbook author and Chinese cuisine expert Fuchsia Dunlop. Her recipe is modeled on a classic Cantonese method in which hot oil is poured over lightly blanched greens. We scattered fresh ginger, scallions and serrano chilies over our greens and found the hot oil bloomed the flavors beautifully. Instead of julienning the ginger, as is traditional, we used a wand-style grater to finely grate it, which distributed it better, was faster and released more of the aromatics. Bonus: No fibrous pieces in the finished dish. For the oil, we found the clean flavor and light texture of grapeseed oil was ideal, but vegetable oil worked well, too. We added toasted sesame oil for a savory touch. To finish the dish, soy sauce alone is fine, but even better was a blend of soy sauce and unseasoned rice vinegar, which added a gentle acidity and light sweetness.

Don't use the chard stems, but also don't throw them away. The stems are tougher than the leaves and won't cook through in the short time it takes to wilt the leaves. Chard stems do have good flavor, however, and can be sauteed, pickled or added to soups and stews.

1. In a large skillet over medium-high, bring the water and salt to a boil. Pile the chard into the pan and cover (the lid may not close completely). Cook until the chard is wilted, about 5 minutes, stirring halfway through. Remove the lid and cook, stirring occasionally, until most of the liquid has evaporated, 1 to 3 minutes. Transfer the chard to a serving platter and wipe out the skillet.

2. Distribute the scallions, ginger and chili evenly over the chard. Add both oils to the skillet and return to medium-high heat until very hot, 1 to 2 minutes. Pour the oils directly over the greens and aromatics (you should hear them sizzle) and toss to distribute. Drizzle the vinegar and soy sauce over the chard and toss again. Sprinkle with the sesame seeds, if using.

ADD SIZZLE
TO YOUR GREENS

Sizzling oil enhances ingredients such as scallions and grated fresh ginger because it draws out their flavors and aromas, yet leaves them tasting fresh. We used Swiss chard here, but this technique works for all manner of vegetables, from broccoli and cauliflower to tender green beans, shredded carrots and julienned sugar snap peas. More robust vegetables should be blanched first in salted water until just tender, then drained. This method also works on poached fish, shrimp, chicken or tofu.

CHINESE VEGETABLE CLEAVERS

American home cooks typically are told the triangular Western chef's knife is the one knife to rule them all. But most of Asia favors rectangular cleaver-like knives, such as the Chinese cai dao. They typically have blades about 8 inches long and 4 inches deep and are surprisingly light. Though proficiency with them involves a learning curve, we were impressed with the way they sliced, diced, chopped, smashed, pulverized and pounded. They also were arguably the most effective bench scraper we've used.

If you're game to try one, keep a few things in mind:

• The forward weight of the blade is different from the neutral balance of a Western knife. The knife leads you rather than you leading it.

• The blade's height changes the spatial relationship between the hand you keep on the knife and the hand you keep on the cutting board. With Western knives, both hands operate on similar planes. It can be disconcerting for them to be so far apart.

• Western blades work best with a rocking motion. Asian cleaver blades are mostly flat and require more of a push or chop.

• Handle a cai dao similar to a Western chef's knife. For the best control you should pinch the blade between your thumb and forefinger while the rest of your fingers wrap around the handle.

Cracked Potatoes with Vermouth, Coriander and Fennel

Start to finish: **35 minutes (10 minutes active)** / Servings: 4

1½ pounds small Yukon Gold potatoes (1½ to 2 inches in diameter)

2 tablespoons extra-virgin olive oil, divided

1 teaspoon kosher salt

¼ teaspoon ground black pepper

1 tablespoon salted butter

2 teaspoons coriander seeds, cracked

1 teaspoon fennel seeds, cracked

1 cup dry vermouth

As much as we like them, crispy, smashed potatoes are a bother. First you boil, then flatten, then crisp in fat. And half the time our potatoes fall apart. We wanted a one-stroke solution, which we found in potatoes afelia, a Cypriot dish that calls for cracking the potatoes when raw, then braising them. Our starting point was a recipe from London chefs Sam and Sam Clark of Moro. They whack raw potatoes, causing them to split and fracture slightly, but not break apart. Next, they cook them in a covered pan with oil and coriander seeds, a traditional afelia flavoring. Red wine, added at the end, simmers into a flavorful sauce. Back at Milk Street we got cracking. Hit too hard and the potatoes break; too gently and they're merely dented. A firm, controlled hit with a meat mallet was the answer. We preferred dry vermouth to red wine. We hate opening a bottle of wine just to cook with and almost always have an open bottle of dry vermouth, which as a fortified wine lasts longer and adds a clean, herbal flavor.

Don't use a skillet with an ill-fitting lid. If the moisture evaporates too quickly, the bottom of the pan can scorch. If the pan looks dry after 10 minutes, add water 2 tablespoons at a time.

1. Using a meat mallet or the bottom of a heavy skillet, whack the potatoes one at a time to crack them until slightly flattened but still intact. In a bowl, toss the potatoes with 1 tablespoon of the oil and the salt and pepper.

2. In a 12-inch stainless steel skillet over medium-high, heat the remaining 1 tablespoon of oil and the butter. Add the potatoes in a single layer, reduce heat to medium, then cook without moving until well browned, 6 to 8 minutes. Flip and cook until well browned on the other side, about 5 minutes.

3. Add the coriander and fennel. Cook, shaking the pan constantly, until fragrant, about 1 minute. Add the vermouth. Cover and reduce heat to medium-low. Cook until the potatoes are just tender and the liquid has nearly evaporated, 12 to 14 minutes, flipping the potatoes halfway through. Transfer to a serving bowl, scraping the sauce and seeds on top.

Sweet Potato Gratin with
Vanilla Bean and Bay Leaves

Start to finish: **3 hours (50 minutes active), plus cooling** / Servings: **8**

5 pounds sweet potatoes

1 cup heavy cream

4 bay leaves

1 vanilla bean

⅓ cup plus 1 tablespoon packed dark brown sugar, divided

1¼ teaspoons kosher salt

¾ teaspoon ground black pepper

⅓ cup white sugar

Pinch cayenne pepper

Sweet potato casserole is a Thanksgiving staple, but our version is delicious all year. We start by ditching the marshmallows and upping the flavor with a dash of spice. For ease, we roasted the sweet potatoes, a hands-off process that can be done a day ahead. Roasting rather than boiling produces cleaner, deeper flavors and a better, less watery texture. In lieu of marshmallows we infuse cream with vanilla bean and bay leaves and add a dusting of black pepper. A crunchy topping of dark brown and white sugar with a touch of cayenne keeps the dish appropriate for the adults' table.

Don't get distracted while the gratin is broiling; all broilers are different, and the difference between browned and burnt can be a matter of seconds.

1. Heat the oven to 400°F with one rack in the middle and another 6 inches from the broiler. Pierce the sweet potatoes with a fork and arrange on a rimmed baking sheet. Bake on the middle rack, turning once, until tender, 1 to 1½ hours. Let cool. Increase oven to 425°F.

2. Meanwhile, in a medium saucepan, combine the cream and bay leaves. With a paring knife, split the vanilla bean lengthwise, then scrape out the seeds. Add the seeds and pod to the cream and bring to a simmer over medium-high. Set aside, covered, for 30 minutes. Strain out and discard the solids.

3. Once the potatoes have cooled, scrape the flesh from the skins; discard the skins. In a food processor, combine half the flesh and half the infused cream. Add 1 tablespoon of the brown sugar, the salt and pepper. Process until smooth, about 1 minute, scraping the

bowl halfway through; transfer to a large bowl. Repeat with the remaining potatoes and cream, then add to the first batch. Mix well, then transfer to a 13-by-9-inch broiler safe baking dish. Smooth the top.

4. In a bowl, stir together the remaining ⅓ cup of brown sugar, the white sugar and the cayenne. Transfer to a medium mesh strainer, then evenly sift the mixture over the surface of the potatoes (or do by hand). Brush any sugar off the rim of the baking dish.

5. Bake on the middle rack until bubbling at the edges, about 20 minutes. Remove from the oven, then heat the broiler. When ready, place the dish on the upper rack and broil until deeply browned and crisp, 2 to 7 minutes. Let sit for 20 minutes before serving.

Celery Root Puree

Start to finish: **45 minutes** / Servings: **8**

2 pounds celery root, peeled and cut into 1-inch pieces

1 pound Yukon Gold potatoes, peeled and cut into 1-inch pieces

2 cups half-and-half

2 cups whole milk

4 garlic cloves, peeled and smashed

4 sprigs fresh thyme

Kosher salt

8 tablespoons (1 stick) salted butter

Ground black pepper

Chopped fresh chives

We give mashed potatoes a sophisticated spin with an unlikely candidate: celery root. Also known as celeriac, this vegetable gets little attention in American kitchens—perhaps because of its less than beautiful appearance. When cooked and processed, however, the knobby, gnarled root transforms into a subtler, version of mashed potatoes with a light, fresh celery flavor. To balance that lightness, we paired celery root with Yukon Golds, producing a medium-bodied puree. We cooked the vegetables in a mixture of milk and half-and-half, a combination that won't dilute or mask celery root's flavor. A stick of butter gave the puree a silky texture. We liked the flavors of thyme and garlic, but small amounts of sage, rosemary and marjoram worked, too. The cooled puree can be refrigerated for two days; rewarm in a saucepan over low heat and check the seasoning before serving.

Don't add too much cooking liquid right away as the moisture content of starchy vegetables can vary. If your puree is loose, start with just a splash and go from there.

1. In a large saucepan over high, combine the celery root, potatoes, half-and-half, milk, garlic, thyme and 1½ teaspoons salt. Bring to a boil, then cover, leaving the lid slightly ajar, and reduce heat to low. Simmer, stirring occasionally, until the vegetables are tender, about 25 minutes. The mixture will froth and foam and may appear curdled; watch carefully to prevent boiling over.

2. Drain the vegetables, reserving the liquid. Remove and discard the thyme sprigs, then transfer the solids to a food processor. Process until smooth, about 1 minute. Return to the pan along with the butter. Set over low heat and cook, stirring occasionally, until the butter is melted. Starting with ½ cup, gradually stir in the reserved cooking liquid until the puree reaches the desired consistency. The puree should be not quite pourable. Taste and season with salt and pepper. Sprinkle with chives.

THE MATTER OF THE ROOT

Between its lumpy shape, thick skin and gnarly tangle of roots, celery root can be a real challenge, but not an insurmountable one. To start, use a strong knife to chop off the bottom (root end) of the bulb. Use a Y-style peeler to peel and discard the skin (you may need to use a paring knife for thicker skins). Cut out any discolored veins that may be left. Once peeled, cut the root into chunks to be used as is—as we do in our celery puree—or thinly slice using a mandolin or food processor to use fresh in a salad, such as a classic French remoulade.

Sweet-and-Spicy Ginger Green Beans

Start to finish: **10 minutes** / Servings: 4

2 tablespoons packed
light brown sugar

1 tablespoon fish sauce

1 tablespoon soy sauce

3 tablespoons grapeseed
or other neutral oil, divided

1 pound green beans, stemmed
and halved crosswise on a bias

¼ cup water

1 tablespoon finely grated
fresh ginger

½ teaspoon red pepper flakes

2 tablespoons unseasoned
rice vinegar

Ground white pepper

The challenge of stir-frying green beans is that, more often than not, the frills slide off and you're left biting into a bland bean. The key is cooking them in a sauce that actually sticks. Chef Charles Phan, owner of The Slanted Door, a popular Vietnamese restaurant in San Francisco, caramelizes sugar, then stir-fries string beans in the blistering heat of a wok. A final toss with sake and fish sauce coats the charred beans with a dark, bittersweet sauce. We adjusted the recipe to work without a wok. Phan's recipe calls for blanching the beans first. We simplified by adding the beans to a very hot pan with a small amount of oil, then making a sauce around them as they cooked. We found a Dutch oven worked best to control splattering—drying the beans thoroughly also helped (though a large skillet works in a pinch). Cutting the beans on a bias gave us more surface area for better browning. To re-create Phan's flavorful sauce—itself a take on nuoc mau, or Vietnamese caramel sauce—we used brown sugar instead of taking the time to caramelize white sugar. It gave us comparable depth and flavor.

Don't use an ill-fitting lid. A proper seal is key to this recipe, whether you cook the beans in a Dutch oven or a skillet. Have the lid ready as soon as you add the water.

1. In a small bowl, stir together the sugar, fish and soy sauces. Set aside.

2. In a large Dutch oven or 12-inch skillet over medium-high, heat 2 tablespoons of the oil until beginning to smoke. Add the beans and cook, without stirring, until beginning to color, about 3 minutes. Add the water and immediately cover the pan. Cook until the beans are bright green and barely tender, about 2 minutes.

3. Clear a space in the center of the pan, then add the remaining 1 tablespoon of oil to the clearing. Stir in the ginger and pepper flakes, then cook until fragrant, about 30 seconds. Stir the the sugar-fish sauce mixture then pour it into the skillet and cook, stirring occasionally, until the liquid has thickened and coats the beans, about 1 minute. Off heat, stir in the vinegar. Taste and season with pepper.

Cauliflower with Tahini

Start to finish: **35 minutes** / Servings: **4**

½ cup tahini

1 teaspoon grated lemon zest,
plus 2 tablespoons lemon juice,
divided

2 tablespoons extra-virgin
olive oil, plus more to serve

2 garlic cloves, grated

1½ teaspoons kosher salt

1 teaspoon sweet paprika

¼ to ½ teaspoon cayenne pepper

1 large head cauliflower
(about 2½ pounds), cut into
1½- to 2-inch florets

⅓ cup roasted, salted cashews,
chopped

⅓ cup chopped fresh cilantro

Cauliflower's been getting the celebrity treatment lately, but we liked it before it was cool for its mild, nutty flavor. In this take, we roasted florets with a tahini sauce brightened with lemon juice and cayenne. We used cilantro in our sauce, but flat-leaf parsley worked as a substitute. When buying cauliflower, look for a head with densely packed florets. Medium florets, about 1½ to 2 inches, were best in this dish; smaller pieces became mushy. And having a hot oven and heated baking sheet were key to browning the cauliflower before it overcooked. For a crunchy, nutty alternative, substitute ⅓ cup dukkah (see sidebar) for the cashews.

Don't forget to line the baking sheet with foil before heating. The tahini mixture makes a mess of an unlined pan.

1. Heat the oven to 500°F with a rack in the lowest position. Line a rimmed baking sheet with foil and set on the rack to heat. In a large bowl, whisk together the tahini, lemon zest, 1 tablespoon of the lemon juice, the oil, garlic, salt, paprika and cayenne. Add the cauliflower and toss, massaging the dressing into the florets.

2. Working quickly, remove the baking sheet from the oven and carefully spread the cauliflower on it in an even layer, scraping any remaining tahini onto the florets.

Reserve the bowl. Roast until well browned in spots and just tender, 15 to 18 minutes, stirring and turning the florets and rotating the pan halfway through.

3. Transfer the roasted florets to the reserved bowl. Add the remaining 1 tablespoon of lemon juice and toss. Add half of the nuts and the cilantro and toss. Sprinkle with the remaining cashews and serve drizzled with more oil, if desired.

EGYPTIAN NUT-AND-SEED SEASONING (DUKKAH)

The Egyptian seasoning mixture known as dukkah—a rich blend of seeds, nuts and spices—adds welcome texture and complexity to dips and salads, and even can be used as a rub for meat or fish. It began as peasant fare, used to give flavor to coarse bread. In the U.S., dukkah has found popularity with restaurant chefs. It can be bought ready-made from spice shops (and Trader Joe's), but the best way to enjoy it is to make your own. Store in an airtight container at room temperature for up to a week. Freeze for longer use.

Start to finish: **15 minutes**
Makes **about 1 cup**

½ cup raw cashews

2 tablespoons sesame seeds

2 tablespoons coriander seeds

2 tablespoons cumin seeds

1 tablespoon caraway seeds

1 teaspoon dried oregano

½ teaspoon kosher salt

½ teaspoon ground black pepper

In a large skillet over medium, toast the cashews, stirring, until beginning to brown, 3 to 4 minutes. Add the sesame seeds and toast, stirring, until golden, 1 to 2 minutes. Add the coriander, cumin and caraway, and toast, stirring, until fragrant, about 1 minute. Transfer to a food processor and let cool for 5 minutes. Add the oregano, salt and pepper. Pulse until coarsely ground, 12 to 15 pulses.

Harissa Roasted Potatoes

Start to finish: **1 hour (10 minutes active)** / Servings: 4

2 pounds Yukon Gold potatoes, peeled and cut into 1½-inch pieces

4 ounces shallots (about 4 small), peeled and quartered

2 tablespoons extra-virgin olive oil

1 teaspoon kosher salt

½ teaspoon ground black pepper

6 tablespoons harissa, divided (recipe p. 250)

⅓ cup chopped flat-leaf fresh parsley

1 tablespoon lemon juice, plus lemon wedges to serve

Harissa (pronounced ha-REE-sah) may well be one of the original hot sauces. It's generally believed to have originated in Tunisia, where it's often served with couscous and brik, a tuna-and-egg turnover. This recipe uses our piquant, homemade harissa sauce (p. 250) to give potatoes a sweet-spicy kick, but harissa also can be found online and in the grocer's international aisle. Tossing the raw potatoes with harissa before roasting muted the chili paste's flavor, so we crisped "naked" potatoes on the bottom rack first, then tossed them with a portion of the harissa and returned them to the oven. That gave the potatoes the right texture and a spicy crust. A final hit of the remaining harissa, along with parsley and lemon juice, kept the flavors bright.

Don't forget to taste your harissa for heat and pungency before tossing the potatoes. A harissa with gentle heat and smooth texture, like Milk Street's recipe (p. 250), worked best here. If your variety is particularly spicy, you may want to reduce the total amount to ¼ cup, reserving 1 tablespoon to finish the dish.

1. Heat the oven to 400°F with racks in the middle and lowest positions and a rimmed baking sheet on the bottom rack. In a large bowl, toss the potatoes and shallots with the oil, salt and pepper.

2. Working quickly, remove the baking sheet from the oven, add the potato-shallot mixture and spread in an even layer; reserve the bowl. Roast on the bottom rack until the potatoes are well browned on the bottoms, about 20 minutes, rotating the sheet halfway through.

3. Use a thin metal spatula to transfer the potatoes to the reserved bowl, scraping up any browned bits. Add 4 tablespoons of the harissa and toss until evenly coated. Return the potatoes to the sheet, spreading in an even layer and reserving the bowl. Roast on the middle rack until tender, 18 to 22 minutes, rotating the sheet halfway through.

4. Return the potatoes to the reserved bowl, scraping up any browned bits from the pan. Add the parsley, the remaining 2 tablespoons of harissa and the lemon juice. Toss to coat. Serve with lemon wedges.

Austrian Potato Salad

Start to finish: 30 minutes / Servings: 4

2 pounds Yukon Gold potatoes, peeled, halved and sliced ¼-inch thick

2 cups low-sodium chicken broth

Kosher salt

¼ cup finely chopped cornichons, plus 1 tablespoon brine

2 tablespoons red wine vinegar, divided

Ground black pepper

½ cup diced red onion (about ½ medium)

½ teaspoon caraway seeds

¼ cup grapeseed or other neutral oil

1 tablespoon Dijon mustard

½ cup diced celery (about 2 medium stalks)

2 hard-boiled eggs, chopped (optional)

¼ cup chopped fresh dill

Our ongoing quest to take potato salad from humdrum to humming took us to Austria, where they don't drown their potato salads in mayonnaise. In this version, the flavor starts early as the potatoes are simmered in a mixture of chicken broth and water. Onions and caraway seeds also go into the pot, softening the flavors of both. Always loath to flush flavor down the drain, we save some of the seasoned, starchy cooking liquid to help thicken a dressing made tangy with mustard, oil and vinegar. If your potatoes are quite large, quarter them instead of halving before slicing. To add crunch, we used celery; you also could add chopped hard-boiled eggs. A handful of fresh dill made for a bright finish.

Don't overcook—or undercook—the potatoes. They should be firm but not grainy, creamy in the center and just starting to fall apart at the edges. This texture is important, as some of the potatoes will break down into the salad. But if they're too soft, they will turn into mashed potatoes.

1. In a medium saucepan, combine the potatoes, broth and 2 teaspoons salt. Add enough water to just cover the potatoes. Bring to a boil over medium-high. Reduce heat to medium-low and simmer until just tender, 8 to 10 minutes. Drain, reserving ½ cup of the cooking liquid, and transfer to a large bowl. Sprinkle with the cornichon brine, 1 tablespoon of the vinegar and ½ teaspoon pepper.

2. In the empty pan, combine the reserved cooking liquid with the onion and caraway seeds and bring to a simmer over medium-high. Pour the mixture over the potatoes and stir well. Let sit, stirring occasionally, until the liquid is absorbed and thickened, about 10 minutes.

3. Meanwhile, in a liquid measuring cup, whisk together the oil, mustard, the remaining 1 tablespoon of vinegar, ¾ teaspoon salt and ½ teaspoon pepper until emulsified. To the potatoes, add the dressing, celery, eggs, if using, cornichons and dill, then fold until evenly coated. Taste and season with salt and pepper. Serve at room temperature.

Grains

5

Quinoa Pilaf with Dates, Almonds and Carrot Juice

Start to finish: 40 minutes (15 minutes active) / Servings: 4

___

2 tablespoons salted butter

1 medium carrot, peeled and diced (about ½ cup)

1 small yellow onion, diced (about ½ cup)

Kosher salt

1 cup white quinoa

1 tablespoon finely grated fresh ginger

1 teaspoon ground cumin

½ cup carrot juice

¾ cup water

4 medjool dates, pitted and diced

⅓ cup chopped almonds or cashews, toasted

2 scallions, trimmed and chopped

3 tablespoons chopped fresh dill, plus more to garnish

1 teaspoon grated lemon zest, plus 1 tablespoon lemon juice

Ground black pepper

Extra-virgin olive oil, for drizzling (optional)

We like the nutty, earthy flavor and gentle crunch of quinoa, but too often salads made with this seed—it's technically not a grain—end up mushy and flavorless. For a better way, we looked to Deborah Madison, author of "Vegetarian Cooking for Everyone." She cooks her quinoa in carrot juice, a winning combination that perked up its natural sweetness and tempered its tendency to muddiness. We also likea a quinoa by Erik Ramirez of Brooklyn's Llama Inn. He makes a famously madcap quinoa pilaf studded with bananas, bacon, cashews and avocado, which showed us that texture and contrast can make the often insipid seed exciting. We liked a simple combo of chewy-sweet dates and crunchy almonds. We took a three-step approach to keeping our pilaf light and fluffy: first toasting the quinoa, then cooking it with less liquid than typically called for, and finally letting the cooked quinoa rest before fluffing. For texture, we added dates and almonds or cashews; both worked. Finishing with scallions, lemon and fresh dill brightened the final dish. Eat this as is or pair it with sautéed shrimp, broiled salmon or fried tofu.

Don't worry about rinsing the quinoa. Most varieties sold in the U.S. are pre-rinsed. Just check the packaging.

___

1. In a medium saucepan over medium, melt the butter. Add the carrot, onion and ¼ teaspoon salt. Cook, stirring, until softened, 3 to 5 minutes. Add the quinoa and cook, stirring, until fragrant and beginning to pop, about 5 minutes. Stir in the ginger and cumin. Cook, stirring, for 1 minute. Add the carrot juice, water and ½ teaspoon salt. Bring to a boil. Cover, reduce to medium-low and cook until the liquid is absorbed, 11 to 13 minutes.

2. Remove the pan from the heat and uncover. Sprinkle in the dates, cover the pan with a kitchen towel and replace the lid. Let sit for 10 minutes. Fluff the quinoa with a fork, then add the almonds or cashews, scallions, dill, lemon zest and juice. Stir gently to combine, season with salt and pepper, then garnish with dill and a drizzle of olive oil, if desired.

LIKE CARROT JUICE FOR WATER

Substituting another liquid for water
when cooking lets you nudge the flavor
factor up a notch with little effort. In
our quinoa pilaf, for example, we cook
the seeds in diluted carrot juice, which
mitigates their subtle bitterness. And
for our Chinese white-cooked chicken
(p. 144), we recommend cooking an
accompanying pot of rice in the warm
broth generated by the cooked bird,
infusing the meal with every bit of
meaty flavor. This works for sweets, too.
Our caramel oranges (p. 222) get added
depth by swapping fresh orange juice
for the water typically used to dissolve
the sugar for the caramel sauce. Try
this different ways. Use broth or diluted
vegetable juices to cook grains, or puree
soft fresh herbs and a garlic clove or
two in water, then use that to cook rice or
bulgur. Be mindful that acidic ingredients
can change the rate at which starches
cook. You can add tomato flavor to rice
as we do in our Indian tomato rice
(p. 101), but don't try to cook rice in
tomato juice; the rice will turn out mushy
and unevenly cooked.

Thai Fried Rice

Start to finish: **20 minutes** / Servings: 4

1 tablespoon fish sauce

1 teaspoon soy sauce

1 teaspoon water

1 teaspoon white sugar

4 cups cooked and chilled jasmine rice

1 tablespoon peanut or vegetable oil

2 eggs, lightly beaten

4 ounces thinly sliced pancetta, chopped

4 scallions, white and green parts thinly sliced, reserved separately

1 large shallot, minced

1 garlic clove, minced

¼ cup chopped fresh cilantro

Sliced cucumber and lime wedges, to serve

Cooked in under five minutes in the open-air kitchen of his home in Thailand, chef Andy Ricker's fried rice was speedy, simple—and delicious. Pork belly, shallot and garlic added bold flavors. Soy and fish sauces added savory depth. Fresh herbs kept everything bright and light. We returned to Milk Street and got to work deconstructing Thai cooking, which is perfectly suited to home kitchens in the U.S. Ricker prefers to use a wok because it allows him to move food away from the hot oil at the center to the cooler sides of the pan. In a nod to the Western kitchen, we began with a large nonstick skillet, though you can use a wok if you have one (and a burner powerful enough to heat it). Pork belly can be hard to find in the U.S.. Looking for a substitute we found ground pork too greasy and bacon too smoky. Pancetta—if culturally odd—was just right, which makes sense since it's cured pork belly. In a skillet, we had to reverse-engineer the process and move foods in and out, starting with the eggs, then the pancetta. We liked the aromatic flavor of jasmine rice, but long-grain white or basmati work, too. If you have no leftover rice, follow our recipe (see sidebar). Thai restaurants offer condiments for fried rice, including sliced green chilies in white vinegar. We came up with our own (p. 273). Use it with the fried rice or any dish that needs a hit of gentle heat and acid.

Don't use hot or warm rice. The fried rice will be clumpy and gummy (see sidebar).

1. In a bowl, stir together the fish sauce, soy sauce, water and sugar. Set aside. Use your hands to break up the rice so no clumps remain. Set aside.

2. In a 12-inch nonstick skillet over medium-high, heat the oil until just smoking. Pour in the eggs and cook, stirring, until just set. Transfer the eggs to a plate. Add the pancetta to the skillet and cook over medium until crisp. Using a slotted spoon, transfer to the plate with the eggs.

3. Pour off all but 1 tablespoon of the fat from the skillet and return to medium-high. Add the scallion whites, shallot and garlic and cook until softened, about 1 minute. Add the rice and cook, stirring occasionally, until heated through, about 2 minutes.

4. Stir the fish sauce mixture, then pour over the rice. Cook, stirring, until well mixed. Stir in the egg and pancetta, breaking up the eggs. Transfer to a large platter and sprinkle with cilantro and scallion greens. Serve with cucumber, lime wedges and fish sauce–pickled chilies (p. 273), if desired.

RICE AT THE READY

While our Thai fried rice takes just minutes to prepare, it does require cooked-and-cooled plain rice. Warm, freshly cooked rice won't work; it sticks to the pan and turns gummy. For rice to fry, its starches must first cool and recrystallize. Fresh rice needed two hours minimum to chill adequately, but it can be prepared up to three days in advance and kept refrigerated. For real make-ahead convenience, cooked rice also can be frozen. Make a batch or two, then freeze in zip-close plastic bags.

Rice for Thai Fried Rice

Start to finish: 20 minutes, plus cooling
Makes 4 cups

2 cups water

1½ cups jasmine rice, rinsed

½ teaspoon kosher salt

Line a rimmed baking sheet with kitchen parchment and lightly coat it with vegetable oil. In a large saucepan, combine the water, rice and salt. Bring to a simmer, then reduce to low, cover and cook until tender and fluffy, 15 to 18 minutes. Fluff with a fork, then spread on the prepared baking sheet. Let cool, then cover and refrigerate until cold.

Coconut Rice

Start to finish: **35 minutes (10 minutes active)** / Servings: **4**

2 tablespoons coconut oil

½ cup unsweetened shredded coconut

1½ cups jasmine rice, rinsed

¾ cup water

14-ounce can coconut milk, shaken

1 teaspoon kosher salt

Plain rice needs to be paired with a flavorful counterpoint, otherwise it's just a bowl of bland. Fiery curries, for example, are a great partner. But what if you're not into (or in the mood for) heat? We found our flavor in coconut rice, a dish popular in India and Southeast Asia, where it appears in many forms. It's quick and easy to assemble and has layers of flavor. We start by toasting unsweetened coconut in coconut oil, which gave us a pleasant texture as well as flavor. The rice went in next and we added unsweetened coconut milk at two stages: as the rice cooked and at the very end. We chose jasmine rice for its aromatic flavor. Gentle heat ensured the liquid wouldn't boil over and the rice wouldn't burn on the bottom. Our finished rice made the perfect accompaniment to grilled or roasted meats and fish. We like to cook extra and use leftovers in fried rice, salads or to pair with fried eggs for breakfast. It's even good as a sweet snack with a sprinkle of brown sugar or drizzle of honey.

Don't use a small saucepan. If the cooking liquid bubbles over, the sugar will cause it to smoke and burn. A medium or large heavy-bottomed saucepan was best.

1. In a medium saucepan over medium, combine the oil and shredded coconut. Cook, stirring, until lightly toasted, 1 to 2 minutes. Add the rice and cook, stirring, until some of the grains are translucent and a few begin to pop, about 2 minutes. Stir in the water, all but 2 tablespoons of the coconut milk and the salt.

2. Bring to a simmer, stirring and scraping the bottom of the pan frequently. Reduce heat to low, cover and cook until the liquid is absorbed, 15 to 18 minutes. Remove from the heat and let sit, covered, for 5 minutes. Drizzle in the reserved coconut milk, then fluff and stir.

Herb-and-Pistachio Couscous

Start to finish: **30 minutes** / Servings: 6

1 cup couscous

3 tablespoons dried currants

½ teaspoon ground cumin

Kosher salt and ground black pepper

¾ cup boiling water

6 tablespoons extra-virgin olive oil, divided, plus more for serving

2 cups lightly packed fresh cilantro leaves and tender stems

2 cups lightly packed fresh flat-leaf parsley leaves

2 tablespoons finely chopped pickled jalapenos, plus 2 teaspoons brine

2 ounces baby arugula, coarsely chopped (about 2 cups)

½ cup shelled pistachios, toasted and chopped

2 scallions, trimmed and thinly sliced

Couscous may be fast and convenient to prepare, but it's also pretty dull. And the traditional method of infusing it with flavor—steaming it in a special pot over a flavorful liquid—just isn't happening. We found a better way by undercooking—technically underhydrating—the couscous by preparing it with less water than typically called for. We then combine the couscous with a flavorful paste made from oil and pureed fresh herbs. The "thirsty" couscous absorbs tons of flavor as it finishes hydrating. Inspired by a recipe from Yotam Ottolenghi, we piled on the herbs—2 cups each of cilantro and flat-leaf parsley plus another 2 cups of arugula. We also added currants as we doused the couscous with boiling water, giving them time to plump. Jalapenos brought a spicy kick; we used pickled peppers, which have more consistent heat and contributed welcome piquancy. Toasted pistachios and thinly sliced scallions added a finishing crunch. The couscous pairs well with most any meat, though it is particularly good with salmon.

Don't use Israeli (also called pearl) couscous, which won't hydrate sufficiently in this recipe.

1. In a large bowl, combine the couscous, currants, cumin and ¼ teaspoon each salt and black pepper. Stir in the boiling water and 1 tablespoon of the oil, then cover and let sit for 10 minutes.

2. Meanwhile, in a food processor, combine the cilantro, parsley, the remaining 5 tablespoons of oil, the jalapeno brine and ¼ teaspoon salt. Process until a smooth paste forms, about 1 minute, scraping down the bowl 2 or 3 times.

3. Fluff the couscous with a fork, breaking up any large clumps, then stir in the herb paste until thoroughly combined. Fold in the jalapenos, arugula, pistachios and scallions, then let sit for 10 minutes. Season with salt and pepper. Serve at room temperature, drizzled with oil.

Indian Tomato Rice

Start to finish: 35 minutes (15 minutes active) / Servings: 4

1 cup white basmati rice, rinsed

1¼ cups water

2 tablespoons tomato paste

2 tablespoons grapeseed or other neutral oil

1 teaspoon cumin seeds

1 teaspoon coriander seeds

1 teaspoon brown or black mustard seeds

2 bird's eye chilies, stemmed and halved lengthwise (optional)

1 garlic clove, finely grated

1 teaspoon finely grated fresh ginger

1½ teaspoons kosher salt

½ pound cherry or grape tomatoes, quartered

¼ cup chopped fresh cilantro leaves

Robust tomato flavor is key to this popular southern Indian dish, typically prepared when there is an abundance of ripe, red tomatoes and leftover basmati rice. It can be eaten as a light meal with a dollop of yogurt or pairs well with seafood, poultry or even a simple fried egg. We needed a year-round recipe, so we concentrated on finding the best way to impart deep tomato flavor. A combination of cherry or grape tomatoes and tomato paste was best. We also focused on making sure the rice was cooked properly, fluffy and tender with each grain separate. We were inspired by Madhur Jaffrey's tomato rice recipe in "Vegetarian India," though we upped the intensity of both the spices and tomato flavor. We preferred brown or black mustard seeds for their pungency; if you substitute yellow mustard seeds, increase the volume to 1½ teaspoons. Serrano chilies can be used in place of bird's eye chilies, also called Thai bird or Thai chilies. Or you can leave them out entirely. If your pan does not have a tight-fitting lid, cover it with foil before putting the lid in place.

Don't skip soaking the rice. This traditional approach to cooking the rice gives it time to expand gently and cook up in tender, separate grains.

1. In a bowl, combine the rinsed rice with enough cold water to cover by 1 inch. Let soak for 15 minutes. Drain the rice very well. In a 2-cup liquid measuring cup, combine the 1¼ cups water and the tomato paste and whisk until dissolved. Set aside.

2. In a large saucepan over medium, combine the oil, cumin, coriander, mustard seeds, chilies, garlic and ginger. Cook until the seeds begin to pop and the mixture is fragrant, about 1 minute.

3. Stir in the rice and salt and cook, stirring, until coated with oil, about 30 seconds. Stir in the water-tomato paste mixture and bring to a simmer. Cover, reduce heat to low and cook until the water has been absorbed, about 15 minutes. Remove from the heat, add the tomatoes and let sit, covered, for 5 minutes. Stir in the cilantro, fluffing the rice with a fork.

Suppers

Punjabi Chickpeas with Potato (*Chole*)

Start to finish: **45 minutes** / Servings: **4**

1 large red onion

4 tablespoons grapeseed or other neutral oil, divided

1½ teaspoons ground coriander

1 teaspoon ground cardamom

1 teaspoon sweet paprika

½ teaspoon cinnamon

¼ teaspoon ground cloves

¼ teaspoon nutmeg

⅛ teaspoon cayenne pepper

Kosher salt and ground black pepper

1 teaspoon cumin seeds

¾ pound russet potatoes (about 2 medium potatoes), peeled and cut into ½-inch cubes

1 tablespoon finely grated fresh ginger

3 garlic cloves, finely grated

1 tablespoon tomato paste

1½ cups water

Two 15½-ounce cans chickpeas, drained

1 tablespoon lime juice, plus lime wedges, to serve

¼ cup coarsely chopped cilantro leaves, plus more to garnish

Chopped fresh tomato, thinly sliced bird's eye or serrano chilies and whole-milk Greek-style yogurt, to serve (optional)

Seasoning blends known as masalas are the backbone of much of Indian cooking. But they often involve intimidatingly long lists of spices, each requiring toasting and grinding. Buying prepared blends is easier, but they can taste faded and stale. For our chole (pronounced CHO-lay)—a chickpea curry popular in India and Pakistan—we mix our own garam masala, a warm seasoning blend that features cayenne pepper and cinnamon. To make the sauce, we started with onion cooked until it practically melted. Grating the onion before browning to help it cook faster and gave it a better texture. Amchoor powder made from dried green mangoes gives traditional chole its characteristic tang, but we found lime juice was a good—and more convenient—substitute. When preparing this dish, make sure your potato pieces are no larger than ½ inch thick so they cook in time. Chole typically is eaten with flatbread, such as roti or nan.

Don't use a nonstick skillet for this recipe; the fond (browned bits on the bottom of the pan) won't form, which will alter the chole's flavor. And don't be deterred by the lengthy list of spices here. Most are pantry staples and are key to producing the dish's complex flavor.

1. Using the large holes of a box grater, grate the onion, then transfer to a mesh strainer and drain. In a small bowl, stir together 1 tablespoon of the oil with the coriander, cardamom, paprika, cinnamon, cloves, nutmeg, cayenne, 1¼ teaspoons salt and ½ teaspoon pepper.

2. In a 12-inch skillet over medium-high, heat the remaining 3 tablespoons of oil. Add the cumin seeds and cook, shaking the pan, until the seeds are fragrant and darken, 30 to 60 seconds. Add the drained onion and cook, stirring frequently, until the moisture has evaporated, 1 to 3 minutes. Add the potatoes, reduce heat to medium and cook, stirring frequently, until the onions begin to brown and a fond forms on the bottom of the pan, 6 to 8 minutes. Add the ginger, garlic and tomato paste, then cook for 1 minute, stirring constantly.

3. Clear the center of the pan, then add the spice paste to the clearing and cook, mashing and stirring until fragrant, about 15 seconds. Stir into the vegetables. Add the water and bring to a boil, scraping up all the browned bits. Add the chickpeas and return to a boil, then cover, reduce heat to low and cook until the potatoes are tender and the oil separates from the sauce at the edges of the pan, 13 to 15 minutes.

4. Off the heat, stir in the lime juice and cilantro. Taste and season with salt and pepper. Serve with lime wedges, chopped tomato, chilies and yogurt, if desired.

Spanish Spice-Crusted **Pork Tenderloin Bites** (*Pinchos Morunos*)

Start to finish: **50 minutes (25 minutes active)** / Servings: **4**

1½ teaspoons ground coriander

1½ teaspoons ground cumin

1½ teaspoons smoked paprika

¾ teaspoon each kosher salt and coarsely ground black pepper

1-pound pork tenderloin, trimmed and cut into 1- to 1½-inch pieces

1 tablespoon lemon juice, plus lemon wedges for serving

1 tablespoon honey

1 large garlic clove, finely grated

2 tablespoons extra-virgin olive oil, divided

1 tablespoon chopped fresh oregano

Loosely translated as "Moorish bites impaled on thorns or small pointed sticks," pinchos morunos is a Basque dish of seared pork tenderloin rubbed with a blend of spices, garlic, herbs and olive oil. The recipe dates back generations, boasting influences from Spain and North Africa. Classic versions skewer the meat, which is seasoned with ras el hanout, a Moroccan spice blend, among other flavorings. We streamlined, nixing the skewers. And since ras al hanout can be hard to find, we went with a blend of cumin, coriander and black pepper. A bit of smoked paprika added the requisite Basque touch. We finished with a drizzle of honey, which heightened the flavor of the pork and seasonings. Don't cut the tenderloin too small. Cutting it into 1- to 1½-inch pieces produced more surface area, allowing the spice rub to quickly penetrate and season the meat. Any smaller and the meat cooked too quickly.

1. In a medium bowl, combine the coriander, cumin, paprika, salt and pepper. Add the pork and toss to coat evenly, massaging the spices into the meat until no dry rub remains. Let the pork sit at room temperature for at least 30 minutes and up to 1 hour. Meanwhile, in another bowl, combine the lemon juice, honey and garlic. Set aside.

2. In a large skillet over high, heat 1 tablespoon of the oil until just smoking. Add the meat in a single layer and cook without moving until deeply browned on one side, about 3 minutes. Using tongs, flip the pork and cook, turning occasionally, until cooked through and browned all over, another 2 to 3 minutes. Off the heat, pour the lemon juice-garlic mixture over the meat and toss to evenly coat, then transfer to a serving platter. Sprinkle the oregano over the pork and drizzle with the remaining 1 tablespoon of oil. Serve with lemon wedges.

Hot-Smoked Salmon Salad with Arugula, Avocado and Pepitas

Start to finish: **15 minutes** / Servings: 4

¼ cup lemon juice (about 1 lemon)

2 tablespoons whole-grain mustard

1 tablespoon honey

Kosher salt and ground black pepper

6 tablespoons extra-virgin olive oil

8 ounces hot-smoked salmon, plain or black pepper, skin removed

½ cup toasted, salted pepitas, coarsely chopped

2 avocados

10 ounces baby arugula or stemmed watercress (about 10 cups)

Ingredients with contrasting flavors and textures are an easy way to elevate everyday meals. And it's key to one of Nigella Lawson's go-to Tuesday night dinners, which upsells basic poached salmon by pairing it with crunchy and tangy ingredients. Lawson simply flakes the salmon into a salad with some watercress, avocado, pumpkin seeds and tangy vinegar. The lush avocado complements the rich salmon, both of which are balanced by the vinegar and pumpkin seeds. The greens add freshness, while the pepitas lend texture. Our Milk Street version saves time by using hot-smoked salmon, which has a texture similar to cooked salmon, but with an intensely smoky flavor and sweet and salty overtones. We made our dressing with lemon juice and whole-grain mustard. Eat this dish indulgently, as Lawson would want you to. "You know, the whole guilt thing I never quite get," she said. "One of the things I'm asked most often when I'm interviewed is, 'What is your guilty pleasure?' And I get rather prissy and I always say to everyone, 'Look, if you feel guilty about pleasure, you don't deserve to have pleasure.'"

Don't assemble the salad until just before serving. Otherwise, the avocado will brown and the greens will begin to wilt.

1. In a large bowl, whisk together the lemon juice, mustard, honey and ½ teaspoon each salt and pepper. Whisking constantly, add the oil in a stream until emulsified. Into another large bowl, flake the salmon into large chunks. Add half of the chopped pepitas and 2 tablespoons of the dressing. Toss lightly.

2. Halve the avocado lengthwise and discard the pit. Using a paring knife, cut the flesh into ½-inch pieces while still in the skin. Scoop the avocado

chunks into the bowl with the salmon. Stir gently to combine. Taste, then season with salt and pepper.

3. Add the greens to the bowl with the remaining dressing and toss. Transfer the arugula to a serving dish and top with the salmon mixture and remaining pepitas.

Skirt Steak Salad with Arugula and Peppadews

Start to finish: **30 minutes** / Servings: **4**

2 teaspoons ground fennel

Kosher salt and ground black pepper

1 pound skirt steak, trimmed

7 tablespoons extra-virgin olive oil, divided

3 tablespoons lemon juice

½ cup chopped Peppadew peppers, drained

1 large garlic clove, thinly sliced

8 cups baby arugula

1½ ounces Parmesan cheese, shaved (½ cup)

Our steak salad takes inspiration from classic Italian tagliata, then skips across continents with the addition of Peppadews, a tangy pepper from South Africa. A popular dish in Tuscany, tagliata is a simple presentation of thinly sliced, rare steak, extra-virgin olive oil, arugula and shaved Parmesan. We made ours work with an inexpensive skirt steak seasoned with a dry rub of salt, pepper and ground fennel. We then whipped up a simple lemon juice-olive oil vinaigrette. The steak got a quick sear then, while it rested, we added thinly sliced garlic and chopped Peppadew peppers to the pan. In an unusual touch, we used half the vinaigrette to dress the arugula and the other half to deglaze the pan, creating a warm, sweet-and-sour garlicky sauce that blended with the steak's juices. Pay attention to how you slice the steak. Cuts like skirt steak have longer, thicker muscle fibers than sirloin and tenderloin; they are relatively tough unless cut against the grain, which results in shorter fibers. Skirt steaks can sometimes come as long pieces; if needed, cut the meat in half to fit the pan. If you can't find skirt steak, flank, flat iron and bavette steaks all work well.

Don't cook the steak beyond medium-rare or it will be tough.

1. In a small bowl, combine the fennel, 1 teaspoon salt and 2 teaspoons pepper. Coat the steak with the seasoning, then let sit for 15 minutes. Meanwhile, in a liquid measuring cup, whisk together 6 tablespoons of the oil, the lemon juice, ¾ teaspoon salt and ½ teaspoon pepper. Set aside.

2. In a large skillet over medium-high, heat the remaining tablespoon of oil until beginning to smoke. Add the steak and sear, without moving, until well browned, about 3 minutes. Flip and brown on the second side, about another 2 minutes for rare to medium-rare.

3. Transfer to a plate and let rest for 10 minutes. Return the skillet to the heat. Add the Peppadews and garlic, then cook for 30 seconds. Stir the dressing, then add half of it to the skillet, along with any juices from the meat on the plate, scraping the pan to deglaze.

4. In a large bowl, toss the arugula with the remaining dressing and half of the Parmesan, then divide among serving plates. Thinly slice the steak against the grain, then arrange slices over the arugula. Spoon some warm pan sauce over each serving. Top with the remaining Parmesan.

Welsh **Rarebit**

Start to finish: **15 minutes** / Servings: 4

8 ounces sharp cheddar
cheese, grated

2 tablespoons all-purpose
flour, divided

2 tablespoons salted butter

Ground black pepper

⅛ teaspoon cayenne pepper

1 teaspoon Dijon mustard

1 teaspoon Worcestershire sauce

1 cup brown ale or amber beer

Kosher salt

4 slices thick bread, toasted

2 tablespoons minced fresh chives

Nothing in the refrigerator but beer and cheese? There's a supper for that. We found it by way of 18th-century Britain and the oddly named dish Welsh rarebit. With such a simple dish—basically cheese melted with beer and poured on bread—the challenge was to make each ingredient shine. The beer was key, adding flavor but also helping the cheese melt smoothly because its acid helps loosen the proteins in cheese. We preferred a mild brown ale. We tried variations such as adding eggs or sour cream for smoothness, but weren't won over. But tossing the cheese with flour before mixing it, a technique we borrowed from another cheese classic, fondue, did help with emulsification, producing a smoother sauce. For the cheese, we used blocks of sharp (extra-sharp was nice, too) cheddar grated on a box grater. White bread was the best match for our flavorful rarebit— ideally, thick slices of toast, cut diagonally. But high-quality supermarket sandwich bread worked, too. For a simple supper, spoon the rarebit on toast topped with sauteed mushrooms (see sidebar), sliced tomatoes and turkey or ham. The cooled sauce can be refrigerated for up to four days. To reheat, allow to come to room temperature, then spread on toast and broil until browned and bubbling.

Don't use pre-shredded cheese. It has additives that give it a plasticky texture.

1. In a bowl, toss the cheese with 1 tablespoon of the flour. In a medium saucepan over medium, melt the butter. Add the remaining 1 tablespoon of flour, ½ teaspoon black pepper and the cayenne. Cook, whisking constantly, for 1 minute. Stir in the mustard and Worcestershire, then slowly stir in the beer. Bring to a simmer and cook over medium-low, stirring, until thickened, about 3 minutes.

2. Reduce the heat to low and add the cheese a handful at a time, whisking until smooth after each addition. Off heat, season with salt and pepper. To serve, spoon the sauce over the toast and sprinkle with the chives.

BISTRO MUSHROOMS

Start to finish: **10 minutes**
Servings: 4

Welsh rarebit is great on its own, but topping it with a quick mushroom saute makes it a complete meal. We liked cremini mushrooms, but white button work, too. Salting the mushrooms helps draw out some of the moisture, which encourages browning. In addition to accompanying Welsh rarebit, these mushrooms are delicious as a topping for steak or burgers or served on hot buttered toast.

Don't add the mushrooms to the skillet until it is very hot. If it's not, the mushrooms will steam rather than brown.

2 tablespoons salted butter

1 pound cremini mushrooms, cleaned, trimmed and thinly sliced

Kosher salt and ground pepper

2 garlic cloves, finely chopped

1 teaspoon minced fresh rosemary

½ cup dry white wine

2 teaspoons whole-grain mustard

In a 12-inch nonstick skillet over medium-high, melt the butter. Add the mushrooms and ½ teaspoon salt. Cook, stirring, until the mushrooms are browned, about 10 minutes. Add the garlic and rosemary, then cook another 30 seconds. Add the wine and cook until mostly evaporated, about 2 minutes. Off heat, stir in the mustard, then taste and season with salt and pepper.

Chinese Chili-and-Scallion **Noodles**

Start to finish: **40 minutes (20 minutes active)**
Servings: 4

---

12 ounces udon noodles,
lo mein or spaghetti

5 tablespoons soy sauce

3 tablespoons unseasoned
rice vinegar

3 tablespoons packed dark
brown sugar

1 tablespoon toasted sesame oil

¼ cup grapeseed or other
neutral oil

5 teaspoons sesame seeds

1¼ teaspoons red pepper flakes

12 scallions, white and green parts
separated and thinly sliced on a bias

4 fried eggs, to serve (optional)

Every cook needs a few back-pocket recipes that can be thrown together
quickly from pantry staples. Think spaghetti carbonara, the Italian pasta
dish of bacon and eggs. Or Fuchsia Dunlop's game-changing "midnight
noodles," a fresh spin on a Chinese staple. The simple sauce comes
together in the time it takes the noodles to cook. Our version swaps out
some of the hard-to-find Chinese ingredients and creates a simple chili
oil that can be adjusted to taste. We cooked scallion whites in the hot oil to
soften their bite and used the milder green parts to add brightness at the
end. While we preferred udon noodles, chewy Chinese wheat noodles such
as lo mein were fine substitutes. Even spaghetti worked in a pinch. These
noodles also are great topped with a fried egg, see our recipe (p. 23.)

*Don't walk away while heating the oil. The sesame seeds can burn in an instant,
and the red pepper flakes will blacken and become bitter. The seeds should be
just turning golden, and the pepper flakes should be pleasantly fragrant.*

1. Bring a large pot of well-salted water
to a boil. Add the noodles and cook until
al dente, then drain. Meanwhile, in a
large bowl whisk together the soy sauce,
vinegar, sugar and sesame oil.

2. In a large nonstick skillet over
medium, heat the grapeseed oil, sesame
seeds and pepper flakes until the pepper
flakes are fragrant and the sesame seeds
begin to brown, 3 to 5 minutes. Off heat,
stir in the scallion whites, then transfer
the oil mixture to the bowl with the soy
sauce mixture.

3. Add the cooked pasta to the sauce
and toss. Add the scallion greens,
reserving some for garnish, and toss.
Divide among 4 serving bowls and top
each with more scallion greens and a
fried egg, if desired.

Gemelli Pasta with Chevre, Arugula and Walnuts

Start to finish: **45 minutes** / Servings: 4

12 ounces gemelli or casarecce pasta

4 ounces chevre (fresh goat cheese)

5 tablespoons extra-virgin olive oil

Kosher salt

Red pepper flakes

4 ounces baby arugula (about 4 cups)

¾ cup walnuts, toasted and chopped

⅓ cup finely chopped fresh chives

Creamy pasta sauces pose two problems: They are finicky to make and they quickly decompose into a stringy or grainy mess. So when we came across a recipe that suggested using fresh goat cheese instead of the Parmesan called for in classic Alfredo and carbonara, we were intrigued. The notion was simple. The heat of freshly cooked pasta and a splash of its cooking water would dissolve the soft chevre into a rich, smooth sauce in no time. Except it didn't work. The ingredients quickly broke down into a chalky mess. Then we discovered a technique by Marcella Hazan in which you first mix the cheese with oil. It worked wonderfully, but why? Goat's milk has more fat than cow's milk, so turning it into cheese requires the addition of acid. The acid forms the cheese curds but also creates strong water-insoluble bonds between the proteins. Hence our clumpy mess. But add oil to the chevre and those bonds slip apart, and the cheese melts easily. The same trick works for any acid-set cheese, such as ricotta, cottage and feta.

1. Bring a large pot of well-salted water to a boil. Add the pasta and cook until al dente. Meanwhile, in a medium bowl, combine the cheese, oil and ¼ teaspoon each salt and red pepper flakes, stirring and mashing with a fork until smooth. Drain the pasta, reserving ¾ cup of the cooking water, then return the pasta to the pot.

2. Add the arugula, the goat cheese mixture and the reserved pasta cooking water, then toss until the cheese mixture is evenly distributed and the arugula begins to wilt.

3. Stir in the walnuts and chives, reserving a tablespoon of each for garnish, if desired, then season with additional salt and red pepper flakes. Transfer the pasta to a warmed serving bowl, then garnish with the remaining walnuts and chives.

Peruvian Pesto (*Tallarines Verdes*)

Start to finish: **45 minutes** / Servings: **4**

12 ounces linguine
or fettuccine

1 yellow onion chopped
(1 cup)

½ cup extra-virgin olive oil

¼ cup water

3 garlic cloves, smashed

Kosher salt and ground
black pepper

12 ounces baby spinach
(about 12 cups)

¼ cup heavy cream

2 ounces Parmesan cheese,
grated (about 1 cup)

4 ounces queso fresco,
crumbled (about 1 cup)

Lime wedges, to serve

The origin of Peruvian pesto, or tallarines verdes, dates to the 19th century, when a wave of Italian immigrants settled in Peru. Many came from Genoa—the birthplace of pesto—and they adapted the recipe to the available ingredients. A shocking amount of spinach replaces the basil, and crumbled queso fresco supplements (and sometimes entirely replaces) salty Parmesan cheese. "It became a kind of dialogue or maybe a love story" between two worlds, says Gastón Acurio, Peruvian culinary star, founder of the La Mar restaurants, and champion of his country's food. For bright color and fresh flavor, we pureed ¾ pound of spinach for this pesto, along with onion and garlic. A quick simmer in a skillet took the raw edge off the onion and spinach, giving a depth and complexity lacking in traditional raw Italian pestos. Once the sauce thickened, we added reserved pasta cooking water, followed by undercooked pasta. The starch-infused water gave the pesto body, and the pasta finished cooking in the sauce, absorbing more of its flavor.

Don't be alarmed if the skillet seems very full after adding the pasta. Use tongs to gently lift and stir the noodles, and a rubber spatula to scrape the edges of the pan.

1. Bring a large pot of well-salted water to a boil. Add the pasta and cook until just tender but not fully cooked, about 2 minutes less than package directions. Drain the pasta, reserving 1½ cups of the cooking water.

2. Meanwhile, in a food processor, combine the onion, oil, ¼ cup water, garlic and 1 teaspoon each salt and pepper. Add a third of the spinach and process until smooth, about 30 seconds. Add the remaining spinach in 2 batches, processing until smooth after each.

3. Transfer the spinach mixture to a 12-inch nonstick skillet over medium-high. Bring to a boil and cook, stirring occasionally, until it begins to thicken, 3 to 5 minutes. Add the reserved pasta water and return to a simmer, then add the pasta and stir to coat. Simmer, stirring occasionally, until the pasta is al dente and the pesto no longer appears watery, 3 to 5 minutes. Stir in the cream. Off the heat, stir in the Parmesan, then taste and season with salt and pepper. Transfer to a serving dish, sprinkle with the queso fresco and serve with lime wedges.

PISCO SOUR

Start to finish: **5 minutes**
Makes **2 drinks**

This Peruvian staple is traditionally made with lime juice, but we preferred a brighter blend of lemon and lime. "Dry shaking" the cocktail with one ice cube (to seal the shaker) helps create the sour's signature foam.

3½ ounces pisco

1 egg white

½ ounce lemon juice

½ ounce lime juice

½ ounce simple syrup

Angostura bitters

In a cocktail shaker, combine the pisco, egg white, both juices and the syrup. Add 1 ice cube and shake vigorously for 15 seconds. Fill the shaker with ice, then shake vigorously for 15 seconds. Strain into chilled glasses and sprinkle 3 to 4 dashes of bitters over each.

Soba Noodles with Asparagus, Miso Butter and Egg

Start to finish: **25 minutes** / Servings: 4

___

1 pound medium asparagus, tough ends trimmed

5 tablespoons white miso

4 tablespoons (½ stick) salted butter, softened

1½ tablespoons finely grated fresh ginger

12 ounces soba noodles

3 scallions, chopped, plus thinly sliced scallions to garnish

4 fried eggs (p. 23)

Shichimi togarashi rice seasoning, to serve (optional)

Lemon wedges, to serve

Asparagus has a built-in challenge; the sturdy, fibrous stalks need to be cooked to a different degree than the feathery tips. How to handle both? We cut the spears in two—stalks and tips—and simply toss the stalks into the noodle cooking water first, and a minute later add the tips. Stalks that measured about ½ inch at the thickest end were best. To flavor our asparagus and noodles, we liked savory-sweet miso, but we needed a fat to draw out the flavors. We turned to Momofuku's David Chang, who famously blends miso and butter. We liked that combination, particularly when balanced with grated fresh ginger. For the noodles, we preferred those made from a blend of whole-wheat and buckwheat flours; 100 percent buckwheat noodles were fragile and expensive. A sunny-side up egg proved the perfect topper. (p. 23.) Most soba noodles cook in 4 minutes. For noodles that need longer, adjust the timing for adding the asparagus. Assembling and preparing all the ingredients before cooking the noodles was essential for proper timing. While the soba cooks, heat the skillet, then fry the eggs while tossing the noodles with the miso butter. To finish, we liked a sprinkle of shichimi togarashi, the Asian rice seasoning (p. 10.)

Don't add salt to the soba cooking water. While we usually salt our pasta water, miso can be quite salty and sodium levels vary widely by brand. Skipping the salt gave us better control over seasoning.

1. Bring a large pot of water to a boil. Meanwhile, snap or cut off the tender tips of the asparagus. Set aside. Slice the stalks on a bias into ½-inch pieces. Set aside separately. In a large bowl, combine the miso, butter and ginger, stirring and mashing.

2. Add the noodles to the boiling water. Cook for about 1 minute. Add the asparagus stalks and cook for another minute. Add the tips, then cook for 2 minutes. Drain the noodles and asparagus, reserving ½ of the cup cooking water. The noodles should be just tender. Add the noodles, asparagus and minced scallions to the miso butter. Add enough reserved cooking water to reach a creamy consistency, using tongs to toss until the butter melts and coats the noodles.

3. Divide the noodles among 4 serving bowls and top each with a fried egg. Sprinkle with sliced scallions and shichimi togarashi, if using. Serve with lemon wedges.

Trapani Pesto

Start to finish: **30 minutes** / Servings: 4

4 ounces slivered almonds
(about 1 cup), toasted

1 small garlic clove

¼ teaspoon red pepper flakes

1 pound cherry tomatoes

¾ ounce fresh basil leaves
(1 cup lightly packed)

Kosher salt

½ cup extra-virgin olive oil

1 ounce grated pecorino Romano
cheese (½ cup), plus more to serve

12 ounces short, sturdy pasta, such
as gemelli, casarecce or rigatoni

Ground black pepper

We hear "pesto" and see shades of green, but the word refers to prep, not pigment. It stems from pestare, to pound—this Italian sauce traditionally was made with a mortar and pestle. The basil-heavy, and therefore green, version we know best comes from northwestern Italy. In Sicily, you'll find pesto Trapanese (named for the town of Trapani), a sauce also known as mataroccu. It has less basil than the northern version and adds tomatoes, garlic and almonds, the latter a nod to Sicily's Arabic heritage. To make this a truly year-round recipe we ruled out standard winter tomatoes and instead settled on cherry tomatoes, though grape or small plum tomatoes worked, too. For ease, we used a food processor, though we found it was best to incorporate the olive oil or cheese (pecorino) by hand at the end. Raw almonds are common, but we found them a little dull. When we toasted them, however, we were wowed by how they brought out the sweetness of the tomato, added a crispier crunch and improved the balance of the dish. We preferred blanched, slivered almonds, which were easiest to toast and grind, but any variety is fine.

Don't add the cooking water to the sauce right away. While we always reserve some starchy cooking water before draining pasta, this sauce has so much moisture from the tomatoes that it wasn't always necessary.

1. Bring a large pot of salted water to a boil. Meanwhile, in a food processor, combine the almonds, garlic and pepper flakes. Process until coarsely ground, 20 to 30 seconds. Add the tomatoes, basil and ¾ teaspoon salt. Pulse until uniformly ground but still chunky, 10 to 12 pulses. Transfer to a large bowl and stir in the oil and cheese.

2. Cook the pasta until al dente. Drain, reserving 1 cup of the cooking water. Add the pasta to the bowl with the pesto and toss. If the sauce is too thick, add a bit of the reserved pasta water. Taste and season with salt, pepper, red pepper flakes and more cheese.

Spaghetti with Lemon, Anchovies and Capers

Start to finish: **30 minutes (15 minutes active)** / Servings: 4

12 ounces spaghetti

¼ cup extra-virgin olive oil

6 garlic cloves, thinly sliced

¾ teaspoon red pepper flakes

12 anchovies, minced (2-ounce can)

3 tablespoons drained capers, chopped, plus 2 tablespoons caper brine

2 teaspoons lemon zest, plus 3 tablespoons lemon juice (1 to 2 lemons)

¾ cup chopped fresh parsley leaves

2 ounces grated Parmesan cheese (about 1 cup)

Kosher salt and ground black pepper

Lidia Bastianich reminds us that the water we cook our pasta in is worth saving. She uses the starchy liquid to thicken quick, flavorful sauces made from potent pantry staples such as anchovies and capers. Our quick pasta dish, inspired by Bastianich, draws its intense flavor from anchovies, capers, garlic, lemon and red pepper flakes. We intentionally undercooked the pasta to leave it underhydrated and ready to absorb more flavor when cooking in the sauce.

Don't salt the pasta water as much as usual; the other ingredients provide plenty of salt. One tablespoon kosher salt for 4 quarts of water worked for this recipe.

1. Bring a large pot of lightly salted water to a boil. Add the pasta and cook until just tender but not fully cooked, about 2 minutes less than package directions. Reserve 2 cups of the cooking water, then drain.

2. In a large skillet over medium, combine the oil, garlic, pepper flakes, anchovies and capers. Cook, stirring occasionally, until fragrant and the garlic is golden, about 5 minutes. Add the reserved pasta water and bring to a simmer. Add the pasta and stir. Cook, stirring occasionally, until the pasta is al dente, 3 to 5 minutes.

3. Off heat, stir in the lemon zest and juice, the caper brine, parsley and half of the cheese. Taste, then season with salt and pepper. Serve topped with the remaining cheese.

Whole-Wheat Pasta with Yogurt and Tahini

Start to finish: **25 minutes** / Servings: 4

2 garlic cloves, finely grated

1 teaspoon grated lemon zest, plus 3 tablespoons lemon juice (1 to 2 lemons)

½ cup walnuts, finely chopped

1½ teaspoons cumin seeds

2 scallions, trimmed and finely chopped

Kosher salt

12 ounces whole-wheat pasta

1 cup plain whole-milk Greek-style yogurt

⅓ cup tahini

2 tablespoons extra-virgin olive oil

With its earthy flavor and dense chew, whole-wheat pasta often gets passed over. But with the right ingredients it can be a star. Take our Greek-inspired pasta tossed with a simple, creamy sauce of thick yogurt and nutty tahini. While we recommend whole-grain, the dish also is delicious with traditional pasta. Chunky pastas such as orecchiette, farfalle and penne worked as well as long noodles, such as fettuccine and tagliatelle. To add interest to our sauce we toasted cumin seeds and finely chopped walnuts—they also provided the basis for a garnish. The ratio of tahini to yogurt—1:3 as it turned out—was key to a full-flavored, creamy sauce; a bit of olive oil helped with emulsification. For a tangy touch, we added lemon zest to both the toasted walnuts and the tahini sauce, giving us a double layer of flavor.

Don't substitute traditional yogurt for Greek-style or the sauce will be too thin.

1. Bring a large pot of salted water to a boil. Meanwhile, in a medium bowl combine the garlic and lemon juice and let sit for 10 minutes. In a small skillet over medium-low, toast the walnuts and cumin seeds, stirring frequently, until golden brown and fragrant, 3 to 5 minutes. Transfer to a small bowl and stir in the scallions, ½ teaspoon of the lemon zest and ¼ teaspoon salt.

2. Cook the pasta until al dente. Drain, reserving 1 cup of the cooking water, then return the pasta to the pot. To the lemon juice–garlic mixture, whisk in the yogurt, tahini, oil, the remaining ½ teaspoon of lemon zest, ½ teaspoon salt and ½ cup of the reserved pasta water. Add the sauce to the pasta and toss until evenly coated. Stir in half of the walnut mixture. Transfer the pasta to a platter or individual bowls, then garnish with the remaining walnut mixture.

Spicy Stir-Fried Cumin Beef

Start to finish: 1 hour (35 minutes active)
Servings: 4

___

1 pound sirloin tips, trimmed

3½ tablespoons soy sauce, divided

½ teaspoon ground black pepper

12 dried red chilies (such as arbol
or Japones), stemmed

1½ tablespoons cumin seeds,
toasted

5 large garlic cloves, minced

6 teaspoons grapeseed or
other neutral oil, divided

1 large yellow onion, thinly
sliced lengthwise

4 teaspoons unseasoned
rice vinegar

1 teaspoon white sugar

2 teaspoons toasted sesame oil

1½ cups coarsely chopped fresh
cilantro leaves and tender stems

Cumin is rarely used in Chinese cooking, but when it is, it shows up boldly. Hunan beef and Sichuan lamb are two such dishes from neighboring regions in which an abundance of whole cumin seeds is combined with whole chilies and aromatics to great effect. Don't be deterred by the whole seeds; they soften in the heat and provide a textural counterpoint to the tender meat. Beware the chilies, though. Despite being perfectly edible, they retain a fiery heat. While we specify beef here, we also loved this made with 1½ pounds of lamb leg or shoulder, trimmed and thinly sliced (freeze the lamb for about 30 minutes before slicing). Once cooking begins, things move along quickly, so have all your ingredients prepared and a serving platter nearby. Serve with steamed white rice.

Don't make this dish in a tight space. Toasting the chilies and searing the meat produced a fair amount of smoke and fumes. Turn your hood vent to high before beginning, or open a window.

1. **Cut the meat** into 2-inch pieces, then thinly slice each piece against the grain. In a medium bowl, combine the beef, 1 tablespoon of the soy sauce and the pepper. Stir to coat evenly. Set aside.

2. **Meanwhile, break open** about half of the chilies, then transfer all of them to a 12-inch nonstick skillet. Toast over medium, pressing the pods against the skillet, until fragrant and darkened in spots, 1 to 3 minutes. Transfer to a large bowl and add the cumin seeds. In a small bowl, stir together the garlic and 2 teaspoons of the grapeseed oil to form a paste.

3. **Add 2 teaspoons of the** remaining grapeseed oil to the empty skillet and heat over high until shimmering. Add the onion and cook, stirring occasionally, until charred in spots and partially softened, 3 to 5 minutes. Transfer to the bowl with the cumin seeds and

chilies. Return the skillet to high heat. Add 1 teaspoon of grapeseed oil, then arrange half of the beef in a single layer in the skillet and cook, undisturbed, until deeply browned on the bottom, 1 to 2 minutes. Stir, scraping the bottom of the pan, and cook until no pink remains, 60 to 90 seconds. Transfer to the bowl with the onion. Repeat with the remaining grapeseed oil and beef.

4. **In the skillet over low,** cook the garlic paste, mashing the mixture, until aromatic, about 1 minute. Add the beef mixture. Stir in the remaining 2½ tablespoons of soy sauce, the vinegar and sugar. Increase the heat to medium-high and cook, stirring constantly and scraping up any browned bits, until the liquid is thickened, about 1 minute. Off heat, stir in the sesame oil and cilantro.

Turkish Beans with Pickled Tomatoes

Start to finish: 3 hours (15 minutes active)
Servings: 6

5½ cups water

1 pound dried cannellini beans, soaked overnight and drained

12- to 16-ounce beef or lamb shank

1 large yellow onion, chopped (about 2 cups)

4 tablespoons (½ stick) salted butter

8 garlic cloves, peeled and smashed

4 sprigs fresh thyme

2 bay leaves

1 teaspoon paprika

1 teaspoon red pepper flakes

14½-ounce can diced tomatoes, drained

Kosher salt

½ cup chopped fresh parsley leaves

2 tablespoons chopped fresh dill, plus more to serve

2 tablespoons pomegranate molasses, plus more to serve

Ground black pepper

Whole-milk yogurt and extra-virgin olive oil, to serve

Pickled tomatoes (see sidebar), to serve

This hearty white bean stew was inspired by the Turkish dish kuru fasulye, basically beans stewed in a spicy tomato sauce. We also borrowed a bit of flavor from the Middle Eastern pantry, using pomegranate molasses, a syrup of boiled pomegranate juice, to add a unique and fruity sweetness. You'll find it in the grocer's international section or near the honey, maple syrup and molasses. This dish calls for dried beans, which means an overnight soak for evenly cooked beans. We found the creamy texture of dried cannellini beans was best, but Great Northern beans worked, too. We maximized meaty flavor—without using a lot of meat—by using a collagen-rich beef or lamb shank. Serve these beans as is or with a drizzle of extra-virgin olive oil and a spoonful of whole-milk yogurt. We also loved the bright contrast provided by pickled tomatoes (see sidebar). The beans can be made up to two days ahead. Reheat over low, adding water to reach your desired consistency.

Don't forget to salt the beans' soaking water. The salt tenderizes and seasons the beans. We liked a ratio of 1½ tablespoons kosher salt to 3 quarts water.

1. Heat the oven to 325°F with a rack in the middle position. In a large oven-safe pot or Dutch oven over high, combine the water, beans, shank, onion, butter, garlic, thyme, bay leaves, paprika and red pepper flakes. Bring to a boil, then cover and transfer to the oven. Bake for 1 hour 15 minutes.

2. Remove the pot from the oven. Stir in the tomatoes and 2 teaspoons salt. Return, uncovered, to the oven and bake until the beans are fully tender and creamy and the liquid is slightly thick-ened, another 1 hour 15 minutes. Transfer the pot to a rack. Remove the shank and set aside. Discard the thyme sprigs and bay leaves.

3. When cool, remove the meat from the bone, discarding fat, gristle and bone. Finely chop the meat and stir into the beans. Stir in the parsley, dill and molasses. Taste and season with salt and pepper. Serve with yogurt, oil, pickled tomatoes and additional pomegranate molasses and dill.

PICKLED TOMATOES

Start to finish: **5 minutes, plus chilling**
Servings: **1½ cups**

These pickled tomatoes are delicious with our Turkish beans, but also can be used on sandwiches or in hearty soups. Make them up to two days ahead. Be sure to seed the tomatoes. Seeds gave the final product an unpleasant texture.

3 plum tomatoes (12 ounces), cored, seeded and diced

3 tablespoons cider vinegar

1 tablespoon chopped fresh dill

1 teaspoon crushed Aleppo pepper (or ½ teaspoon red pepper flakes)

1 teaspoon white sugar

½ teaspoon kosher salt

In a medium bowl, stir together all ingredients. Refrigerate for at least 1 hour. Will keep, refrigerated, for 3 days.

Lentil Salad with Gorgonzola

Start to finish: 1½ hours (30 minutes active)
Servings: 6

½ cup white balsamic vinegar

2 medium shallots, peeled, halved lengthwise and thinly sliced

Kosher salt

1 garlic head

6 cups water

2 medium carrots, halved crosswise

1 celery rib, halved crosswise

1 tablespoon yellow mustard seeds

6 sprigs fresh thyme, tied together

2 bay leaves

1½ cups (10 ounces) French green lentils, sorted and rinsed

1 tablespoon extra-virgin olive oil

2 ounces Gorgonzola cheese, crumbled (about ¾ cup)

½ cup chopped fresh parsley leaves

½ cup walnuts, toasted and chopped

Ground black pepper

Green lentils du Puy, also known as French lentils, cook quickly, hold their shape well and do a great job at soaking up flavors in a rich broth or stew. But it can be a bit of a race to develop that flavor before the lentils overcook and become mushy. Our solution: Simmer vegetables and aromatics in advance, then add lentils. To really punch up the flavor we turned to one of our favorite seasoning shortcuts and simmered a whole head of garlic with the herbs until it was mellow and tender; the cloves became soft enough to be mashed and formed the basis of a richly savory dressing. Pungent Gorgonzola cheese gave the salad sharp contrast, while toasted walnuts added crunch.

Don't use brown lentils here. They are larger and have a different cooking time from peppery green lentils.

1. In a liquid measuring cup, combine the vinegar, shallots and 1 teaspoon salt. Let sit for 10 minutes. Meanwhile, cut off and discard the top third of the garlic head, leaving the head intact. In a 2-quart saucepan over medium-high, combine the garlic, water, carrots, celery, mustard seeds, thyme, bay leaves and 1 teaspoon salt. Bring to a boil, then cover, reduce heat to low and simmer for 30 minutes. Remove and discard the carrots, celery, thyme and bay leaves.

2. Return the pot to medium-high and stir in the lentils. Return to a boil, then cover and reduce heat to low. Simmer until the lentils are tender but still hold their shape, 30 to 35 minutes. Remove the garlic and set aside. Drain the lentils, reserving the liquid, and transfer to a large bowl. Stir in the vinegar-shallot mixture and let cool to room temperature.

3. Squeeze the pulp from the garlic into a bowl and mash with a fork. Stir in ¼ cup of the reserved cooking water, the oil and ½ teaspoon salt. Stir the garlic mixture, half of the cheese, the parsley and half of the walnuts into the lentils. Taste and season with salt and pepper. Transfer to a platter and top with the remaining cheese and walnuts.

Sichuan Chicken Salad

Start to finish: 1 hour 20 minutes (20 minutes active)
Servings: 4

___

Two 10- to 12-ounce bone-in,
skin-on split chicken breasts

6 scallions, white parts coarsely
chopped, green parts thinly sliced
on a bias, reserved separately

1-inch piece fresh ginger,
cut into 4 pieces and smashed

2 large garlic cloves, smashed

Kosher salt

4 cups water

¼ cup dry sherry (optional)

2 tablespoons chili oil

2 tablespoons tahini

1½ tablespoons white sugar

1½ tablespoons toasted sesame oil

1 tablespoon soy sauce

2 tablespoons unseasoned
rice vinegar

1 teaspoon Sichuan peppercorns,
toasted and finely ground (optional)

⅛ to ¼ teaspoon cayenne pepper

1 large English cucumber, halved
lengthwise, seeded and thinly
sliced crosswise on a bias

⅓ cup dry-roasted peanuts, chopped

Chicken salad generally is pretty mediocre—all mayonnaise and no substance. We retooled this American staple by taking a cue from Sichuan bang-bang chicken salad, which skips the mayo and turns up the heat. The name stems from the sound of the traditional prep technique in which the chicken is pounded to shreds, allowing it to soak up a flavorful dressing. We didn't raise quite such a ruckus, finding that a sturdy wooden spoon and bowl got us the results we needed (be sure not to use a fragile bowl). To get our chicken ready, we poached it along with scallion whites and ginger, infusing it with flavor. Then we stirred together a vibrant dressing that included rice vinegar, chili oil and tongue-tingling Sichuan peppercorns. We worked some of the dressing into the chicken shreds, using our spoon-bowl method, and served the rest over the finished salad. The peppercorns are optional; leave them out if you don't want the extra heat, but we loved their floral, piney notes. We toasted the peppercorns in a skillet over medium heat—they took about 2 minutes—before grinding them to a fine powder with a spice grinder or mortar and pestle.

Don't boil the chicken for too long; the meat will dry out. Residual heat gently poaches the chicken, guaranteeing it stays moist and tender.

1. In a large saucepan, place the chicken skin side down, then add the scallion whites, ginger, garlic and 1½ teaspoons salt. Add the water and sherry, if using, fully submerging the chicken. Bring to a boil over medium-high, then cover, turn off the heat and let sit until the chicken registers 160°F, 15 to 20 minutes. Uncover the pan and let the chicken cool in the liquid for 30 to 45 minutes.

2. Meanwhile, in a small bowl, whisk together the chili oil, tahini, sugar, sesame oil, soy sauce, rice vinegar, 1½ teaspoons salt, Sichuan peppercorns, if using, and cayenne.

3. Remove the chicken from the cooking liquid. Remove and discard the skin and bones, then transfer the meat to a large bowl. Add 2 tablespoons of the dressing, then use a wooden spoon to smash the meat, working the dressing into the chicken and shredding it. Use your fingers to pull the shreds into bite-size pieces. Add the cucumber and three-quarters each of the peanuts and scallion greens. Drizzle with the remaining dressing and toss until evenly coated. Transfer to a serving bowl and sprinkle with the remaining peanuts and scallions.

HIGH FIBER, HIGH FLAVOR

The key to a flavorful chicken salad turns out to be all about fiber. Like other animal muscle tissue, the muscle fibers in chicken, especially breast meat, are long and occur in bundles surrounded by thin sheets of connective tissue. Think electrical wires wrapped in plastic. The fibers must be exposed to absorb dressing, and one way to do that is to cut the meat across the grain, as in cubing. Shredding is an even more effective way to achieve this, as it exposes the most muscle fiber.

Turkish Meatballs with Lime-Yogurt Sauce

Start to finish: 20 minutes, plus cooling
Servings: 6

3 tablespoons extra-virgin
olive oil, divided

1 medium shallot, finely chopped

1 garlic clove, grated

½ teaspoon ground cumin

½ teaspoon cinnamon

½ teaspoon dried oregano

One 8-inch pita bread, torn into
small pieces (about 3 ounces)

¼ cup plain whole-milk yogurt

¼ cup water

1 cup packed fresh mint leaves
(1-ounce), finely chopped

1½ pounds 90-percent lean
ground beef

1½ teaspoons kosher salt

1 teaspoon ground black pepper

Lime-yogurt sauce, to serve
(see sidebar)

There are many variations (and spellings) of kofta across the Middle East and North Africa, but essentially they're seasoned patties, often made from ground lamb or a blend of beef and lamb. It's the rest of the world's answer to the Italian meatball. We particularly liked Turkish kofta, which sometimes are squashed flat and can be grilled, fried or even cooked on a skewer. We went with an all-beef version using 90 percent lean beef, though this recipe also works with a blend of lamb and beef. We pan-fried our patties, which gave us a deliciously crispy crust. To stop our meat mixture from getting tough in the middle we borrowed the French technique known as panade. It involves mixing a bread and dairy paste into the ground meat to bind it together and keep it moist during cooking. Since we already were serving pita bread with the patties, we used crumbled pita for our panade. We served the cooked patties in pita pockets with sliced tomato, cucumber, red onion and parsley. They also would be good over rice pilaf and served with a simple salad.

Don't use stale bread for the meatballs. The fresh pita added a lighter texture and fresh flavor. Likewise, use plain whole-milk yogurt, not Greek-style, to get the right consistency in both the meatballs and the sauce.

---

1. In a small bowl, stir together 2 tablespoons of the oil, the shallot, garlic, cumin, cinnamon and oregano. Microwave until fragrant, about 30 seconds, then set aside to cool.

2. In a large bowl, combine the pita bread, yogurt and water. Use your hands to mash the mixture to a smooth paste. Add the reserved oil mixture, the mint, beef, salt and pepper. Use your hands to thoroughly mix. Divide the meat into 12 portions, then use your hands to roll each into a smooth ball. Refrigerate for 15 minutes.

3. In a 12-inch nonstick skillet, heat the remaining tablespoon of oil over medium-high until just beginning to smoke. Add the meatballs and use a metal spatula to press them into ½-inch-thick patties. Cook over medium, adjusting the heat as necessary, until the meatballs register 140°F at the center and are cooked through and well browned on both sides, 5 to 7 minutes per side. Transfer to a platter, tent with foil and let rest for 5 minutes.

LIME-YOGURT SAUCE

Start to finish: 5 minutes
Servings: 1½ cups

1 cup plain whole-milk yogurt

3 tablespoons tahini

3 tablespoons lime juice

½ teaspoon kosher salt

¼ teaspoon cayenne pepper

In a small bowl, whisk together all ingredients until smooth.

Refried Beans

Start to finish: **15 minutes**
Servings: 4

Two 15½-ounce cans pinto
or black beans, drained

4 tablespoons lard, olive oil
or vegetable oil, divided

1 large yellow onion, quartered
and thinly sliced

2 garlic cloves, thinly sliced

Kosher salt

1 teaspoon ground cumin

1 teaspoon ground coriander

¾ teaspoon dried oregano

2 chipotle chilies in adobo sauce,
plus 1 tablespoon adobo sauce

⅓ cup water, plus extra for
thinning beans as needed

½ cup minced fresh cilantro leaves

1 tablespoon lime juice

Traditional refried beans involve an overnight soak followed by cooking, stirring and mashing the beans to the desired consistency. It is a bit more of a commitment than most of us can make on a weeknight. So we came up with a fast—as in 15 minutes—and simple approach that uses canned beans and lets the food processor do most of the work. We found pinto beans slightly sweeter and creamier than black beans, but both worked in this recipe. We loved the rich flavor lard gave the beans, but if you'd rather keep this vegetarian, olive or vegetable oil worked, too. For a smoother texture, process the beans longer after removing 1 cup in the first step. For a thinner consistency, stir in more water. Serve as a side with shredded cheese, sliced scallions or chopped onion, or spread into a torta, folded into a quesadilla or burrito, or spooned over nachos.

Don't remove the remaining beans from the food processor after measuring out 1 cup. Set aside until needed later.

1. In a food processor, pulse the beans until coarsely chopped, about 7 pulses. Transfer 1 cup of the beans to a bowl and set aside. In a 12-inch nonstick skillet over medium, heat 2 tablespoons of the lard until shimmering. Add the onion, garlic and 1 teaspoon salt. Cook until the onion is lightly browned, about 5 minutes. Stir in the cumin, coriander and oregano; cook until fragrant, about 30 seconds. Stir in the chilies and adobo sauce and cook, breaking up the chilies with a spatula, until fragrant, about 30 seconds.

2. Transfer the onion mixture to the processor, reserving the skillet; pulse until coarsely chopped, about 7 pulses. Add the water and pulse until the onions and beans are coarsely pureed, 7 to 12 more pulses. Set aside.

3. Add the remaining 2 tablespoons of lard to the empty skillet and heat over medium until just starting to smoke. Add the reserved cup of beans and cook until they begin to brown and most of the lard has been absorbed, 1 to 2 minutes. Stir in the pureed beans, then spread the mixture to the edges of the skillet. Cook, without stirring, until the beans begin to brown at the edges, 1 to 2 minutes. Stir the beans well and repeat the process twice more. Off heat, stir in the cilantro and lime juice. Taste and season with salt. Adjust the consistency with additional water.

Israeli Hummus (Hummus Masabacha)

Start to finish: 1 hour (15 minutes active), plus soaking
Makes 4 cups

___

Water

8 ounces (227 grams) dried chickpeas

2 tablespoons plus 1 teaspoon kosher salt

½ teaspoon baking soda

¾ cup sesame tahini, room temperature

3½ tablespoons lemon juice

1 to 2 tablespoons extra-virgin olive oil

1 tablespoon chopped fresh parsley

½ teaspoon ground cumin

½ teaspoon paprika

In Israel, hummus is breakfast, not a party dip. Our education began in Tel Aviv at Abu Hassan, the country's premier hummus shop, where customers get wide, shallow bowls of hummus topped with whole chickpeas, a sprinkle of parsley, pops of red paprika and amber cumin. The hummus is light, almost sour cream smooth—and warm. Back at Milk Street, we found small chickpeas worked best. The Whole Foods Market 365 Everyday Value brand worked very well. Cook larger chickpeas for 10 to 15 minutes longer, or until almost starting to break down. Soak the chickpeas for at least 12 hours. We liked the Kevala brand tahini, but Soom and Aleppo were good, too. We didn't like the Joyva brand, which had a bitter taste and grainy texture. Processing the chickpeas while warm ensures the smoothest, lightest hummus, as will processing it for a full three minutes in the first stage. Hummus traditionally is served warm and garnished with paprika, cumin, chopped fresh parsley and a drizzle of extra-virgin olive oil. Sometimes a sliced hard-boiled egg is added. Leftover hummus can be refrigerated for up to five days. To reheat, transfer to a microwave-safe bowl, cover and gently heat, adding a few tablespoons of tap water as needed to reach the proper consistency, 1 to 2 minutes.

Don't forget to stir the tahini very well. Some brands separate and can become quite thick at the bottom of the container.

1. In a large bowl, combine 8 cups water, the chickpeas and 2 tablespoons of salt. Soak for at least 12 hours.

2. In a stockpot over high, bring another 10 cups water and the baking soda to a boil. Drain the soaked chickpeas, discarding the soaking water, and add to the pot. Return to a simmer, then reduce heat to medium and cook until the skins are falling off and the chickpeas are very tender, 40 to 50 minutes.

3. Set a mesh strainer over a large bowl and drain the chickpeas into it; reserve ¾ cup of the chickpea cooking water. Let sit for 1 minute to let all liquid drain. Set aside about 2 tablespoons of the chickpeas, then transfer the rest to the food processor. Add the remaining

1 teaspoon of salt, then process for 3 minutes.

4. Add the tahini. Continue to process until the mixture has lightened and is very smooth, about 1 minute. Use a rubber spatula to scrape the sides and bottom of the processor bowl. With the machine running, add the reserved cooking liquid and the lemon juice. Process until combined. Taste and season with salt.

5. Transfer the hummus to a shallow serving bowl and use a large spoon to make a swirled well in the center. Drizzle with olive oil, then top with the reserved chickpeas, the parsley, cumin and paprika.

SPICED BEEF TOPPING (KAWARMA)

Start to finish: **25 minutes**
Makes **about 2 cups**

Warm ground meat toppings lend rich, savory notes to hummus, and make it a more robust meal.

½ pound lean ground beef

2 teaspoons sweet paprika

¾ teaspoon kosher salt

½ teaspoon cinnamon

½ teaspoon ground cumin

½ teaspoon dried oregano

½ teaspoon cayenne pepper

2 garlic cloves, grated

¾ cup water

½ small yellow onion, chopped

1 tablespoon extra-virgin olive oil

2 tablespoons tomato paste

2 tablespoons chopped fresh parsley or mint

1½ teaspoons lemon juice

Tahini, to serve

1. In a medium bowl, mix together the beef, paprika, salt, cinnamon, cumin, oregano, cayenne, garlic and 2 tablespoons of the water.

2. In a 10-inch skillet over medium-high, add the ground beef mixture, the onion and oil. Cook until the onion is softened and the beef is no longer pink, 6 to 8 minutes. Stir in the tomato paste and cook until fragrant, about 30 seconds.

3. Add the remaining water and cook, scraping the pan, until the water has evaporated and the mixture sizzles, about 5 minutes. Off heat, stir in the parsley and lemon juice. salt. Spoon over hummus, then drizzle with tahini.

Dinners

7

Chinese White-Cooked **Chicken** with Ginger-Soy Dressing

Start to finish: **2 hours (30 minutes active)** / Servings: **4**

For the chicken and poaching broth:

3½- to 4-pound chicken, giblets discarded

1 bunch fresh cilantro

6 scallions, trimmed and halved crosswise

4½ quarts water

2 cups dry sherry or mirin

4-inch piece fresh ginger, cut into 4 pieces and smashed

3 tablespoons kosher salt

For the dressing:

4 scallions, thinly sliced on a bias

3 tablespoons soy sauce

2 tablespoons grapeseed or other neutral oil

4 teaspoons finely grated fresh ginger

1 tablespoon unseasoned rice vinegar

1 tablespoon toasted sesame oil

½ teaspoon white sugar

½ pound (½ small head) napa or savoy cabbage, thinly sliced (4 cups)

Cooked white rice, to serve (optional)

It's easy to take a skin-deep approach to chicken, paying lots of attention to getting a golden brown crust only to end up with dull, bland—and too often overcooked—meat. We avoid that trap by adopting the Chinese technique of whole-bird poaching to create a chicken with simple, clean flavors and a silky, tender-but-firm meat primed for a variety of vibrant sauces. Simmered without soy sauce (and therefore white), the classic Cantonese dish is known as white-cooked or white-cut chicken. Poaching—in which the chicken is slowly cooked in liquid just below a simmer—delivers heat evenly, so no worries about dry breasts or pink thighs. The whole process takes about the same amount of time as roasting, most of it hands-off. In fact, the last 30 minutes of cooking occurs off the heat entirely. Poaching results in blond skin that most Americans will want to discard (though Chinese cooks leave it on and consider it perfectly tasty). The bright aromatics of raw scallions and ginger worked best in a soy sauce–based dressing, which we thinned with some of the poaching liquid.

Don't use cooking sherry for this recipe; it usually has added sodium and little, if any, actual sherry flavor. Look for a high-quality (but affordable) dry sherry.

1. Remove the chicken from the refrigerator and let sit at room temperature while making the broth. Reserving a few sprigs for garnish, cut the cilantro bunch in half crosswise, separating the stems and leaves. Use kitchen twine to tie the stems and scallions into a bundle. Chop enough of the cilantro leaves to measure ½ cup and set aside. (The remaining cilantro leaves are not needed.)

2. In a large pot (at least 8 quarts) over high, combine the cilantro-scallion bundle with the remaining broth ingredients and bring to a boil. Using tongs, lower the chicken into the broth breast side up, letting the liquid flow into the cavity. If the chicken isn't fully submerged in the broth after flooding the cavity, weigh it down with a plate.

3. Allow the broth to return to a boil, then reduce heat to medium and cook for 25 minutes, adjusting the heat to maintain a bare simmer; flip the chicken to be breast side down after 15 minutes. Turn off the heat, remove the pot from the burner and let the chicken sit in the hot broth for 30 minutes. Transfer the chicken to a carving board and let rest for 15 minutes.

4. While the chicken rests, prepare the dressing. In a small bowl, stir together ¼ cup of the poaching broth, the scallions, soy sauce, grapeseed oil, ginger, vinegar, sesame oil and sugar.

PUT YOUR POACHING BROTH TO WORK

While the poached chicken cools before carving, use the hot, seasoned broth to cook rice to round out the meal. Use the broth 1:1 for any water called for by the variety of rice you use. For long-grain white rice, for example, combine 1½ cups rinsed rice with 2 cups of the broth. Bring to a simmer, then reduce heat to low, cover and cook until the rice is fluffy and tender, 15 to 18 minutes. And be sure to save any remaining broth for use in rice, soup, sauces and braises. We freeze it in 2-cup portions in zip-close freezer bags.

5. Using a sharp knife, remove the legs from the chicken by cutting through the thigh joints, then separate the thighs from the drumsticks. Carve the breast meat from the bone and slice each breast crosswise into 4 pieces. Discard the chicken skin, if desired. Spread the cabbage on a serving platter, then arrange the chicken pieces on top. Pour the dressing over the chicken and sprinkle with the reserved ½ cup chopped cilantro. Garnish with cilantro sprigs.

Brown Ale Turkey with Gravy

Start to finish: 3½ hours (30 minutes active), plus cooling
Servings: 10

---

2 medium yellow onions
(1 to 1¼ pounds), cut into
8 wedges each

4 large sprigs fresh thyme

2 large sprigs fresh rosemary

2 large sprigs fresh sage

2 bay leaves

2 garlic cloves, crushed

Two 12-ounce bottles brown ale,
such as Newcastle Brown Ale

4 tablespoons (½ stick) salted
butter, cut into 4 pieces

¼ cup fish sauce

Kosher salt and ground black pepper

12- to 14-pound turkey, neck
and giblets discarded

2 stalks celery, quartered

Low-sodium turkey or chicken stock,
as needed

¼ cup instant flour, such as Wondra

Roasting a turkey, whether for Thanksgiving, Christmas or just because, can be an ordeal. The debate over brining alone is enough to make one consider going vegetarian. And, of course, there is the finicky business of how to get the thigh and breast meat to cook to perfect—yet different—temperatures simultaneously. We skipped the culinary gymnastics in favor of a tried-and-true method—basting. Then we made it better with beer. We doused our turkey—but only twice, so no worries about having to babysit the bird–with a reduction of brown ale, onions, garlic and fresh herbs, which combined to form a rich, malty base. Avoid hoppy beers, which turned unpleasantly bitter when reduced. We also used a secret ingredient: fish sauce. It adds savory depth to the baste that is reflected in the umami-rich gravy made from pan drippings. Relax, it doesn't taste at all fishy.

1. Heat the oven to 350°F with a rack in the lower middle position. In a 12-inch skillet, combine the onions, thyme, rosemary, sage, bay leaves, garlic and beer. Bring to a boil, then reduce heat to medium and simmer until reduced to ⅔ cup, about 20 minutes.

2. Strain the mixture into a large bowl, pressing on the solids. Reserve the solids. The liquid should measure ⅔ cup. If not, either reduce further or add water. Return reduction to the skillet, add the butter, and whisk until melted. Stir in the fish sauce and ½ teaspoon each salt and pepper.

3. Pat the turkey dry inside and out with paper towels. Tuck the wings underneath. Spread the reserved solids and celery in a large roasting pan and place the turkey breast side up over the mixture. Pour half of the beer reduction over the turkey; use your hands to coat it evenly. Cover loosely with foil, then roast for 1½ hours.

4. Remove the foil. Whisk the remaining beer reduction, then pour over the turkey. Roast until the breast registers 160°F and the thigh registers 175°F, 1 to 1 hour 45 minutes. If the turkey gets too dark, cover with foil.

5. Transfer the turkey to a platter or carving board, letting the juices run into the pan, then tent with foil and let rest for 30 minutes. Strain the pan drippings into a 4-cup liquid measuring cup, pressing on the solids; discard the solids.

6. Skim the fat from the drippings. If you have less than 3 cups of defatted drippings, add stock to measure 3 cups, then return to the roasting pan. Whisk in the flour, then set the pan on the stovetop and bring to a boil over medium. Simmer, whisking constantly and scraping the bottom, until thickened, 1 to 3 minutes. Season with salt and pepper. Carve the turkey, adding any accumulated juices to the gravy, then serve with gravy.

Easy-Bake Herbed Dressing

Start to finish: 2 hours 15 minutes (30 minutes active), plus cooling
Servings: 8

1 cup finely chopped celery

8 tablespoons (1 stick) salted butter, melted

8 ounces shallots, peeled

⅓ cup lightly packed fresh sage leaves

2 tablespoons fresh thyme leaves

1½ teaspoons kosher salt

1 teaspoon ground black pepper

1½ pounds sturdy white sandwich bread, cut into ¾-inch cubes

3 cups low-sodium chicken broth

½ cup heavy cream

½ cup chopped fresh flat-leaf parsley leaves

Let's face it, stuffing is basically a flavorful sponge to soak up gravy and any stray melting butter that escapes a vegetable. But mincing and sauteing the aromatics that help turn bland bread tasty is a chore. We sped things up—and maximized flavor—by giving butter, fresh herbs and raw shallots a whiz in the food processor, then using the resulting paste to season bread cubes as they toast in the oven. We found that any sturdy, high-quality sliced sandwich bread worked well. As the bread bakes, the raw bite of the shallots cooks off, leaving behind a mellow tang. Chopped celery was tossed with melted butter and mixed into the bread, softening as the cubes toast. The mixture then was moistened with chicken broth and a touch of cream before being baked to create a relatively carefree stuffing that will satisfy even the strictest traditionalists.

Don't use regular chicken broth. Make sure to use low-sodium, otherwise you'll end up with an over salted stuffing.

1. Heat the oven to 325°F with racks in the upper- and lower-middle positions. In a bowl, toss the celery with 1 tablespoon of the butter; set aside. In a food processor, combine the shallots, sage, thyme, salt, pepper and the remaining butter. Process to form a smooth paste, about 30 seconds.

2. In a large bowl, combine the bread and shallot-herb paste, tossing gently. Fold in the celery, then divide the mixture between 2 rimmed baking sheets. Bake until the celery is tender and the bread is crisp and golden, 50 to 60 minutes, stirring the bread and switching and rotating the pans halfway through. Let cool slightly. At this stage the bread mixture can be cooled, bagged and stored for a day.

3. When ready to proceed, increase the oven temperature to 400°F. Transfer the bread mixture to a large bowl, scraping any browned bits off the sheet pans. Fold in the broth, cream and parsley; let sit for 10 minutes, stirring occasionally. Transfer to a 13-by-9-inch baking dish and spread evenly. Bake on the upper- middle rack until well browned on top, 40 to 45 minutes, rotating the dish halfway through. Let sit for 20 minutes before serving.

Japanese Fried Chicken (*Karaage*)

Start to finish: 1 hour 45 minutes (15 minutes active), plus resting
Servings: 4

For the chicken:

3-ounce chunk unpeeled fresh ginger, coarsely grated

¼ cup sake

¼ cup tamari

1 tablespoon grated lemon zest

2 pounds boneless, skinless chicken thighs, trimmed and cut into thirds

227 grams (2 cups) cornstarch

1 tablespoon shichimi togarashi

1 teaspoon ground black pepper

2 quarts peanut or vegetable oil

For the dipping sauce:

¼ cup tamari

¼ cup unseasoned rice vinegar

1 teaspoon finely grated peeled fresh ginger

¼ teaspoon toasted sesame oil

We love crispy, juicy fried chicken, but getting it right can be hard. Too often, the breading is heavy and dull, masking the flavor of the meat. And coating the chicken can be a messy three-step process. We found a better way in karaage (kah-rah-ah-gay), the Japanese bite-sized fried chicken that starts with a zesty marinade and is coated with potato starch or potato flour, which creates a thin, crispy crust. We chose boneless, skinless chicken thighs and soaked them briefly in a slurry featuring fresh ginger. We also used tamari, a Japanese soy sauce. Tamari has a bolder flavor and darker color than Chinese-style soy sauces, but if you can't find it any soy sauce will work. For our coating, we tried potato starch, which was good but tricky to work with. Cornstarch proved easier to handle—and find at the store—and produced good results. If you can't find shichimi togarashi, add ½ teaspoon red pepper flakes to 2½ teaspoons sesame seeds. A large Dutch oven, at least 7 quarts, was essential for frying. We finished with a dipping sauce that mirrored the marinade with tamari, unseasoned rice vinegar, grated fresh ginger and toasted sesame oil.

Don't let the chicken sit for longer than an hour after coating it before frying. It will get gummy.

1. To make the chicken, gather the ginger in your hands and squeeze as much juice as possible into a large bowl. Add the ginger solids to the bowl and stir in the sake, tamari and lemon zest. Add the chicken and stir to coat. Refrigerate for at least 30 minutes or up to 1 hour.

2. Set a wire rack in a rimmed baking sheet. In a large bowl, combine the cornstarch, shichimi togarashi and pepper. Working 1 piece at a time, remove the chicken from the marinade, letting excess drip off, then dredge in the cornstarch mixture, pressing evenly to adhere on all sides. Transfer to the rack and refrigerate, uncovered, for at least 30 minutes and up to 1 hour.

3. In a 7-quart Dutch oven, heat the oil to 375°F. Add a third of the chicken to the hot oil and fry, stirring to prevent sticking, until the chicken is deep golden brown, 5 to 7 minutes. Transfer the chicken to a clean wire rack, return the oil to 375°F and repeat twice with the remaining chicken.

4. For the dipping sauce, whisk together all ingredients.

No-Sear Lamb or Beef and Chickpea Stew

Start to finish: 2 hours 15 minutes (40 minutes active)
Servings: 4

___

1 tablespoon sweet paprika

2 teaspoons ground cumin

1 teaspoon ground cardamom

¼ teaspoon cinnamon

Kosher salt and ground black pepper

1¼ pounds boneless lamb shoulder, trimmed of fat and cut into ¾-inch pieces

1 head garlic

2 tablespoons salted butter

1 large yellow onion, diced (about 2 cups)

2 tablespoons tomato paste

6 cups water

½ pound carrots (2 to 3 medium), peeled, halved lengthwise and cut crosswise into ½-inch pieces

15½-ounce can chickpeas, drained

3 ounces baby spinach (about 3 cups)

1 cup chopped fresh cilantro, plus more to garnish

3 tablespoons lemon juice

Plain whole-milk yogurt, to serve (optional)

The mess, time and trouble required to brown meat for a stew left us longing for a better way. Did we really need that step to get big flavor? Then we discovered a world of alternatives from cultures where cooks skip the browning and instead build layers of flavor with spices and condiments. For our no-sear, no-stock stew, based on the Yemeni dish known as maraq, we started with a dry seasoning mix—paprika, cumin, cardamom, cinnamon, salt and pepper. It did double duty, with half the mixture rubbed onto the meat and the rest briefly cooked in the pot with onion, butter and tomato paste. Cooking the seasonings with the fat and tomato paste bloomed their flavors and lightly browned the tomato paste. We wanted the savory sweetness of roasted whole garlic cloves (mincing releases aggressive sulfurous compounds) but not the trouble of roasting a head separately. So, we sliced off the top of the head, then added it whole to the stew to cook alongside the meat. We liked the flavor and texture of lamb shoulder. Boneless beef chuck worked, too (but needs an extra cup of water and must cook longer, 90 minutes total, before adding the carrots).

Don't use old spices. The backbone of the dish is the bold, vibrant spice mixture. Make sure yours are no more than a year old.

1. In a bowl, stir together the paprika, cumin, cardamom, cinnamon, 2 teaspoons salt and ½ teaspoon pepper. Reserve half of the spice mixture, then toss the lamb with the rest until well coated. Set aside. Cut off and discard the top third of the garlic head, leaving the head intact.

2. In a large Dutch oven over medium-high, melt the butter. Add the onion and cook, stirring often, until softened and just beginning to brown around the edges, 5 to 8 minutes. Add the tomato paste and the reserved spice mixture, then cook, stirring constantly, for 1 minute. Add the water and bring to a boil over high, then add the lamb and garlic head, cut side down. Cover, leaving the lid slightly ajar, and reduce heat to low.

3. Simmer for 1 hour, adjusting the heat as necessary to maintain a gentle bubble. Add the carrots and continue to simmer, partially covered, for another 30 minutes. Using tongs, remove the garlic head and squeeze over the stew to release the cloves. Stir in the chickpeas and spinach and cook until the spinach is wilted, about 5 minutes.

4. Stir in the cilantro and lemon juice, then season the stew with salt and pepper. Serve topped with yogurt and sprinkled with cilantro.

Prune, Peppercorn and
Fresh Herb-Rubbed **Roast Beef**

Start to finish: 2 hours 45 minutes, plus 48 hours to marinate
Servings: 10

8 ounces pitted prunes
(about 1½ cups)

½ cup soy sauce

¼ cup ketchup

3 tablespoons kosher salt

2 tablespoons black peppercorns

2 tablespoons chopped
fresh rosemary

2 tablespoons fresh thyme leaves

3 anchovy fillets

5- to 6-pound beef eye round
roast, trimmed

Fresh horseradish sauce,
(see sidebar) to serve (optional)

We challenged ourselves to transform a thrifty, low-cost cut of beef into a lush, celebratory meal. The answer was eye round, a roast often deemed too lean to be tender. The cut is taken from the hind leg of a steer, so there's little marbling, the usual key to keeping meat moist. To roast this tough cut and get succulent, perfectly cooked results, we marinated the meat in ingredients that would do the work for us. We started with a sticky, sweet puree of prunes. That may sound unusual, but prunes are high in hygroscopic sorbitol and fructose, which—along with salt and soy sauce—amplify the way the meat absorbs flavor. The puree also adhered well to the roast, promoting moisture retention and a caramelized crust without the trouble of browning. Ketchup and anchovies added rich umami, while rosemary, thyme and black peppercorns brought an herbal kick. To boost the marinade's effect, we poked the roast repeatedly with a fork. The roast beef tasted best after marinating for 48 hours, but 24 will work.

Don't check the roast too frequently. A succulent roast relied on even cooking at a low temperature; opening the oven door interrupted that process.

1. In a food processor, blend the prunes, soy sauce, ketchup, salt, peppercorns, rosemary, thyme and anchovies until smooth, about 1 minute. Transfer to a 2-gallon zip-close bag. Poke the roast all over with a fork, then place in the bag. Turn to coat, then refrigerate for 48 hours.

2. Heat the oven to 275°F with a rack in the middle position. Set a wire rack in a rimmed baking sheet. Remove the roast from the bag and transfer to the rack. Discard the marinade in the bag and

evenly brush any marinade sticking to the roast's surface. Roast until the meat registers 125°F, 1 hour 45 minutes to 2 hours.

3. Transfer the roast to a carving board, tent loosely with foil and let rest for 30 minutes. Thinly slice and serve with fresh horseradish sauce, if desired.

FRESH HORSERADISH SAUCE

Start to finish: **5 minutes**
Makes **about 1½ cups**

We preferred the brightness and intensity of fresh horseradish in this sauce, but bottled horseradish worked well, too. If you use bottled, reduce the vinegar to 1 tablespoon. Look for fresh horseradish root in the produce aisle, often near the fresh ginger. For maximum flavor, peel and finely grate the root with a wand-style grater. If you have extra horseradish, try grating it into mashed potatoes, or over a warm steak or pork chop.

1 cup sour cream

½ cup freshly grated horseradish root (3-inch piece)

2 tablespoons white wine vinegar

1 tablespoon water

2 teaspoons minced fresh rosemary

1 teaspoon kosher salt

In a bowl, stir together all the ingredients. The sauce can be refrigerated for up to 2 days.

Cuban-Style Pork Shoulder
with Mojo Sauce

Start to finish: 12½ hours (40 minutes active) / Servings: 6

3 tablespoons kosher salt

1 tablespoon smoked sweet paprika

4- to 5-pound bone-in pork butt, fat cap trimmed to ¼ to ½ inch

1 teaspoon grated orange zest, plus ⅔ cup orange juice (2 to 3 oranges)

1 teaspoon grated lime zest, plus ⅓ cup lime juice (2 to 3 limes)

⅓ cup fresh oregano leaves

8 garlic cloves, smashed

2 tablespoons extra-virgin olive oil

1 tablespoon ground cumin

1 teaspoon ground black pepper

½ cup coarsely chopped fresh cilantro

Lime wedges, to serve

A thick, well-marbled pork shoulder shines in pernil asado, a classic Cuban dish in which the meat marinates overnight in salt, spices and sour orange juice before being roasted for many hours. It's impressive, but most recipes call for repeated basting and flipping, or fiddling with oven temperatures, sometimes for five hours or more. We tried low, dry heat but it took too long and our meat was drying out on the surface before it finished cooking inside. So, we ratcheted the oven up to 400°F, put the pork on a roasting rack and surrounded it with a loose wrapping of parchment-lined foil. When we opened our foil packet after three and a half hours, the meat was practically falling off the bone. We sacrificed a crackly crust, but didn't miss it. That's partly because the cooking liquid—a mix of garlic, orange and lime juices, fresh oregano and cumin—gave the meat so much flavor. We also poked holes into the surface of the pork, then covered it with salt and paprika for at least eight hours before roasting. This tenderized the meat and promoted browning. Eight hours seasoning was best, but one hour will suffice. Be careful when forming the packet. Tears or openings will cause the meat to dry out. Flavorful juices pooled in the foil-parchment packet; we combined those with orange and lime juices (to replicate the taste of the sour Seville oranges typically used) and fresh cilantro to make a mojo sauce. Tossing the shredded pork with the sauce ensured every bite had a delicious, tangy flavor.

Don't let the pork or its juices come into contact with the foil during cooking; it can cause a metallic taste and discolor the juices. Make sure the parchment fully lines the bottom of the pan and covers the pork on top.

1. In a small bowl, mix together the salt and paprika. Using a paring knife and a twisting motion, make twelve 1-inch-deep cuts all over the pork. Rub with the salt mixture, then wrap tightly in plastic wrap and refrigerate for 8 to 24 hours.

2. Heat the oven to 400°F with a rack in the lower-middle position. In a liquid measuring cup, combine both juices. In a food processor, combine both zests, the oregano, garlic, oil, cumin and pepper. Process until the garlic is finely chopped, about 1 minute. Add ¼ cup of the juice and process until combined, about 10 seconds.

3. Using 18-inch-wide heavy-duty foil, make a sling in a large roasting pan. Leaving generous overhang on either side, gently press 1 sheet of foil into the pan lengthwise. Press a second sheet over that crosswise, again leaving ample overhang. Using kitchen parchment, repeat the process, setting the parchment sling over the foil. Set a wire roasting rack over the parchment.

4. Unwrap the pork and rub all over with the herb-garlic paste. Place fat side up on the rack in the prepared pan. Pour ¼ cup of the juice into the bottom of the pan. Loosely fold the excess parchment

around the pork, then fold the excess foil up over the pork. Crimp the foil to create a loose but sealed packet. Roast until the meat is tender and registers 190°F in the thickest part, about 3½ hours.

5. Transfer the pork to a carving board, tent loosely with foil and let rest for 30 minutes. Pour the accumulated juices from the pan into a medium saucepan over medium heat, then add the remaining ½ cup of citrus juice. When hot, remove from the heat and stir in the cilantro; cover and keep warm.

6. Using tongs and a knife or carving fork, cut and shred the meat into chunks, discarding the bone and any fat. Transfer to a bowl and toss with ¼ to ½ cup of the sauce. Serve with the remaining sauce and lime wedges.

STEAM COOKING WITH
A FOIL-PARCHMENT PACKET

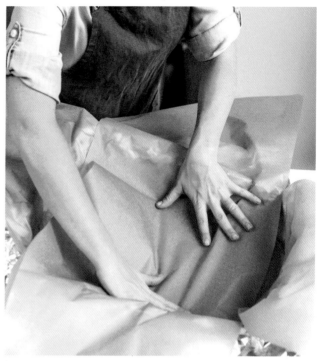

1. Leaving a generous amount of overhang on either side, gently press 1 sheet of 18-inch-wide foil lengthwise into a large roasting pan. Press a second sheet over that crosswise, again leaving ample overhang.

2. Using kitchen parchment, repeat this process, setting the sheets over the foil.

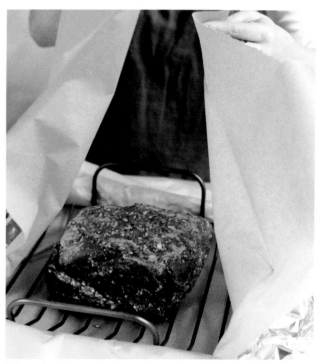

3. Set a wire roasting rack over the parchment.

4. Loosely fold the excess parchment around the pork.

5. Fold the excess foil up over the pork. Crimp the foil together to create a loose but sealed packet.

CHILI-PINEAPPLE MARGARITA

Start to finish: : 1 hour 30 minutes (20 minutes active)
Makes 2 drinks

The smooth, round flavor of reposado tequila worked best with the chilies in this cocktail.

1 cup plus 1½ teaspoons white sugar, divided

1 cup water

Four 1-inch strips lime zest

Four 1-inch strips orange zest, plus 1 orange wedge

1 jalapeno chili, halved

1 habanero chili, halved

1 tablespoon kosher salt

¾ teaspoon chili powder

4 ounces (½ cup) reposado tequila

2 ounces (¼ cup) pineapple juice

1½ ounces (3 tablespoons) lime juice (1 to 2 limes)

1. In a small saucepan, combine 1 cup of the sugar, the water, both zests and both chilies. Bring the mixture to a boil, stirring occasionally, then remove from the heat and steep for 15 minutes. Strain into a jar, discarding the solids. Let cool.

2. While the syrup cools, in a small bowl, stir together the salt, chili powder and the remaining 1½ teaspoons of sugar. Spread the mixture on a small plate. Use the orange wedge to moisten the rims of 2 rocks glasses, then dip in the chili salt, turning to coat.

3. In a cocktail shaker, combine the tequila, pineapple juice, lime juice and 1½ ounces (3 tablespoons) of the chili syrup. Add 2 cups of ice and shake vigorously until chilled, 10 to 15 seconds. Strain into the prepared glasses.

Thai Beef Salad (*Yam Neua*)

Start to finish: **40 minutes** / Servings: **4**

1 large shallot, sliced into very thin rings

3 tablespoons lime juice (about 2 limes)

4 teaspoons packed brown sugar, divided

1½ teaspoons kosher salt

¾ teaspoon ground white pepper

1½ pounds skirt steak, trimmed and cut into 2 or 3 pieces

Canola oil (if using a skillet)

1 to 2 tablespoons fish sauce

1 teaspoon red pepper flakes

1½ cups (about 7 ounces) red or yellow cherry tomatoes, halved

½ cup coarsely chopped fresh cilantro, plus cilantro sprigs to garnish (optional)

½ cup coarsely chopped fresh mint

In the U.S., a steak salad can be just about any dreary salad topped with steak. But in Thailand, the steak is the star of the dish. Thai beef salad, or yam neua, is a tangle of thinly sliced grilled steak, tossed, with a hot, sour, salty and slightly sweet dressing, shallots and a heap of cilantro and fresh mint—and possibly some sliced cucumbers and chopped tomatoes. "Yam" refers to a style of salads that are spicy and slightly sour thanks to the classic Thai combination of fish sauce, lime juice, palm sugar and chilies. For our version of yam neua (pronounced yum n-UH), we started by choosing the right steak—skirt. The thin, well-marbled cut has big beefy flavor that can stand up to the salad's robust dressing. To season the meat, we used white pepper instead of black for its complexity. A couple teaspoons of brown sugar, balanced with salt, approximated the faint maple flavor of palm sugar. A very hot grill or skillet was essential to developing a flavorful crust on the meat. Rubbing the steak with sugar first increased the char.

Don't ignore the steak's grain. Cutting with the grain results in tough slices. Cutting against the grain shortens the muscle fibers, producing tender, juicy meat.

1. In a large bowl, combine the shallots and lime juice and let sit for 10 minutes, stirring occasionally. In a small bowl, combine 2 teaspoons of the sugar, the salt and white pepper. Pat the steak dry with paper towels, then rub all over with the sugar-salt mixture. If using a cast-iron or carbon-steel skillet, cut the steak into 4 to 6 pieces if needed to fit into the pan.

2. Prepare a grill or skillet for very high heat. For a charcoal grill, spread a full chimney of hot coals evenly over half of the grill bed. For a gas grill, set all burners to a high, even flame. Heat the grill for 5 minutes, then clean and oil the cooking grate. For a cast-iron or carbon-steel pan, heat 1 teaspoon canola oil over medium-high until smoking, about 5 minutes.

3. If using a grill, grill the steak (directly over the coals, if using a charcoal grill) until charred all over, 2 to 4 minutes per side. If using a skillet, sear the steak in 2 batches until charred, 2 to 4 minutes per side. Transfer the steak to a carving board and let rest for 10 minutes.

4. Meanwhile, add 1 tablespoon of the fish sauce, the pepper flakes and the remaining 2 teaspoons of sugar to the shallot–lime juice mixture and stir until the sugar has dissolved. Taste, then add additional fish sauce, if desired. Thinly slice the steak against the grain, then transfer to the bowl along with any accumulated juices. Add the tomatoes, cilantro and mint and stir. Transfer to a platter and garnish with cilantro sprigs, if desired.

Shrimp in Chipotle Sauce (*Camarones Enchipotlados*)

Start to finish: **25 minutes** / Servings: 4

4 vine-ripened tomatoes
(1¼ pounds), quartered

4 chipotle chilies in adobo sauce
and the sauce clinging to them

Kosher salt and ground black pepper

4 tablespoons olive oil, divided

1½ pounds extra-large raw shrimp,
peeled, deveined, tails removed and
patted dry

4 tablespoons lime juice, divided

1 medium yellow onion, chopped

3 garlic cloves, thinly sliced

½ teaspoon dried oregano

¼ cup dry white wine

½ cup chopped fresh cilantro,
plus more to serve

Eight 6-inch corn tortillas, warmed

Avocado, sour cream and lime
wedges, to serve

A perfectly cooked shrimp—pink, firm but not tough, curved but not coiled—stymies most of us. The window between done and overdone is narrow. We solved that problem by giving the shrimp very little time over direct heat. Instead, we let the residual heat of a flavorful sauce cook them more gently. For the sauce, we used canned chipotle chilies and the adobo sauce in which they are packed, which give the dish pleasant, lingering heat and deep smoky flavor. The shrimp got a brief sear to start, then finished cooking off the burner in the warm sauce. Perfect results, effortlessly, every time. These shrimp made wonderful tacos when paired with diced avocado, fresh cilantro, lime wedges and sour cream. This dish also is delicious served alongside rice or cold as an appetizer.

Don't worry if your chipotles vary in size. Despite appearances, most weigh about half an ounce.

1. In a food processor, pulse the tomatoes, chilies and any sauce coating them and ¾ teaspoon salt until mostly smooth, 1 minute. Set aside.

2. In a 12-inch nonstick skillet over medium-high, heat 2 tablespoons of the oil until beginning to smoke. Add half the shrimp and cook, stirring, until golden, about 45 seconds. Transfer to a bowl. Repeat with the remaining shrimp, adding them to the bowl. Toss with 2 tablespoons of the lime juice. Set aside.

3. Return the skillet to medium-high and add the remaining 2 tablespoons of oil. Add the onion and cook for 3 to 4 minutes. Add the garlic and oregano and cook until just beginning to brown, 1 minute. Stir in the wine and any accumulated shrimp juice from the bowl. Cook until liquid is nearly evaporated. Add the chipotle mixture and simmer, stirring, until thick enough to coat a spoon, 10 to 12 minutes.

4. Remove the skillet from the heat. Stir in the shrimp, cover and let sit until the shrimp are opaque and cooked through, 2 to 4 minutes. Stir in the cilantro and remaining lime juice. Taste, then season with salt and pepper. Serve with warmed tortillas, avocado, sour cream and lime wedges.

Oven-Poached Salmon with Thyme, Dill and Vermouth

Start to finish: 1½ hours / Servings: 8

½ cup soy sauce

3½- to 4-pound salmon fillet, skin on, pin bones removed

2 medium carrots, finely chopped

1 celery stalk, finely chopped

1 shallot, thinly sliced

8 sprigs fresh thyme

8 sprigs fresh dill, plus 3 teaspoons minced, divided

Kosher salt

1 cup dry vermouth

Ground black pepper

2 tablespoons salted butter

1 tablespoon lemon juice

Lemon wedges, to serve

Ideal for a crowd, a side of salmon is an impressive main course that's as good at room temperature as it is hot from the oven. Trouble is, it can be difficult to cook without drying out and often is flavorless. Our inspiration for a better way came from an oven-poaching method we learned from French chef Michel Bras. He slow cooks smaller cuts of salmon in a 250°F oven over a water-filled baking pan. To adapt the technique for a larger side of salmon, we ratcheted up the heat; surrounded the fish with carrots, celery, shallot and a bit of vermouth; and covered it all tightly with foil. This allowed the salmon to steam and infuse with flavor while cooking faster and staying tender. And for even more flavor, we start by soaking the salmon briefly in soy sauce. A fillet between 1½ and 1¾ inches thick worked best. We found temperature was a better indicator for doneness than cooking time. To test the salmon's temperature, carefully peel back the foil just enough to insert a digital thermometer at the thickest end. The best way to perfectly cook this dish was to remove it from the oven a little before the salmon was fully cooked. The residual heat gently finished the cooking.

Don't marinate the salmon longer than 20 minutes. The soy sauce adds an earthy dimension to the salmon's flavor, but if left too long its saltiness will become overpowering.

1. Heat the oven to 500°F with a rack in the middle position. Pour the soy sauce into a baking dish large enough to fit the salmon. Add the fish, flesh side down. Marinate for 15 to 20 minutes.

2. Meanwhile, in a bowl toss the carrots, celery, shallot, thyme, 8 dill sprigs and 1 teaspoon salt. Set aside. Fold an 18-inch-long sheet of foil lengthwise into a strip wide enough for the salmon to fit on. Lightly coat the foil with oil, then place it, oiled side up, in the center of a rimmed baking sheet. Arrange the carrot-celery mixture around the outside edges of the foil. Drizzle the vegetables with the vermouth. Place the salmon on the foil, flesh side up. Season with pepper.

3. Cover the entire pan tightly with foil, allowing it to dome over the salmon.

Roast until the salmon registers 120°F, 20 to 25 minutes. Remove the pan from the oven, keeping the foil in place, and let the salmon rest until it is between 125°F and 130°F, another 5 to 8 minutes. Remove the top foil, then use the foil under the salmon to lift and transfer it to a serving platter. Let cool for 5 minutes.

4. Meanwhile, strain the liquid and solids on the baking sheet into a saucepan. Discard the solids and all but ¾ cup of the liquid. Over medium heat, bring the liquid to a simmer. Off the heat, stir in the butter, lemon juice and 1 teaspoon of the minced dill. Season with salt and pepper. Pour 3 tablespoons of the sauce over the salmon. Sprinkle the remaining 2 teaspoons dill over the salmon. Serve with lemon wedges and the remaining sauce.

Salmon Packets with Chermoula

Start to finish: **50 minutes (15 minutes active)** / Servings: **4**

Four 6-ounce center-cut skinless
salmon fillets (1 to 1¼ inches thick)

Kosher salt and ground black pepper

1 teaspoon extra-virgin olive oil

Chermoula sauce, to serve
(see sidebar)

Lemon wedges, to serve

Cooking salmon can be a conundrum. Cook it long enough to brown the skin and the inside becomes dry and overcooked. Take it off the heat sooner and the flesh is tender but wanly unappetizing. To get our salmon both browned and delectably moist we use the classic French method of cooking food in a sealed packet. The packet traps the natural moisture of the food inside, puffing impressively and steaming the dish in its own juices. Known as cooking en papillote, variations of the technique, such as cooking food wrapped in leaves, husks or even paper bags, exist around the world. But there's one drawback: The results can be bland because browning—the source of rich caramelized flavors—occurs only above 300°F. But steaming (which is the cooking that occurs inside a packet) never gets above 212°F. So we borrowed a variation we'd seen French chef and restaurateur Jean-Georges Vongerichten use—foil. Encasing a salmon fillet in a foil packet that is cooked on the stovetop allowed us to both brown (because of the direct heat beneath the fish) and steam (because of the trapped moisture) the fish. Six-ounce fillets were the perfect size; if the fillets were thinner than 1 inch or thicker than 1¼ inches, we needed to adjust the cooking time.

Don't hesitate to remove the packet from the skillet a little early if you think it's cooking too quickly. It's easy to return it to the skillet.

1. Remove the salmon from the refrigerator and let sit at room temperature for 20 to 30 minutes.

2. Pat the salmon dry with paper towels and season with salt and pepper. Place a 12-by-24-inch sheet of foil on the counter, shiny side down. Fold in half to form a 12-inch square. Unfold the foil and spread oil evenly over half of it (one 12-inch square), leaving a 3-inch border.

3. Arrange the salmon fillets over the oiled area, leaving at least ½ inch between them. Fold the top square of foil over the salmon and, without pressing down on the fillets, roll and crimp the open sides to create an airtight packet. Fold in the corners of the packet to help it fit in the pan.

4. Heat a 12-inch skillet over high heat for 5 minutes. Carefully place the packet in the skillet and cook 5 minutes for medium and 6 minutes for medium-well, rotating the pan frequently to ensure even cooking. The packet should begin puffing after 2 minutes and be fully inflated after 4 minutes. If the bottom edges of the packet start lifting up, reduce the heat slightly.

5. Using tongs, slide the packet onto a platter and let sit for 1 minute. Carefully open the packet. Spoon the accumulated juices over the salmon and serve topped with chermoula and lemon wedges.

CHERMOULA SAUCE

Start to finish: 10 minutes
Makes enough to top 4 salmon fillets

1 cup lightly packed flat-leaf parsley leaves

2 tablespoons pine nuts, toasted

2 teaspoons grated lemon zest

1 large garlic clove

1 teaspoon ground coriander

1 teaspoon sweet paprika

½ teaspoon kosher salt

½ teaspoon ground cardamom

¼ teaspoon red pepper flakes (optional)

3 tablespoons extra-virgin olive oil

In a food processor, combine all ingredients but the oil. Process until finely ground, about 20 seconds. Scrape down the bowl, add the oil, then process until incorporated, about 10 seconds.

Za'atar Chicken Cutlets and Lemon-Parsley Salad

Start to finish: 30 minutes / Servings: 4

1½ pounds boneless, skinless chicken breast cutlets (4 cutlets), pounded to ¼-inch thickness

Kosher salt

¼ cup plus 1 teaspoon za'atar, divided

3 tablespoons all-purpose flour

¾ teaspoon Aleppo pepper

2 tablespoons plus 1 teaspoon olive oil, divided

¾ cup lightly packed fresh flat-leaf parsley leaves

2 scallions, trimmed and thinly sliced on a bias

½ teaspoon lemon zest, plus 1 tablespoon lemon juice

2 tablespoons pomegranate molasses

3 tablespoons finely chopped walnuts

Our search for ways to spice up weeknight chicken took us to the Middle East where za'atar is a popular seasoning blend that often includes sesame seeds, sumac, thyme, oregano, marjoram and salt. We were influenced by Ana Sortun, who often uses za'atar at her Oleana restaurant in Cambridge, Massachusetts. She calls za'atar "craveable" and jokes, "I can imagine it as the next Doritos flavor." Her recipe for crispy lemon chicken with za'atar calls for making a lemon confit and stuffing it under the skin of whole halves of deboned chicken along with cubes of butter. We took a simpler tack and coated chicken cutlets in a flour-za'atar mixture. We also used lemon zest and juice in our sauce along with tart and smoky Aleppo pepper, which has a fruity, moderate heat. If you can't find Aleppo pepper, a few pinches of paprika and cayenne make a good substitute.

Don't substitute chicken breasts here without pounding the meat first. Boneless, skinless chicken cutlets were ideal for fast cooking and are widely available at grocers. If you have only chicken breasts, use a meat mallet or heavy skillet to flatten them to an even ¼ inch.

1. Season the chicken all over with salt. In a wide, shallow dish, combine ¼ cup of the za'atar, the flour and pepper. In a 12-inch stainless steel skillet over medium-high, heat 2 tablespoons of the oil until shimmering. One cutlet at a time, transfer the chicken to the za'atar mixture, coating and pressing onto all sides. Add the cutlets to the pan and cook until well browned, about 3 minutes per side. Transfer to a platter.

2. In a medium bowl, mix together the parsley, scallions, lemon zest and juice, the remaining 1 teaspoon of oil and a pinch of salt. Drizzle the molasses evenly over the chicken, then mound the greens over the cutlets. Sprinkle with walnuts and the remaining za'atar.

MAKING CHICKEN CUTLETS

1. Start with boneless, skinless chicken breasts that weigh 6½ to 7 ounces each. (If breasts are larger than 8 ounces, halve horizontally after removing the tenderloin. Cutlets will require less pounding but will be smaller.)

2. Remove the tenderloin from the breast using kitchen shears and save for another use, such as chicken fingers.

3. Use a sharp knife or kitchen shears to trim away any fat, then, if necessary, trim the breasts to 6 ounces each.

4. Working with 1 breast at a time, place on a cutting board and lay a sheet of plastic wrap on top. Use a meat mallet or small, heavy skillet to gently but firmly pound the breast to an even, ¼-inch thickness.

Vietnamese Caramel Fish

Start to finish: 30 minutes / Servings: 4

1 tablespoon plus ½ cup coconut water, divided

¼ cup white sugar

3 tablespoons fish sauce

½ cup thinly sliced shallots (about 1 large shallot)

1½-inch piece fresh ginger, halved and smashed

Four 2-inch strips lime zest

Four 5- to 6-ounce cod fillets, about ¾-inch thick

Ground black pepper

¼ cup chopped fresh cilantro leaves

1 jalapeno or serrano chili, thinly sliced

We're always looking for ways to cook moist, flavorful fish with relatively little fuss. And we found a new, unusual way to do that via a sauce we usually associate with dessert. In Vietnam, fish is cooked in a savory-sweet caramel sauce, both seasoning the fish and keeping it moist. To ensure our sauce was dark and savory, not cloying, we cooked the sugar a little longer, creating a darker and slightly bitter caramel. We found that a tablespoon of coconut water helped the sugar caramelize faster, getting us the deep coffee color we were after in just minutes. Keep a close eye on the caramel to prevent it from burning and becoming too bitter. Dark, oily fish are common in this dish, but we liked it better with a firm whitefish. Note that cooking times are for fillets about ¾ inch thick.

Don't use canned coconut milk here. Coconut water is widely available and lends a light sweetness and subtle coconut flavor to the caramel. If you can't find it, use water.

1. In a large Dutch oven over medium-high, bring 1 tablespoon of the coconut water and the sugar to a boil. Cook, stirring occasionally, until the mixture begins to color at the edges, 2 to 3 minutes. Reduce heat to medium-low and cook, stirring often, until the sugar is mahogany-colored, another 1 to 3 minutes. Off heat, add the fish sauce and whisk until smooth (the mixture will steam and bubble vigorously). Add the remaining ½ cup of coconut water and whisk until fully incorporated. Add the shallots, ginger and lime zest. Return to a simmer over medium. Reduce heat to medium-low and simmer gently for 5 minutes.

2. Season the fish with pepper, then nestle it into the pot. Simmer for 3 minutes, then gently turn the fish and continue simmering until just cooked through, 3 to 5 minutes, scraping the edges of the pot as necessary to prevent burning and adjusting the heat to maintain a gentle simmer. (If the caramel darkens too quickly around the edges, reduce the heat to low.)

3. Carefully transfer the fish to a rimmed serving plate. The sauce should be thick and syrupy. If necessary, continue to simmer until the proper consistency is achieved. Off heat, remove and discard the ginger and zest. Drizzle the fish with the sauce, then sprinkle with cilantro and chili.

Filipino Chicken Adobo with Coconut Broth

Start to finish: 1 hour 45 minutes (30 minutes active)
Servings: 4

___

1½ cups unseasoned rice vinegar

¾ cup low-sodium soy sauce

6 garlic cloves, smashed

6 bird's eye chilies, halved lengthwise

4 bay leaves

1 teaspoon black peppercorns

8 bone-in, skin-on chicken thighs
(3 to 3½ pounds)

1 cup coconut milk

⅓ cup chopped fresh cilantro

Steamed white rice, to serve

Thousands of islands make up the Philippines. And there probably are as many recipes for chicken adobo, the classic Filipino dish that turns a handful of ingredients—loads of garlic, black pepper and vinegar—into a bright and tangy meal. The name comes from a Spanish word for sauce. Food historian Raymond Sokolov reasons that the Spaniards, when they arrived in the Philippines, gave the native Filipino dish the name because it resembled the Spanish adobo they knew. We tailored our recipe for weeknight ease, using a hefty dose of rice vinegar blended with soy sauce and aromatics to create a potent marinade for bone-in chicken thighs. For heat, we used bird's eye chilies (sometimes called Thai chilies), but if you can't find them any small chili will do. Look for chicken thighs that are uniform in size. If some are smaller than others, begin to check them early and remove them as they come up to temperature.

Don't use regular soy sauce. As the chicken braises, the cooking liquid reduces, concentrating the flavor—and salt. Low-sodium soy sauce produced a broth that was well seasoned.

1. In a large Dutch oven, combine the vinegar, soy sauce, garlic, chilies, bay leaves and peppercorns. Add the chicken thighs, submerging them. Cover and refrigerate for 30 to 60 minutes.

2. Bring the mixture to a boil over medium-high. Reduce heat to medium-low and cook, turning the thighs occasionally, until the chicken registers 170°F, 25 to 30 minutes, adjusting the heat as necessary to maintain a medium simmer.

3. Heat the broiler with an oven rack 6 inches from the element. Line a rimmed baking sheet with foil. Remove the chicken from the pot and arrange skin side up on the baking sheet. Pat dry with paper towels and set aside.

4. Strain the cooking liquid, discarding the solids, then skim off the fat. Return 1 cup of the defatted liquid to the pot, stir in the coconut milk and bring to a simmer over medium. Take the pan off the heat, stir in the cilantro, then cover and set aside.

5. Broil the chicken until the skin is deeply browned and blackened in spots, 3 to 8 minutes. Serve in shallow bowls with steamed white rice, ladling the broth over the rice.

Burmese Chicken

Start to finish: 30 minutes
Servings: 4

8 ounces plum tomatoes (2 large), quartered

4 tablespoons grapeseed or other neutral oil, divided

3 teaspoons kosher salt, divided

2 teaspoons ground turmeric

¼ teaspoon red pepper flakes

2 stalks lemon grass, trimmed and bottom 5 inches chopped

2 large shallots, quartered

2 ounces fresh ginger, thinly sliced (about ¼ cup)

8 garlic cloves

1½ pounds boneless, skinless chicken thighs, trimmed and cut into 1½-inch pieces

½ cup chopped fresh cilantro

2 tablespoons lime juice, plus lime wedges, to serve

Food writer and photographer Naomi Duguid's stunning books provide keen insight into the people and foods of the countries she visits. One of our favorites, "Burma," includes a terrific recipe called Aromatic Chicken from the Shan Hills. It's simple, yet has deep flavor. We wanted to finesse things to make this even faster and easier for the home cook. We swapped in boneless thighs for Duguid's bone-in chicken and switched to a Dutch oven instead of a wok. She suggests a mortar and pestle, but we used a blender to make a paste of lemon grass, garlic, ginger and shallots. This meant we could skip a marinade and let the chicken season as it cooked. A dose of red pepper flakes added moderate heat, but traditional Burmese food can be fairly spicy; if you want more heat, increase the red pepper flakes or stir in a slivered jalapeno, serrano or bird's eye chili with the cilantro. We liked the chicken over steamed rice or thin rice noodles. It also would be excellent with our coconut rice (p. 96).

Don't use the fibrous outer layers of the lemon grass. You want only the white, slightly tender (but still firm) inner bulb. Trim the root and all but the bottom 5 inches of the stalk, then peel off the first few layers. If you buy lemon grass in a plastic clamshell container, it likely already has been trimmed.

1. In a blender, combine the tomatoes, 1 tablespoon of the oil, 1 teaspoon of the salt, the turmeric, pepper flakes, lemon grass, shallots, ginger and garlic. Blend until a thick paste forms, about 1 minute, scraping down the blender as needed.

2. In a large Dutch oven over medium-high, add the remaining 3 tablespoons of oil, the chicken and the remaining 2 teaspoons of salt. Cook, stirring occasionally, until the chicken is no longer pink, about 5 minutes. Add the spice paste and cook, stirring occasionally, until fragrant and the paste coats the chicken, 2 to 3 minutes.

3. Cover, reduce heat to medium-low and cook, stirring occasionally, for 10 minutes. Uncover, increase heat to medium-high and simmer until the chicken is cooked through and the sauce is thickened, 7 to 9 minutes. Off heat, stir in the cilantro and lime juice. Serve with lime wedges.

Caramelized Pork with Orange and Sage

Start to finish: **25 minutes** / Servings: **6**

2 pounds of pork tenderloin, trimmed, cut into 6 pieces

Kosher salt and ground black pepper

½ cup turbinado sugar

3 strips orange zest, chopped (1 tablespoon), plus ½ cup orange juice (1 to 2 oranges)

2 tablespoons chopped fresh sage, divided

¼ teaspoon cayenne pepper

2 tablespoons olive oil

2 tablespoons cider vinegar

Looking for a way to add flavor to all-too-often utilitarian pork tenderloin, we drew inspiration from Francis Mallmann, the Argentine chef best known for pushing the limits of browning—using live fire to cook vegetables, meat and fruit until they're almost burnt. Mallmann tops pork tenderloin with brown sugar, thyme and a fruity orange confit tinged by bay leaves and black peppercorns. The flavorful coating is seared onto the surface in a cast-iron griddle until the orange and thyme are crispy and charred. We loved the flavors, but the technique wasn't home cook friendly. To simplify and preserve the flavors, we started by streamlining the orange confit: Orange zest and fresh sage, coarsely chopped, gave a similar texture and fragrance. Gently pounding the tenderloin ensured a flat surface for a sugar mixture to adhere. Instead of searing the pork, we opted to broil it, making it easier to maintain the topping. Brown sugar became a sticky mess under the broiler, so we used coarse turbinado sugar, which kept its shape and crunch. If the sugar gets too dark before the meat comes to temperature, turn off the oven; the pork will finish cooking in the residual heat.

Don't tent the pork with foil after removing it from the oven. It will lose its candy-like crust. For the same reason, don't spoon the sauce over it.

1. Heat the broiler with a rack 6 inches from the element. Pat the pork dry, then use a meat mallet or a small heavy skillet to gently flatten the pieces to an even 1-inch thickness. Season with salt and pepper. In a small bowl, rub together the sugar, orange zest, 1 tablespoon of the sage and the cayenne. Set aside.

2. In a 12-inch oven-safe skillet over medium-high, heat the oil until just beginning to smoke. Add the pork and cook until deep golden brown on one side, about 3 minutes. Transfer the pork browned side up to large plate; reserve the skillet. Press the sugar mixture onto the tops of the pork pieces in an even layer. Return the meat to the skillet, sugar side up. Set under the broiler until the meat registers 135°F at the center and the sugar mixture is golden brown, 5 to 7 minutes, rotating the pan halfway through. Transfer to a carving board and let rest.

3. Meanwhile, return the skillet to medium-high heat on the stovetop. Add the orange juice and the remaining 1 tablespoon of sage. Cook, scraping up any browned bits, until the sauce is syrupy, 2 to 3 minutes. Stir in the vinegar. Taste and season with salt and pepper. Serve the pork over the sauce.

Red Chili Spatchcocked Roast Chicken

Start to finish: 1 hour 45 minutes (30 minutes active)
Servings: 4

¼ cup grapeseed or other neutral oil

2 ounces whole dried ancho chilies, stemmed and seeded

⅔ cup water

1 tablespoon dried oregano, Mexican if available

2 garlic cloves, smashed

2 tablespoons packed light brown sugar

1 tablespoon cider vinegar

Kosher salt and ground black pepper

½ teaspoon ground cumin

¼ teaspoon cinnamon

3½- to 4-pound whole chicken, backbone cut out

¼ cup lime juice, plus lime wedges to serve

Warmed corn tortillas, to serve (optional)

How to cook a whole chicken quickly and evenly? Remove it's backbone and flatten the bird—a technique called spatchcocking or butterflying. Our next challenge was adding flavor that doesn't stop at the skin. Our solution was to slide a chili-herb-spice mixture between the skin and meat. Our flavoring rub was based on a classic adobado, a seasoning common in Mexican cooking, revamped for indoor cooking without a long marination. Roasting and coarsely grinding the dried chilies before rehydrating them meant we could use less water, giving the resulting chili paste deeper flavor. If you prefer a milder heat, remove the seeds after stemming the chilies.

1. Heat the oven to 375°F with a rack in the middle position. In a 12-inch oven-safe heavy skillet over medium-high, heat the oil until shimmering. Add the chilies and toast until lightly browned, about 20 seconds per side. Transfer to a food processor, reserving the pan and oil. Process until coarsely chopped, about 30 seconds. In a small saucepan, bring the water to a boil. Add the chilies, oregano and garlic, then cover, remove from heat and let sit for 15 minutes.

2. In the food processor, combine the sugar, vinegar, 2½ teaspoons salt, ¼ teaspoon pepper, cumin, cinnamon and 2 tablespoons of the reserved chili oil from the skillet. Add the chili-water mixture and process until smooth, about 1 minute, scraping the bowl as needed. Reserve a third of the mixture, about 5 tablespoons.

3. With the breast side up, flatten the chicken by pressing on the center of the breast with your palms. Carefully lift the skin from the meat of the breasts and legs, avoiding tears. Spoon the remaining chili paste under the skin, massaging the skin to evenly distribute. Rub the skin of the chicken with the remaining reserved chili oil, then season with salt and pepper. Tuck the wing tips under the breasts, then place the chicken breast side up in the empty skillet. Transfer to the oven and roast until the breast registers 160°F, 45 to 50 minutes.

4. Transfer the chicken to a carving board, tent with foil and let rest for 15 minutes. Meanwhile, place the empty skillet over medium heat on the stovetop, then add the reserved chili paste and lime juice. Cook until warmed through. Taste and season with salt and pepper. Carve the chicken, adding any juices to the sauce, and serve with the sauce, lime wedges and warmed tortillas, if desired.

HOW TO SPATCHCOCK A CHICKEN

1. With the chicken sitting breast side down on a cutting board, use sturdy kitchen shears to cut along both sides of the backbone. Discard the backbone or save it for another use (freeze it for stock).

2. Flip the chicken breast side up. Place the heels of your hands on the center of the breast-bone and press down firmly to flatten the chicken.

TEQUILA AT HIGH NOON

Start to finish: **5 minutes**
Makes **2 drinks**

For our take on the classic tequila sunrise, we substituted the mildly bittersweet Italian spirit Aperol for the typical (and often too sweet) grenadine. And we loved the way a dose of chocolate bitters—½ teaspoon's worth—complemented the orange juice.

4 ounces tequila blanco

4 ounces orange juice

1 ounce lemon juice

1 ounce Aperol

½ teaspoon chocolate bitters

In a cocktail shaker, combine all ingredients. Fill the shaker with ice, then shake vigorously for 15 seconds. Strain into chilled rocks glasses.

Chiang Mai Chicken (*Ki Yang*)

Start to finish: 3 hours (20 minutes active)
Servings: 4

---

1 cup lightly packed fresh cilantro leaves and tender stems

½ cup fish sauce

½ cup soy sauce

¼ cup packed light brown sugar

1 lemon grass stalk, trimmed, bottom 8 inches chopped (optional)

4 garlic cloves, smashed

1 tablespoon coriander seeds

1 tablespoon black peppercorns

1 teaspoon white peppercorns

Two 10- to 12-ounce whole chicken legs

Two 10- to 12-ounce bone-in, skin-on chicken breasts, ribs trimmed

1 cup kosher salt

Lime wedges, to serve (optional)

We first tried this chicken at a sidewalk restaurant in Chiang Mai in northern Thailand. The spatchcocked birds were stuck with two bamboo skewers set in a V shape that were used first to turn the chicken, then toelevate it above the heat. The chicken had started the day before with a marinade of fish sauce, coconut milk, lemon grass, crushed coriander and peppercorns, garlic, cilantro root, palm sugar and, perhaps, a touch of MSG—a respectable ingredient in this part of the world. The marinade had actually flavored the chicken, a rare event. The barbecue sauce was another surprise, a tamarind-based concoction that included dried chilies, galangal (a relative of ginger), salt and more fish sauce. Our version uses brown sugar in place of harder-to-find palm sugar. We opted for the ease of chicken parts; you can buy leg quarters and breasts. Use four whole legs or four split breasts, or break down a whole chicken. It's optional, but lemon grass added bright, citrusy flavor that's characteristic of Thai food. The lemon grass paste sold in tubes near the fresh herbs worked in a pinch; substitute 2 tablespoons of paste for the fresh lemon grass. Cooking the chicken over a bed of salt prevented the marinade from burning as it dripped off the chicken. While a simple squeeze of lime was enough to dress the meat, we also liked dipping it in tangy tamarind (p. 256) or chili-lime sauce (see sidebar).

Don't marinate the chicken longer than two hours. The salt in the marinade can toughen the meat and overwhelm its flavor.

1. In a blender, combine the cilantro, fish sauce, soy sauce, sugar, lemon grass, if using, garlic, coriander and both peppercorns. Blend until smooth, about 1 minute. Reserve ¼ cup of the marinade for the glaze.

2. Place the chicken in a large zip-close plastic bag. Pour in the remaining marinade and seal. Set in a bowl and refrigerate for 2 hours.

3. Heat the oven to 400°F with the rack in the middle position. Line a rimmed baking sheet with foil and spread the salt over it. Mist a wire rack with cooking spray, then set over the salt. Arrange the chicken on the rack. Bake for 30 minutes. Brush the chicken with the reserved marinade and continue to bake until the thighs register 175°F and the breasts register 160°F, another 10 to 15 minutes. Transfer the chicken to a carving board and let rest for 15 minutes. Serve with lime wedges or dipping sauce, if desired.

CHILI-LIME DIPPING SAUCE

Start to finish: **5 minutes**
Makes **about ¾ cup**

Chili-garlic sauce has a coarser
texture, fuller body and more
pronounced garlic flavor than
Sriracha. Look for it in the grocer's
Asian foods aisle.

½ cup lime juice (4 to 6 limes)

3 tablespoons fish sauce

2 tablespoons packed light brown
sugar

2 teaspoons chili-garlic sauce

In a bowl, stir together all ingredients until the sugar dissolves. Use
immediately or refrigerate for up to
3 days.

Mussels with Chorizo and Slow-Roasted Tomatoes

Start to finish: **20 minutes** / Servings: 4

4 ounces Spanish chorizo, halved lengthwise and sliced into ½-inch pieces

3 tablespoons extra-virgin olive oil

1 small red onion, thinly sliced

1 small fennel bulb, halved, cored and thinly sliced crosswise

8 garlic cloves, smashed

2 bay leaves

1 teaspoon fennel seeds

16 slow-roasted tomato halves chopped

1½ cups dry vermouth

½ cup water

3 pounds blue mussels, scrubbed

4 tablespoons (½ stick) salted butter, chilled

½ cup chopped fresh flat-leaf parsley

1 tablespoon lemon juice

Kosher salt and ground black pepper

Mussels have a reputation as being tricky, but actually are quick and easy to cook. And as a bonus, they generate their own broth, producing maximum taste in minutes. Our take on mussels turns up the taste by adding Spanish chorizo, giving this dish its smoky, savory flavor. Then we took it a step further by adding our slow-roasted tomatoes (p. 259). Buy mussels from a reliable fishmonger and refrigerate them in a loosely covered colander set over a bowl. You may need to remove the "beard" from the mussels if they aren't cleaned already. Be sure to discard any mussels that are partially opened or broken. Larger black mussels will take a bit longer to cook than blue mussels. Keep a close eye on the mussels; once they start to open, take them off the burner to finish cooking in the residual heat. When buying chorizo for this recipe look for Spanish style, which is cured, smoked and quite firm. Mexican chorizo is soft and crumbles easily. Our favorite brand is Palacios, which is available at many grocers or online. If you can't find it, andouille or linguica are good alternatives. If you don't have any slow-roasted tomatoes, substitute a 14½-ounce can of fire-roasted tomatoes with juice. We liked this dish served with crusty bread and extra-virgin olive oil.

Don't fully cook the mussels on the stove. They continue to cook as they sit off the heat.

1. In a large pot over medium, cook the chorizo in the olive oil until the chorizo begins to brown, about 3 minutes. Stir in the onion, fennel, garlic, bay leaves and fennel seeds. Cover and cook until the onion softens, about 5 minutes. Stir in the tomatoes, vermouth and water, then bring to a simmer. Cover and cook, stirring occasionally, until the fennel is tender, about 7 minutes.

2. Add the mussels and stir. Cover and cook until the mussels just begin to open, about 3 minutes. Remove the pot from the heat and let the mussels continue to cook, covered, until all mussels open, another 3 to 5 minutes, quickly stirring once halfway through.

3. Using a kitchen spider or slotted spoon, transfer the mussels to a serving platter, leaving the sauce in the pot. Return the sauce to a simmer over low, then remove from the heat. Whisk in the butter until melted. Stir in the parsley and lemon juice. Taste and season with salt and pepper. Pour the sauce over the mussels.

Chicken Tagine with Apricots, Butternut Squash and Spinach

Start to finish: **1 hour (30 minutes active)** / Servings: 4

___

4 tablespoons extra-virgin olive oil, divided

Kosher salt and ground black pepper

2 teaspoons cinnamon

2 teaspoons ground cumin

2 teaspoons sweet paprika

1 teaspoon ground coriander

¼ teaspoon pepper cayenne

1½ pounds boneless, skinless chicken thighs, trimmed and cut into 1½-inch pieces

1 large yellow onion, thinly sliced lengthwise

4 garlic cloves, peeled and smashed

4 teaspoons grated fresh ginger

2½ cups low-sodium chicken broth

14½-ounce can diced tomatoes

¾ cup dried apricots, quartered

8 ounces peeled butternut squash, cut into ¾-inch cubes (about 2 cups)

1 cup Greek green olives, pitted and halved

1 cup chopped fresh cilantro, divided

¼ cup pistachios, toasted and chopped

2 teaspoons grated lemon zest, plus 3 tablespoons lemon juice (1 to 2 lemons)

4 ounces baby spinach (about 4 cups)

This spicy, fruity chicken stew is based on tagine, a classic North African dish that cooks meat, vegetables and fruit mostly in their natural juices. We love it because the richness of the dish comes from layers of flavor, not laborious browning. The word tagine refers to both the dish and the clay pot it typically is cooked in. The pot has a shallow pan and a conical top designed to collect condensation from the steam of the cooking food and return the moisture to it. We used a more commonly available Dutch oven, but kept to the spirit of the tagine, using a fragrant spice paste to season the chicken and act as a base for the stew. Apricots added sweetness (we preferred sulfured for their vibrant color) that was balanced by briny green olives. An equal amount of carrots can be substituted for the butternut squash. Serve the tagine with couscous, rice or warmed pita bread.

Don't drain the diced tomatoes. Their liquid adds sweetness and acidity to the stew.

___

1. In a small bowl, stir together 2 tablespoons of the oil, 2½ teaspoons salt, ½ teaspoon black pepper, the cinnamon, cumin, paprika, coriander and cayenne. In a medium bowl, toss the chicken with half the spice paste, rubbing the meat to coat evenly; set aside.

2. In a large Dutch oven over medium-high, combine the onion, garlic, the remaining 2 tablespoons of oil and ¼ teaspoon salt. Cook until the onion is browned and softened, 7 to 9 minutes. Add the ginger and remaining spice paste and cook, stirring constantly, for 1 minute. Add the broth, tomatoes and apricots and bring to a boil, scraping up any browned bits. Add the chicken, return to a boil, then reduce heat to medium-low and simmer for 10 minutes.

3. Add the squash and olives, return to a simmer and cook, partially covered, until the liquid has thickened and the squash is tender, 20 to 25 minutes, stirring occasionally and adjusting the heat to maintain a medium simmer.

4. Meanwhile, in a medium bowl, stir together ½ cup of the cilantro, the pistachios and lemon zest. Stir the spinach into the stew and cook until wilted, 1 to 2 minutes. Stir in the remaining ½ cup of cilantro and the lemon juice, then taste and season with salt and pepper. Serve topped with the cilantro-pistachio mixture.

Curry-Coconut Braised Fish

Start to finish: **20 minutes** / Servings: 4

14-ounce can coconut milk

2 medium carrots, peeled, halved lengthwise and cut into ½-inch pieces

1 medium yellow onion, halved and thinly sliced

6 garlic cloves, finely grated

2 teaspoons turmeric

2 teaspoons curry powder

½ teaspoon red pepper flakes

1 cup low-sodium chicken broth

1½ pounds firm whitefish, cut into 2-inch chunks

Kosher salt and ground white pepper

Steamed white rice, to serve

Lime wedges, to serve

Comfortingly creamy with a little hit of heat, this easy weeknight dish was inspired by chef Edward Lee, author of "Smoke & Pickles," which explores his philosophy of finding innovative ways to blend Southern cuisine and Asian flavors. The coconut milk curry evokes traditional Thai flavors as well as fish amok, the Cambodian classic fish curry often served steamed in a banana leaf. And assembly couldn't be simpler—dump everything but the fish into a pot for about 10 minutes, then add the fish to gently cook for another 10. Any thick, firm whitefish, such as cod, hake or Chilean sea bass, will work. Avoid a thin fillet such as sole or tilapia, which will break down in the braising liquid. Using full-fat coconut milk was important, as it will not break as the vegetables cook. Low-sodium chicken broth gave us better control over the dish's final seasoning.

Don't cook the fish too long or it will fall apart.

1. In a large Dutch oven over medium-high, combine the coconut milk, carrots, onion, garlic, turmeric, curry powder and pepper flakes. Cook over medium heat, uncovered and stirring occasionally, until thickened and the vegetables are softened, about 10 minutes.

2. Stir in the broth and bring to a simmer. Season the fish with salt and white pepper, then stir into the pot. Cover and cook over low until the fish flakes easily when poked with a fork but remains intact, 7 to 10 minutes. Taste and season with salt and pepper. Serve over steamed white rice with lime wedges.

Breads

Italian Flatbread (*Piadine*)

Start to finish: 30 minutes / Makes four 10-inch flatbreads

½ cup water, divided

¼ cup plain whole-milk yogurt

311 grams (2 cups) bread flour

2 teaspoons kosher salt

1½ teaspoons baking powder

63 grams (⅓ cup) lard, room temperature

Flatbread is among the quickest of quick breads. Leavened or not, folded, topped or used as a scoop, it appeals with promises of warm, fresh dough. Fast. One of our favorite variations originated in Romagna, in northern Italy. There they throw together flour, salt, water or milk, and lard or olive oil to make a quick dough. After a short rest, the flatbread—a piadina—is cooked on a griddle or skillet. The cooked piadine then are stuffed with sweet or savory fillings and folded in half to make a sandwich. We started by finding the right fat for our dough. Butter was wrong. Olive oil gave us a pleasant texture and flavor, but something still was missing. So we gave lard a shot. And what a difference. The piadine were tender with just the right chew. But we wanted yet more suppleness and found our answer in nan, a tender flatbread from India that adds a scoop of yogurt to the dough. It seemed heretical in an Italian bread, but fat hinders gluten development, keeping bread soft. It worked well in our piadine and gave the dough more complex flavor. Though it was not as flavorful, vegetable shortening worked as a substitute for lard. If the dough doesn't ball up in the processor, gather it together and briefly knead it by hand. For a simple topping, brush the cooked piadine with our spicy garlic oil (p. 274), or try one of the fillings on the following page.

1. In a liquid measuring cup, whisk together ¼ cup of the water and the yogurt. In a food processor, combine the flour, salt and baking powder. Process for 5 seconds. Add the lard and process until combined, about 10 seconds. With the processor running, add the yogurt mixture. With the processor still running, add the remaining water 1 tablespoon at a time until the dough forms a smooth, moist ball, about 1 minute.

2. Divide the dough into 4 pieces. Roll each into a ball, then cover with plastic wrap. Let rest for 15 minutes. Meanwhile, prepare toppings.

3. Roll each dough ball into a 10-inch round. Poke the surfaces all over with a fork. Heat a 12-inch cast-iron skillet over medium until a drop of water sizzles immediately, 4 to 6 minutes. One at a time, place a dough round in the skillet and cook until the bottom is charred in spots, 1 to 2 minutes. Using tongs, flip and cook for 30 seconds. Transfer to a plate and cover loosely with foil.

Piadine **Toppings**

LAHMAJOUN

Start to finish: 30 minutes
Makes 4 piadine

Made with ground meat, tomatoes and spices, lahmajoun is a common topping for flatbread in Armenia. If you prefer, swap in ground lamb.

8 ounces 80 percent lean ground beef

½ large yellow onion, finely chopped (about ¾ cup)

1 large red bell pepper, cored and finely chopped

2 teaspoons red pepper flakes

1 teaspoon smoked paprika

1 teaspoon ground cumin

Kosher salt and ground black pepper

14½-ounce can fire-roasted crushed tomatoes

½ cup plain whole-milk Greek-style yogurt

4 tablespoons lemon juice (1 to 2 lemons), divided

2 cups lightly packed fresh flat-leaf parsley leaves

2 cups lightly packed fresh mint leaves, torn

1. In a 12-inch nonstick skillet over medium, cook the beef, stirring and breaking up the meat, until beginning to brown, 2 to 3 minutes. Add the onion, bell pepper, pepper flakes, paprika, cumin, 2 teaspoons salt and 1 teaspoon pepper. Cook, stirring occasionally, for 5 minutes. Add the tomatoes and cook until most of the liquid has evaporated, about 8 minutes.

2. In a small bowl, whisk together the yogurt and 2 tablespoons of the lemon juice. In a medium bowl, combine the parsley, mint and the remaining 2 tablespoons of lemon juice. Season with salt and pepper. Spread the lamb mixture evenly over half of each piadina. Drizzle with the yogurt mixture, top with the herbs and fold in half.

PROSCIUTTO, ARUGULA AND RICOTTA

Start to finish: 10 minutes
Makes 4 piadine

In Romagna, piadine often are served with cured meats, greens and fresh cheeses that soften with the warmth of the freshly cooked bread. If possible, purchase fresh-cut prosciutto, sliced as thinly as possible, and allow it to come to room temperature. The flavor and texture of ricotta cheese varies widely by brand; we like Calabro.

¾ cup whole-milk ricotta cheese

½ teaspoon grated lemon zest,
plus 2 tablespoons lemon juice

Kosher salt and ground black pepper

8 slices prosciutto, room temperature

4 ounces baby arugula (about 4 cups)

3 tablespoons extra-virgin olive oil

In a medium bowl, stir together the ricotta and lemon zest. Taste and season with salt and pepper. Spread the ricotta mixture evenly over half of each piadina, then top with 2 slices of the prosciutto. In a medium bowl, toss the arugula with the lemon juice and a pinch of salt. Mound on top of the prosciutto. Drizzle with the oil and fold.

Multigrain Soda Bread

Start to finish: 1 hour 20 minutes (10 minutes active), plus cooling
Makes 2 small loaves

2 cups plain whole-milk yogurt

161 grams (1 cup) 10-grain
hot cereal mix

312 grams (2 cups) whole-wheat flour

142 grams (1 cup) all-purpose flour

37 grams (3 tablespoons packed)
brown sugar

1½ teaspoons kosher salt

1 teaspoon baking powder

1 teaspoon baking soda

½ cup pepitas, toasted (optional)

10 tablespoons (1¼ sticks) salted
butter, melted

Soda bread by definition already is a quick bread, but a few shortcuts helped us make it even faster. Our goal was a flavorful mixed grain soda bread—minus the chore of a long, expensive and hard to find ingredient list. Our solution was premixed multigrain porridge, which gave us 10 grains in one package. We saved even more time by soaking the cereal in yogurt—a convenient replacement for the more classic buttermilk—before mixing it into the dough. This softened the grains and meant we didn't have to cook the porridge on its own. For a little more texture and toasted flavor, we added pepitas. Some recipes call for working cold butter into the dough. We stayed in the fast lane on that step, too, borrowing a technique from scone making and stirring melted butter into our dry ingredients. It was fast, easy and less messy. If you can't find 10-grain cereal mix (Bob's Red Mill makes one), use a five- or seven-grain hot cereal or porridge mix instead. .

Don't use Greek-style yogurt for this recipe; it won't mix with and hydrate the grains. We liked whole-milk yogurt, but low-fat will work, too.

1. Heat the oven to 350°F with a rack in the middle position. Line a baking sheet with kitchen parchment. In a medium bowl, stir together the yogurt and cereal; let sit for 15 minutes. Meanwhile, in a large bowl, whisk together both flours, the sugar, salt, baking powder, baking soda and pepitas, if using.

2. Whisk 8 tablespoons of the butter into the yogurt mixture. Add the mixture to the dry ingredients and fold until no dry flour remains; the dough will be thick and look wet and slightly sandy. Pile the dough into 2 even mounds on the prepared pan. Dampen your hands, then shape into 6-inch rounds.

3. Use a sharp serrated knife to cut a ½-inch-deep X into the top of each loaf. Bake until lightly browned and hollow-sounding when tapped, 50 to 60 minutes. Immediately brush the loaves all over with the remaining 2 tablespoons of butter. Transfer to a wire rack and let cool completely.

Potato-and-Herb Focaccia

Start to finish: 3½ hours (30 minutes active) / Makes one 13-by-9-inch loaf

---

3 cups water

8 ounces Yukon Gold potatoes (about 2 small or 1 large), cut into ¾-inch pieces

6 sprigs fresh rosemary or thyme, plus 2 tablespoons chopped fresh herbs

3 garlic cloves, smashed

3½ teaspoons kosher salt, divided

468 grams (3 cups) bread flour

4 tablespoons extra-virgin olive oil, divided

2 teaspoons instant yeast

2 teaspoons white sugar

½ cup Kalamata olives, pitted and slivered (optional)

1½ ounces Parmesan cheese, grated (about ¾ cup) (optional)

Ground black pepper

Common to the Puglia region of Italy, potato focaccia is a particularly moist version of the classic Italian bread. We embedded ours with deep herbal flavors by seasoning the cooking water for the potatoes with rosemary or thyme, as well as garlic. Then we made the starchy, herb-infused cooking liquid do double duty, using it in the dough, too. Yukon Gold potatoes gave the focaccia color and texture, and didn't require peeling (the soft skins disappeared into the dough). For our herbs, we liked a combination of rosemary and thyme, but oregano and bay leaves worked, too. After the dough comes together, you may need to add more cooking liquid (up to ¼ cup) to achieve the proper texture; the dough should be soft and sticky, and just barely clear the sides of the bowl. The focaccia is delicious with a sprinkling of herbs and black pepper, but Kalamata olives and Parmesan cheese were welcome additions. Flaky sea salt, such as Maldon, was a nice touch, as well.

Don't use a glass baking dish. The bread won't brown and crisp properly. If you don't have a metal baking pan, stretch the focaccia into a rough 13-by-9-inch rectangle and bake on a rimmed baking sheet.

1. In a medium saucepan over high, combine the water, potatoes, herb sprigs, garlic and 2 teaspoons salt. Cover and bring to a boil. Uncover, reduce heat to medium and simmer until the potatoes are tender, 12 to 14 minutes. Drain, reserving the cooking liquid. Discard the herb sprigs, then return the potatoes, garlic and any loose herb leaves to the pan. Use a potato masher or fork to mash until smooth and creamy. Transfer to the bowl of a stand mixer fitted with a dough hook attachment; let the cooking liquid cool until just barely warm, 20 to 30 minutes (it should be no more than 115°F). Meanwhile, oil a large bowl.

2. To the stand mixer bowl, add the flour, 2 tablespoons of the oil, the yeast, the sugar and remaining 1½ teaspoons of salt. Add 1¼ cups of the reserved cooking water, then mix on low speed until the dough comes together, about 1 minute. Increase to medium-high and mix until the dough clears the sides of the bowl but sticks to the bottom, 3 to 5 minutes, adding more cooking liquid 1 tablespoon at a time as needed (dough should be very soft and sticky and just clear the sides of the bowl). Use an oiled silicone spatula to transfer the dough to the prepared bowl. Cover with plastic wrap and let sit in a warm, draft-free area until puffed but not quite doubled, 30 to 60 minutes.

3. Spread the remaining 2 tablespoons of oil over the bottom and sides of a 13-by-9-inch metal baking pan. Transfer the dough to the pan and use oiled fingers to spread in an even layer, pressing into the corners. Cover and let sit in a warm, draft-free area until puffed, 30 to 60 minutes.

4. Heat the oven to 400°F with a rack in the middle position. Use a chopstick to poke the dough all over, then sprinkle with the chopped herbs, olives and Parmesan, if using, and a few grinds of pepper. Bake until the edges are browned and crisp and the top is golden, 35 to 40 minutes. Cool in the pan on a wire rack for 10 minutes, then remove from the pan and cool on the rack. Serve warm or at room temperature.

Whipped Cream **Biscuits**

Start to finish: 30 minutes, plus cooling / Makes 8 biscuits

283 grams (2 cups) all-purpose flour

1½ tablespoons white sugar, divided

2½ teaspoons baking powder

½ teaspoon kosher salt

¼ teaspoon baking soda

⅔ cup heavy cream, plus more as needed

½ cup sour cream

4 tablespoons (½ stick) salted butter, chilled and cut into ¼-inch cubes, plus 1 tablespoon, melted

We first heard of whipped cream biscuits from a central Pennsylvanian cook, then later found recipes for them in a handful of Southern cookbooks. We think they fall in the same category as whipped cream cake, which gets some of its lift from the cream. Instead of relying exclusively on baking powder or baking soda for leavening, these biscuits benefit from the air trapped in stiffly beaten cream. The result is a particularly fluffy texture that doesn't have the heavy-handed richness of an all-butter biscuit. This recipe is designed to work as a dessert, not a breakfast biscuit, and that makes it an ideal candidate for strawberry shortcake. We wanted a bolder filling than one finds in the average shortcake. To avoid waste—as well as the need to reroll scraps—we cut our biscuits into squares. For a savory variation, decrease the sugar to 2 teaspoons and skip the final sprinkle.

Don't forget to decrease the temperature when you put the biscuits in the oven. Starting the biscuits in a very hot oven helped them rise and brown better, but keeping them at that temperature will overcook them.

1. Heat the oven to 475°F with a rack in the middle position. Line a baking sheet with kitchen parchment. In a large bowl, whisk together the flour, 1 tablespoon of the sugar, the baking powder, salt and baking soda. In a second large bowl, use a whisk or electric mixer to beat the cream and sour cream to soft peaks; set aside. Scatter the butter cubes over the flour. With your fingertips, rub together until the butter is thoroughly and evenly dispersed in the flour.

2. Add the whipped cream mixture to the flour mixture. Use a large rubber spatula to fold and press until large clumps form and no dry flour remains. Use your hand to knead the dough in the bowl until it forms a shaggy mass, adding additional cream 1 tablespoon at a time, if needed.

3. Turn the dough out onto a lightly floured counter and divide in half. Form each piece into a rough 5-inch square about ¾ inch thick. With a bench scraper or chef's knife, cut each square into 4 pieces. Evenly space the biscuits on the prepared baking sheet. Brush the tops with the melted butter and sprinkle with the remaining ½ tablespoon sugar.

4. Place the baking sheet in the oven and immediately reduce the temperature to 425°F. Bake until golden brown on top and bottom, 15 to 18 minutes, rotating the pan halfway through. Let cool on the baking sheet for 10 minutes.

MACERATED STRAWBERRIES WITH LIME

We favored small to medium strawberries for this recipe. If your berries are quite large, cut them into 1-inch pieces instead of quartering them.

Don't hull your strawberries before washing them; they may get water-logged and lose flavor.

Start to finish: **20 minutes**
Makes **about 4 cups**

2 pounds strawberries, washed, dried, hulled and quartered

¼ cup white sugar

4 teaspoons grated lime zest (2 to 3 limes)

½ teaspoon kosher salt

In a large bowl, use a potato masher or fork to mash 2 cups of the strawberries until few chunks remain. Stir in the sugar, lime zest and salt. Fold in the remaining strawberries. Cover and let sit until syrupy, at least 15 minutes or up to 2 hours.

TANGY WHIPPED CREAM

Adding a dollop of sour cream to heavy cream can balance the sweetness of a cake and help define the flavor of mediocre fruit. We also add brown sugar and vanilla, lending a depth and complexity to a treat that typically is one note flat.

Start to finish: **5 minutes**
Makes **about 2 cups**

1 cup heavy cream

¼ cup sour cream

2 tablespoons packed brown sugar

½ teaspoon vanilla extract

Pinch of kosher salt

In the bowl of a stand mixer, combine all ingredients. Using the whisk attachment, mix on low until uniform and frothy, about 30 seconds. Increase speed to medium-high and whip until soft peaks form, 1 to 2 minutes.

French Spice Bread (*Pain d'Épices*)

Start to finish: 1 hour 25 minutes (10 minutes active), plus cooling
Makes one 9-inch loaf

---

248 grams (1¾ cups) all-purpose flour

99 grams (1 cup) almond flour

1½ teaspoons ground cinnamon

1 teaspoon baking soda

1 teaspoon ground ginger

½ teaspoon ground mace

Kosher salt and ground black pepper

8 tablespoons (1 stick) salted butter, melted, plus more for the pan

1 cup honey

½ cup whole milk

2 large eggs

2 tablespoons minced crystallized ginger

1 tablespoon finely grated fresh ginger

2 teaspoons grated orange zest

Honey-based spice breads and cakes have been produced in one form or another throughout Europe since the Middle Ages. For good reason: The hygroscopic honey retains moisture, ensuring the breads remain moist during storage. Its antibacterial properties also act as a preservative. Meanwhile, the spices—and therefore the flavor—only improve with time. We wanted a lighter, less sweet alternative to the more common gingerbread, something that tasted as good straight up as it did toasted and topped with butter and marmalade for a quick breakfast or afternoon-coffee accompaniment. This French version is just that. For a fruitier version, add 1 cup golden raisins, chopped dates, figs or dried apricots. Melting the butter in a liquid measuring cup in the microwave, then using the same cup for the honey, made it easy to measure out and add the honey; it slid right out. For maximum spice flavor, we used pepper and three kinds of ginger. If you can't find crystallized (candied) ginger, just skip it; the cake still will be delicious. And if you can't find ground mace, substitute ¼ teaspoon each of ground nutmeg and allspice.

Don't use baking spray in place of butter. While spray is fine in many situations, butter helps create the dark crust that sets pain d'épices apart from other quick breads. Use melted butter and a pastry brush to liberally coat the inside of the pan.

1. Heat the oven to 325°F with a rack in the upper-middle position. Coat the bottom and sides of a 9-by-5-inch loaf pan with butter. In a medium bowl, whisk together both flours, the cinnamon, baking soda, ground ginger, mace and ½ teaspoon each of salt and pepper. In a large bowl, whisk together the butter and honey until smooth. Add the milk, eggs, crystallized ginger, fresh ginger and orange zest; whisk until thoroughly combined.

2. Add the flour mixture to the wet ingredients and fold only until no dry flour remains. Transfer the batter to the prepared pan. Bake until firm to the touch and a toothpick inserted at the center comes out with a few moist crumbs, 65 to 70 minutes. Let cool in the pan on a wire rack for 10 minutes. Remove from the pan and let cool completely, about 2 hours.

Brown Butter–Cardamom Banana Bread

Start to finish: **1 hour 15 minutes** (25 minutes active)
Makes **one 9-inch loaf**

284 grams (2 cups) all-purpose flour

1 teaspoon baking powder

1 teaspoon baking soda

1 teaspoon kosher salt

8 tablespoons (1 stick) salted butter, plus more for the pan

1¼ teaspoons ground cardamom

2 cups mashed bananas (about 4 very ripe bananas)

149 grams (¾ cup packed) dark brown sugar

2 large eggs

2 teaspoons vanilla extract

1 tablespoon white sugar

Banana bread is one of the most common baked goods made at home. Unfortunately, most taste just that–common. We wanted a revved-up recipe that would produce flavorful results without additional effort. So we paired one of banana's most complementary spices—cardamom—with nutty browned butter. Toasting the cardamom briefly in the hot butter intensified the flavor. For just the right texture, we found we needed two leaveners. Baking powder gave the bread lift; baking soda resulted in a well-browned top and a dense crumb. Measuring the bananas in a 1-cup dry measuring cup was important; the difference in moisture between four small and four large bananas could throw off the balance of the ingredients. While we preferred the deeper flavor of dark brown sugar here, light brown works just as well. Sprinkling granulated sugar over the top of the loaf just before baking created a crisp, brown crust that we loved.

1. Heat the oven to 350°F with a rack in the upper-middle position. Lightly coat a 9-by-5-inch loaf pan with butter. In a large bowl, whisk together the flour, baking powder, baking soda and salt.

2. In a medium saucepan over medium, melt the butter. Once melted, continue to cook, swirling the pan often, until the butter is fragrant and deep brown, 2 to 5 minutes. Remove pan from the heat and immediately whisk in the cardamom. Carefully add the bananas (the butter will sizzle and bubble up) and whisk until combined. Add the brown sugar, eggs and vanilla, then whisk until smooth. Add the banana mixture to the flour mixture and, using a silicone spatula, fold until just combined and no dry flour remains.

3. Transfer the batter to the prepared pan and sprinkle evenly with the white sugar. Bake until the loaf is well browned, the top is cracked and a toothpick inserted at the center comes out clean, 50 to 55 minutes, rotating the pan halfway through. Cool the bread in the pan on a wire rack for 10 minutes, then turn out the loaf and cool completely before serving. Cooled bread can be wrapped tightly and stored at room temperature for up to 4 days or refrigerated for a week.

Small Sweets

Tahini Swirl **Brownies**

Start to finish: **40 minutes** / Makes **16 brownies**

4 tablespoons (½ stick) salted butter plus more for pan

4 ounces bittersweet chocolate, finely chopped

16 grams (3 tablespoons) cocoa powder

3 large eggs

223 grams (1 cup plus 2 tablespoons) white sugar

1 tablespoon vanilla extract

1 teaspoon kosher salt

180 grams (¾ cup) tahini

47 grams (⅓ cup) all-purpose flour

Tired of one-note brownies, we looked to the Middle East for a grown-up version of this American standard. We loved the halvah brownie from Tatte Bakery & Cafe in Cambridge, Massachusetts. Halvah is fudge-like candy from the Middle East made from tahini, a rich sesame seed paste. At Milk Street, we fiddled with how much tahini to use—its fat content was the major problem. To start, we reduced the tahini and the amount of butter, substituted cocoa powder for some of the chocolate and added an egg to cut through the rich brownie base. Then, we reversed our thinking and instead of trying to add tahini to a classic brownie batter, we added chocolate to a tahini base. For a final touch, we swirled reserved tahini batter into the chocolate to create a visual and textural contrast and let the tahini flavor shine. The best way to marble the brownies was to run the tip of a paring knife through the dollops of batter. Be sure to fully bake these brownies—they are extremely tender, even wet, if not baked through. The tahini's flavor and color will intensify over time, so make a day ahead for a more pronounced sesame taste.

Don't skip stirring the tahini before measuring; the solids often sink to the bottom.

1. Heat the oven to 350°F with a rack in the middle position. Line an 8-inch square baking pan with 2 pieces of foil with excess hanging over the edges on all sides. Lightly coat with butter.

2. In a medium saucepan over medium, melt the butter. Off heat add the chocolate and cocoa, whisking until smooth.

3. In a large bowl, whisk the eggs, sugar, vanilla and salt until slightly thickened, about 1 minute. Whisk in the tahini. Fold in the flour until just incorporated. Transfer ½ cup of the mixture to a small bowl. Add the chocolate mixture to the remaining tahini mixture and fold until fully combined.

4. Pour the batter into the prepared pan, spreading evenly. Dollop the reserved tahini mixture over the top, then swirl the batters together. Bake until the edges are set but the center remains moist, 28 to 32 minutes. Cool in the pan on a wire rack for 30 minutes. Use the foil to lift the brownies out of the pan and cool on the rack for at least another 30 minutes; the longer they cool, the better they cut. Cut into 2-inch squares.

Rosemary–Pine Nut Cornmeal Cookies

Start to finish: 1½ hours (30 minutes active), plus cooling
Makes 24 cookies

---

213 grams (1½ cups)
all-purpose flour

85 grams (½ cup) fine cornmeal

99 grams (½ cup) white sugar

1 tablespoon minced fresh rosemary

2 teaspoons grated orange zest

16 tablespoons (2 sticks)
salted butter, softened, divided

1 cup pine nuts

3 tablespoons honey

This cookie is sweet enough to track as a treat, but pairs as well with Parmesan as it does a glass of milk. Our inspiration was a hazelnut-rosemary biscotti by Claudia Fleming, the former pastry chef of New York's Gramercy Tavern who famously blended savory flavorings into classically sweet dishes. We chose to reimagine Fleming's biscotti as crisp, pat-in-the-pan shortbread. Same crunchy texture without the hassle of rolling, slicing and twice-baking. The dough got sticky in a warm kitchen, but 10 minutes in the refrigerator fixed that. Letting the cookies cool completely before cutting produced uneven shards; 15 minutes was the sweet spot for a sturdy but sliceable texture.

Don't use dried rosemary. Fresh has a better flavor and softer texture.

1. Heat the oven to 325°F with a rack in the lower-middle position. Line a 13-by-9-inch baking pan with foil, letting the edges hang over the long sides of the pan. In a bowl, combine the flour and cornmeal; set aside.

2. In the bowl of a stand mixer fitted with the paddle attachment, combine the sugar, rosemary and orange zest. Mix on low until the sugar is moistened and begins to clump, 1 to 2 minutes. Add 14 tablespoons of the butter, increase to medium-high and beat until light and fluffy, 3 to 5 minutes, scraping down the bowl twice. Reduce to low and gradually add the flour mixture (this should take about 30 seconds). Scrape down the bowl and mix on low until the dough forms around the paddle, about 1 minute.

3. Crumble the dough evenly over the bottom of the prepared pan. Coat the bottom of a dry measuring cup with oil, then use it to press the dough into an even layer. Sprinkle the pine nuts over the dough in a single layer and press down firmly.

4. In a small bowl, microwave the remaining 2 tablespoons of butter until melted. Add the honey and stir until combined. Brush the mixture over the bars, then bake until the top is deep golden brown, 40 to 45 minutes.

5. Let the bars cool in the pan for 15 minutes. Using the foil, lift the bars and transfer to a cutting board. Cut into 24 pieces. Let the bars cool completely on a wire rack before serving. The cooled cookies can be stored in an airtight container at room temperature for up to 1 week.

Semolina **Polvorones**

Start to finish: 3 hours (45 minutes active), plus cooling time
Makes 24 cookies

---

50 grams (¼ cup) white sugar

1½ teaspoons grated orange zest

57 grams (½ cup) coarsely chopped walnuts

128 grams (¾ cup) semolina flour

½ teaspoon cinnamon

2 large egg yolks

½ teaspoon vanilla extract

⅛ teaspoon kosher salt

94 grams (⅔ cup) all-purpose flour

10 tablespoons (1¼ sticks) salted butter, cut into ½-inch pieces and chilled

Powdered sugar, to coat

Polvorones are Spanish cookies popular across Latin America, Spain and the Phillipines. They're basically a simple shortbread—and sadly can be simply bland. Our inspiration was a lesser-known Basque variation made with semolina and spiced with orange zest and cinnamon. We also borrowed a Filipino technique of toasting the flour first. In fact, we toasted both our walnuts and semolina to give the cookies deep, complex flavor. Adding the ground cinnamon to the hot semolina bloomed it, bringing out its aroma. Flattening the cookies too much made them delicate; ½-inch-thick discs held up best when tossed in powdered sugar. Likewise, the cookies are fragile when hot out of the oven, so let them cool several minutes before transferring to a wire rack. You can bake both sheets of cookies at once on the upper and lower-middle racks, but we got more even browning baking one sheet at a time.

Don't be alarmed if the semolina smokes slightly during toasting. And don't coat the cookies with powdered sugar until you're ready to serve them; they look best immediately after they're sugared.

1. In a food processor, pulse together the white sugar and orange zest. In a 10-inch skillet over medium, toast the walnuts, stirring, until lightly browned and fragrant, 3 to 5 minutes. Transfer to the food processor. Wipe the skillet clean, then add the semolina and toast, stirring, until beginning to brown, 2 to 3 minutes. Reduce heat to medium-low and toast, stirring constantly, until speckled, golden brown and fragrant, another 2 to 3 minutes. Off the heat, stir in the cinnamon, then transfer to a plate and cool to room temperature.

2. In a small bowl, use a fork to beat the yolks and vanilla. Add the salt to the walnuts and sugar, then process until coarsely ground, about 10 seconds. Add the flour and semolina mixture, then process until combined, about 5 seconds. Add the butter and pulse until the mixture resembles damp sand,

10 to 12 pulses. Drizzle in the yolk mixture and pulse until large clumps gather around the blade. Transfer the dough to the counter and knead briefly, then wrap in plastic wrap and refrigerate for at least 1 hour and up to 2 days.

3. Heat the oven to 325°F with a rack in the middle position. Line 2 baking sheets with kitchen parchment. Roll the dough into 24 balls (1 tablespoon each) and arrange evenly on the baking sheets. Press the balls gently into discs about ½ inch thick.

4. One at a time, bake each sheet until well browned, 23 to 28 minutes, rotating halfway through. Let the cookies cool on the sheet for 10 minutes, then transfer to a wire rack and cool completely. Just before serving, gently drop each cookie into powdered sugar to coat.

Swedish Gingersnaps (*Pepparkakor*)

Start to finish: 3½ hours (30 minutes active), plus cooling
Makes **about 24 cookies**

236 grams (1⅔ cups)
all-purpose flour

¼ teaspoon baking soda

8 tablespoons (1 stick) salted butter

99 grams (½ cup packed)
dark brown sugar

74 grams (6 tablespoons) white sugar

¼ cup dark corn syrup

2½ tablespoons ground ginger

1 tablespoon finely grated
fresh ginger

1 teaspoon cinnamon

¾ teaspoon finely grated orange zest

¾ teaspoon kosher salt

½ teaspoon ground cloves

¼ teaspoon ground black pepper

⅛ teaspoon cayenne pepper

1 large egg

Turbinado sugar, for sprinkling

In search of a cookie that would deliver grown-up gingerbread flavor, we came across Swedish gingersnaps, a cookie that goes as well with wine as coffee. For these cookies, we needed to balance dark brown and white sugars to get a workable dough that crisped properly. Baking soda helped with browning and gave the cookies lift, making them crunchy but not hard. The pepparkakor's distinctive spice came from ground and fresh ginger, black pepper and cayenne, and we pumped up all of them. The dough can be made up to two days in advance. The cookies keep for up to a week in an airtight container.

Don't portion the dough right after mixing; it will be too soft and sticky. Because it is made with melted butter (to avoid using a stand mixer), the dough must chill first.

1. In a large bowl, whisk together the flour and baking soda; set aside. In a medium saucepan over medium, combine the butter, both sugars, the corn syrup, both gingers, the cinnamon, orange zest, salt, cloves, black pepper and cayenne. As the butter melts, whisk until the sugar dissolves and the mixture begins to simmer. Remove from the heat. Cool until just warm to the touch, about 30 minutes.

2. Whisk the egg into the cooled mixture until smooth. Add to the dry ingredients and fold until no dry flour remains. Refrigerate for at least 2 hours or up to 2 days.

3. Heat the oven to 350°F with racks in the upper- and lower-middle positions. Line 2 baking sheets with kitchen parchment. Working with a tablespoon of dough at a time, use dampened hands to roll into balls. Arrange 12 dough balls on each baking sheet, spacing evenly.

4. Lay a sheet of plastic wrap over the balls on each sheet and use the bottom of a dry measuring cup to flatten each to about ¼ inch thick. Remove the plastic and sprinkle each cookie with a generous pinch of turbinado sugar. Bake until richly browned, 14 to 16 minutes, switching and rotating the baking sheets halfway through. Cool on the sheet for 10 minutes, then transfer to a wire rack and cool completely.

Date-Stuffed **Semolina Cookies** (*Ma'amoul*)

Start to finish: 1 hour (30 minutes active), plus cooling
Makes 36 cookies

For the dough:

172 grams (1 cup) semolina flour

142 grams (1 cup) all-purpose flour

66 grams (⅓ cup) white sugar

½ teaspoon kosher salt

10 tablespoons (1¼ sticks) salted butter, cut into 10 pieces and chilled

2 tablespoons plain whole-milk yogurt

2 teaspoons rose water

1 teaspoon vanilla extract

Powdered sugar, for dusting (optional)

For the filling:

5 ounces (1 cup) medjool dates, pitted

4 ounces (1 cup) walnut pieces, lightly toasted and cooled

1 tablespoon honey

2 teaspoons grated orange zest

½ teaspoon ground cardamom

¼ teaspoon kosher salt

These semolina-based cookies stuffed with dates, nuts or other fillings are a popular Middle Eastern treat often served on holidays. Though they are often made using a complex molding technique, we simplified and came up with a rolling method anyone could do. A combination of semolina and all-purpose flours gave our cookies a rich, crumbly texture and complex flavor. Chilled butter prevented the dough from getting overly sticky, but if your kitchen is particularly warm and the dough is soft and shiny after mixing, refrigerate it for 30 minutes before proceeding. Covering the dough with plastic wrap while making the filling and rolling it out between sheets of kitchen parchment further prevented the dough from drying out. If the dough begins to crack while shaping the cookies, gently pinch the cracks back together. You can substitute pistachios for the walnuts, but the filling will take an extra minute or so to form into a paste. While rose water is traditional, a good substitute is 2 teaspoons each of orange juice and orange zest, plus ¼ teaspoon almond extract. These cookies keep for up to three days in an airtight container at room temperature.

Don't use deglet dates. Soft, plump medjool dates were essential to producing the proper consistency of the paste, and they made for a moister, more flavorful filling.

1. Heat the oven to 325°F with racks in the upper- and lower-middle positions. Line 2 baking sheets with kitchen parchment.

2. For the dough, in a food processor combine both flours, the white sugar and salt. Process until combined, about 5 seconds. Add the butter and process until the butter is completely incorporated, 15 to 20 seconds. Add the yogurt, rose water and vanilla, then process until the dough comes together, about 1 minute. Transfer to the counter and knead until the dough is smooth, then cover with plastic wrap and set aside.

3. For the filling, in the processor, combine all filling ingredients and process until a smooth paste forms, 45 to 60 seconds.

4. To assemble the cookies, set the dough between 2 sheets of kitchen

parchment and roll into a 12-by-9-inch rectangle, cutting and patching the dough together as needed. Cut the dough into thirds lengthwise to form three 12-by-3-inch strips. Divide the filling into thirds and roll each portion into a 12-inch rope. Place one rope down the middle of each strip of dough, then wrap the dough completely around the filling. Pinch the seam to seal. Place each roll seam side down and cut each crosswise into 12 rounds, gently reshaping if necessary. Evenly space the cookies seam side down on the prepared baking sheets.

5. Bake until the bottoms are golden but the tops are still pale, 25 to 30 minutes, switching and rotating the sheets halfway through. Cool the cookies on the sheets for 5 minutes, then transfer to a wire rack and cool completely, about 30 minutes. Dust with powdered sugar, if desired.

Australian Oat-Coconut Cookies
(*Anzac Biscuits*)

Start to finish: **30 minutes** / Makes **24 cookies**

100 grams (1¼ cups)
old-fashioned rolled oats

98 grams (1¼ cups) unsweetened
shredded coconut

156 grams (1 cup) whole-wheat flour

10 tablespoons (1¼ sticks)
salted butter

99 grams (½ cup packed)
dark brown sugar

¼ cup brewed coffee

3 tablespoons honey

2 teaspoons vanilla extract

1 teaspoon grated orange zest

1 teaspoon baking soda

In Australia and New Zealand, Anzac Day (April 25) honors servicemen and women past and present. The date marks the day the Australian and New Zealand Army Corps (ANZAC) landed at Gallipoli in Turkey during World War I. There are a number of traditions associated with the day, including the Dawn Service marking the pre-dawn landing on Gallipoli. And there are more lighthearted rituals, such as the drinking of "gunfire coffee"— black coffee with a splash of rum—and the eating of Anzac biscuits, an oat and coconut cookie that is both simple and delicious. We wanted a bolder more modern rendition. Though golden syrup is traditional, we found honey and dark brown sugar were good stand-ins. And toasting the coconut and the oats deepened the flavor of the biscuits. Be sure to have all ingredients measured beforehand; it's important to combine everything as soon as possible after the baking soda has been incorporated into the wet ingredients. Underbaking the cookies gave them chewy centers. An oiled 1 tablespoon measuring spoon helped portion out the cookies.

Don't roll these cookies into balls. It will compress them and result in dense cookies.

1. Heat the oven to 350°F with racks in the upper- and lower-middle positions. Line 2 baking sheets with kitchen parchment. In a large skillet over medium-high, toast the oats, stirring often, until fragrant and beginning to brown, about 5 minutes. Reduce the heat to medium-low and add the coconut. Toast until golden, stirring constantly, 1 to 2 minutes. Transfer to a large bowl. Stir in the flour. Wipe out the skillet.

2. Return the skillet to medium-low and add the butter, sugar, coffee, honey, vanilla and orange zest. Cook, whisking, until the butter melts and the mixture boils. Off heat, add the baking soda and

stir until completely mixed, pale and foamy. Add to the oatmeal mixture and stir until just combined.

3. Scoop or drop heaping tablespoons of dough, spaced about 2 inches apart, onto the prepared baking sheets. Bake until the cookies have risen and are deep golden brown but still soft at the center, 8 to 10 minutes, switching and rotating the pans halfway through. Cool on the pans for 5 minutes, then transfer to a wire rack to cool completely.

Rye Chocolate Chip Cookies

Start to finish: 1 hour (20 minutes active), plus cooling
Makes 24 cookies

142 grams (1 cup) all-purpose flour

¾ teaspoon kosher salt

½ teaspoon baking soda

140 grams (1 cup) rye flour

12 tablespoons (1½ sticks)
salted butter

248 grams (1¼ cups) white sugar

2 large eggs

1 tablespoon molasses

1 tablespoon vanilla extract

210 grams (about 1½ cups) dark
chocolate chips or chopped
bittersweet chocolate

113 grams (1 cup) pecans, toasted
and chopped (optional)

We've eaten plenty of Toll House chocolate chip cookies. And while they're good, we wanted something different—a more complex cookie with a robust flavor that could balance the sugar and chocolate. We found inspiration on a visit to Claire Ptak's Violet bakery in London, where she's a fan of switching things up. Think rye flour for an apricot upside-down cake. Rye is a little bitter, a little savory, and it makes the perfect counterpoint for the sugary high notes of a chocolate chip cookie. First, though, we had to make a few adjustments. Rye has less gluten than all-purpose flour so it bakes differently and requires more liquid. We decided to go nearly fifty-fifty rye and all-purpose flours and recommend that you weigh for best results. Toasting the rye flour added complex, nutty flavor that balanced the sweetness of these cookies. While the cookies can be made with any style of rye flour, light or medium proved the best choice. A touch of molasses (blackstrap, if available) deepened the flavor and added slight bitterness. These cookies continue to firm up after they come out of the oven, so it is best to check them early and err on the side of underbaking.

Don't be afraid to toast the flour until dark—ours was the shade of peanut butter—and fragrant. It should smell nutty.

1. Heat the oven to 350°F with a rack in the middle position. Line 2 baking sheets with kitchen parchment. In a medium bowl, whisk together the all-purpose flour, salt and baking soda. In a 12-inch skillet over medium-high, toast the rye flour until fragrant and a shade or two darker, about 5 minutes, stirring frequently. Off heat, add the butter and stir until melted.

2. In a large bowl, mix together the sugar, egg mixture, molasses and vanilla. When the rye mixture is cool to the touch, slowly stir it into the egg mixture. Add the dry ingredients and stir until combined. Stir in the chocolate chips and nuts, if using.

3. Drop 2-tablespoon mounds of dough about 2 inches apart on the prepared baking sheets. One sheet at a time, bake until the edges are firm and the centers are soft, 8 to 12 minutes, rotating the sheet halfway through. Cool on the sheet for 5 minutes, then transfer to a wire rack and cool for 10 minutes. Repeat with the second sheet.

Desserts

10

Caramel Oranges

Start to finish: 40 minutes, plus chilling / Servings: 6

8 medium navel or Cara Cara oranges
(about 4½ pounds) or a combination

198 grams (1 cup) white sugar

2 cinnamon sticks or star anise pods

2 tablespoons salted butter

Oranges with caramel sauce were the hit of dessert carts across London in the 1960s. The dish never caught on in America and eventually faded overseas. But with its bright flavors and fresh-yet-familiar combination of fruit and caramel, we felt it was a classic worth reviving. Our inspiration was a recipe in Nigella Lawson's cookbook, "Forever Summer." She bathes peeled and sliced oranges in caramel spiked with cardamom, and suggests serving them with yogurt. Cardamom was good, but we preferred cinnamon sticks, as well as star anise. Cara Cara oranges are good if you can find them, but navel work fine. Be sure to remove all the bitter white pith. Substituting fresh orange juice for the water in a traditional caramel amplified the flavor of the dish tremendously.

1. Juice 2 of the oranges to yield ¾ cup juice. If 2 oranges don't yield enough juice, add water to measure ¾ cup total.

2. Slice off the top and bottom ½ inch from each of the remaining 6 oranges. Stand each orange on one of its flat ends and use a sharp knife to cut down and around the fruit, following the contours of the flesh, slicing away the skin and white pith. Turn each orange on its side and thinly slice crosswise into rounds. In a 13-by-9-inch baking dish, shingle the rounds in a single layer.

3. In a medium saucepan, combine the sugar, ¼ cup of the orange juice and the cinnamon or star anise; bring to a boil over medium-high, this should take 2 to 3 minutes. Cook, swirling the pan occasionally, until the sugar begins to color at the edges, another 3 to 5 minutes. The bubbles should go from thin and frothy to thick and shiny.

4. Reduce heat to medium-low and cook, swirling the pan often, until the sugar is coppery-brown, 1 to 3 minutes. Remove the pan from the heat, add the butter, then whisk until melted.

5. Add a splash of the remaining orange juice and whisk until smooth (the mixture will steam and bubble vigorously), then add the remaining orange juice and whisk until fully incorporated. If the caramel separates and sticks to the pan, return it to the heat and simmer until the hardened caramel dissolves.

6. Pour the caramel evenly over the oranges, cover with plastic wrap, then refrigerate for at least 3 hours and up to 6 hours.

7. Allowing the caramel to drip off into the baking dish, use a slotted spoon to transfer the oranges to a serving platter or plates. Remove and discard the cinnamon or star anise from the caramel, then whisk to recombine and mix in any juices. Pour the caramel over the oranges.

ORANGE CARAMEL SAUCE

Don't think about the caramel's color for the first few minutes. The sugar mixture will melt, frothing furiously as the heat increases and moisture evaporates, then finally subside into larger, shinier bubbles before it changes color. If the sugar browns too quickly, slide the pan off the heat and whisk steadily to incorporate air, which cools it.

Chocolate, Prune and **Rum Cake**

Start to finish: **1 hour 20 minutes (30 minutes active), plus cooling**
Servings: **12**

9 tablespoons (1 stick plus
1 tablespoon) salted butter
(1 tablespoon softened)

8 ounces pitted prunes
(about 1½ cups), finely chopped

⅓ cup dark rum

1 tablespoon molasses

12 ounces bittersweet chocolate,
finely chopped

6 large eggs, separated

121 grams (⅓ cup plus ¼ cup)
white sugar, divided

½ teaspoon kosher salt

Claire Ptak has a fairly revolutionary approach to baking—soft-whipped egg whites! undermixed batter!—that sets her apart from most bakers. We were smitten with her chocolate, prune and whiskey cake when we tasted it at her Violet bakery in East London. When we got the recipe back to Milk Street, we knew we needed to adjust it to be more approachable for the American home cook. Ptak uses almond flour in her batter, but we preferred the lighter, more mousse-like texture we got by leaving it out. We followed her lead in under whipping the egg whites and just barely mixing them into the batter. We found dark rum was delicious warm or cool and better complemented the molasses than whiskey. We preferred bar chocolates with 60 to 70 percent cacao. Chocolate chips contain stabilizers that can change the cake's texture; it's best to avoid them. We liked this served with whipped cream.

1. Heat the oven to 325°F with a rack in the middle position. Coat the bottom and sides of a 9-inch springform pan evenly with the 1 tablespoon of softened butter.

2. In a 2-cup microwave-safe liquid measuring cup, combine the prunes, rum and molasses. Microwave until the rum is bubbling, 45 to 60 seconds. Let sit for 15 minutes, stirring occasionally.

3. In a medium saucepan over medium, melt the remaining 8 tablespoons of butter. Remove the pan from the heat and immediately whisk in the chocolate until melted and completely smooth. In a large bowl, whisk together the egg yolks and ⅓ cup of the sugar until pale and glossy, about 30 seconds. Slowly add the melted chocolate mixture and whisk until smooth. Stir in the prune mixture.

4. Using a stand mixer with a whisk attachment, whip the egg whites and salt on medium-high until light and foamy, about 1 minute. With the mixer running, slowly sprinkle in the remaining ¼ cup of sugar and continue to whip until the whites are thick and glossy and hold soft peaks, about 1 minute.

5. Whisk a third of the whipped egg whites into the chocolate mixture to lighten it. Gently fold in the remaining whites with a rubber spatula until the batter is marbled but not fully blended.

6. Pour the batter into the prepared pan. If needed, smooth the top with a spatula. Bake until the edges of the cake are firm and cracked, 35 to 40 minutes. The center will be just set, but will jiggle. Cool the cake in the pan on a wire rack for at least 1 hour before serving. The cake will settle and sink as it cools.

Foolproof Single-Crust Pie Dough

Start to finish: 2½ hours (30 minutes active), plus cooling
Makes one 9-inch pie shell

---

3 tablespoons water

2 teaspoons cornstarch

159 grams (1 cup plus 2 tablespoons) all-purpose flour

2 teaspoons white sugar

¼ teaspoon kosher salt

10 tablespoons (1 stick plus 2 tablespoons) salted butter, cut into ½-inch pieces and chilled

2 tablespoons sour cream

Finding that sweet spot in pie dough can be a challenge. Drier doughs are less likely to shrink during blind baking, but they can be stiff and difficult to roll out. Moist doughs are easier to work with, but tend to slump in the oven. We stabilize our basic but excellent pastry dough by borrowing a technique known as tangzhong that is used to make Japanese milk bread, the soft, pillowy staple of Asian bakeries. Moisture makes dough easier to work with, but it also activates gluten, which makes pie dough tough. We wanted to add moisture without activating gluten. The tangzhong technique does this by mixing a small portion of the flour with boiling water to make a paste that then gets mixed into the dough. The paste adds moisture, but also traps it, preventing it from triggering the gluten. Inspired by this, we used cornstarch blended with water for the paste, heating it briefly to create a gel. The gel trapped the water, preventing it from reacting with the proteins in the flour. We also added sour cream to the dough, which contains a small peptide called glutathione. This peptide can be a baker's secret weapon because it reduces the ability of the proteins in wheat to react and form gluten. Result: a softer, more forgiving dough that rolls out easily and resists slumping in the pan during prebaking.

Don't skimp on the pie weights. Use enough to come three-quarters of the way up the sides. We like ceramic pie weights, but 1 pound dry beans or rice works, too. Avoid glass pie weights; they are too heavy and retain heat too long. And don't remove the foil and weights until the dough is set and dry. A moist or partially set crust can slump or shrink after the weights are removed. To check, lift up some of the foil and feel the edge of the pie or tart with your finger.

1. In a small bowl, whisk together the water and cornstarch. Microwave until set, 30 to 40 seconds, stirring halfway through. Chill in the freezer for 10 minutes.

2. Once the cornstarch mixture has chilled, in a food processor, combine the flour, sugar and salt, then process until mixed, about 5 seconds. Add the chilled cornstarch mixture and pulse until uniformly ground, about 5 pulses. Add the butter and sour cream, then process until the dough comes together and begins to collect around the blade, 20 to 30 seconds. Pat the dough into a 4-inch disk, wrap in plastic wrap and refrigerate for at least 1 hour and up to 48 hours.

3. When ready to bake, heat the oven to 375°F with a rack in the middle position. On a well-floured counter, roll the dough into a 12-inch circle. Hang the dough over the rolling pin and transfer to a 9-inch pie pan. Gently ease the dough into the pan by lifting the edges while pressing down into the corners of the pan. Trim the edges, leaving a ½-inch overhang, then tuck the overhang under itself so the dough is flush with the rim of the pan. Crimp the dough with your fingers or the tines of a fork, then chill in the freezer for at least 15 minutes.

4. To blind bake, line the chilled crust with heavy-duty foil and fill with enough pie weights to come three-quarters up. Bake until the edges are light golden brown, about 25 minutes, rotating the pan halfway through. Remove the foil and weights and bake until the bottom of the crust just begins to color, another 5 to 7 minutes. Let cool on a wire rack for 1 hour before filling. Once baked and cooled, the crust can be wrapped in plastic wrap and kept at room temperature for up to 2 days.

Brown Sugar Tart

Start to finish: 1¾ hours (30 minutes active), plus cooling / Servings: 8

---

1 recipe single-crust pie dough (p. 226)

99 grams (8 tablespoons packed) dark brown sugar

1 tablespoon all-purpose flour

⅛ teaspoon kosher salt

4 large egg yolks

1¼ cups heavy cream

2 teaspoons vanilla extract

The inspiration for this simple yet rich tart was a French-Canadian sugar tart that originated in Waterloo, the Belgian town that was the site of Napoleon Bonaparte's 1815 defeat. Our brown sugar tart has two distinct layers: a rich, lightly sweet egg-yolk custard on top, and a thick bed of brown sugar on the bottom. Using just egg yolks in the custard resulted in a silkier, creamier texture than whole eggs, and adding flour prevented the tart from forming a skin on top. We wanted the brown sugar layer to be distinct from the custard layer, but found that adding a few tablespoons of the sugar to the custard mixture rounded out the flavor. While light brown sugar worked fine, we preferred the deep, more robust flavor of dark brown.

Don't use old, hard brown sugar. If your sugar is clumpy and dry, it will never fully incorporate into the custard mixture.

1. Heat the oven to 375°F with racks in the middle and lowest positions. On a well-floured counter, roll the dough into a 12-inch circle. Wrap the dough loosely around the rolling pin and transfer to a 9-inch tart pan with a removable bottom. Gently ease the dough into the corners of the pan, then trim the edges flush with the pan rim. Freeze for 15 minutes.

2. Line the chilled tart shell with heavy-duty foil and fill with enough pie weights to come three-quarters up, then place it on a rimmed baking sheet. Bake on the oven's lowest rack until the edges are light golden brown, 25 to 30 minutes, rotating the pan halfway through. Remove the foil and weights, then bake until the bottom of the crust just begins to color, another 5 to 7 minutes. Remove the pan from the oven and reduce the oven temperature to 325°F.

3. In a medium bowl, combine 2 tablespoons of the sugar with the flour and salt. Add the yolks and whisk until combined. Add the cream and vanilla and whisk until smooth. Sprinkle the remaining 6 tablespoons of sugar over the warm crust and gently press into an even layer.

4. Slowly pour the custard over the sugar. Bake on the oven's middle rack until the edges are set but the center jiggles slightly, about 25 minutes. Cool in the pan on a wire rack for at least 1 hour. Remove the outer metal ring and serve at room temperature.

Chocolate Tart

Start to finish: **1 hour 20 minutes (25 minutes active)**, plus cooling
Servings: 8

1 recipe single-crust pie dough
(p. 226)

6 tablespoons salted butter

6 ounces bittersweet chocolate,
finely chopped

2 large eggs, plus 1 large egg yolk

44 grams (5 tablespoons)
all-purpose flour

50 grams (¼ cup) white sugar

2 teaspoons vanilla extract

⅛ teaspoon kosher salt

When it comes to French-style chocolate tarts, there's a fine line between elegant and unpleasant. There's much to be said for the flavor of fine bitter chocolate, but it can be overwhelming. We aimed for a balance with more richness than is common. Flour and eggs provided structure, preventing the filling from being too gooey or pudding-like, while butter and an extra egg yolk added richness.

Don't be alarmed by how soft the center is when you remove the tart from the oven. The edges will be set, but the center still will be quite soft.

1. Heat the oven to 375°F with racks in the middle and lowest positions. On a well-floured counter, roll the dough into a 12-inch circle. Wrap the dough loosely around the rolling pin and transfer to a 9-inch tart pan with a removable bottom. Ease the dough into the pan, then trim the edges flush with the rim. Freeze for 15 minutes.

2. Line the chilled tart shell with heavy-duty foil and fill with enough pie weights to come three-quarters up, then place it on a rimmed baking sheet. Bake on the oven's lowest rack until the edges are light golden brown, 25 to 30 minutes, rotating the pan halfway through. Remove the foil and weights, then bake until the bottom of the crust just begins to color, another 5 to 7 minutes. Set aside. Leave the oven on.

3. In a medium saucepan over medium, melt the butter. Remove from the heat and add the chocolate, whisking until smooth. Whisk in the remaining ingredients until fully incorporated; the filling should appear shiny. If the mixture separates during whisking, don't worry. Just keep whisking; it will smooth out again. Pour into the warm crust and smooth the top. Bake on the baking sheet on the middle rack until the edges are just set, 8 to 10 minutes. Cool in the pan on a wire rack for at least 15 minutes. Serve warm or at room temperature.

Pumpkin **Tart**

Start to finish: 1 hour 40 minutes (40 minutes active), plus cooling
Servings: 8

1 recipe single-crust pie dough
(p. 226)

15-ounce can pumpkin puree

149 grams (¾ cup packed)
dark brown sugar

¼ cup bourbon

8-ounce container (1 cup)
crème fraîche

3 large eggs

¼ teaspoon kosher salt

We love pumpkin pie, but we don't love how dense and cloying it can be. We wanted a lighter, fresher take with a pronounced pumpkin flavor. Canned pumpkin puree was a great place to start, but we intensified the flavor by giving it a quick sauté with dark brown sugar. This simmers off excess moisture and adds caramel flavors. Deglazing the pan with bourbon added a complexity we loved, but an equal amount of orange juice worked well, too. Crème fraîche gave the filling tang and richness that other dairy products couldn't match.

Don't use canned pumpkin pie filling for this recipe. Look for unsweetened canned pumpkin puree; the only ingredient listed should be pumpkin.

1. Heat the oven to 375°F with racks in the middle and lowest positions. On a well-floured counter, roll the dough into a 12-inch circle. Wrap the dough loosely around the rolling pin and transfer to a 9-inch tart pan with a removable bottom. Ease the dough into the pan, then trim the edges flush with the rim. Freeze for 15 minutes.

2. Line the chilled tart shell with heavy-duty foil and fill with enough pie weights to come three-quarters up, then place it on a rimmed baking sheet. Bake on the oven's lowest rack until the edges are light golden brown, 25 to 30 minutes, rotating the pan halfway through. Remove the foil and weights, then bake until the bottom of the crust just begins to color, another 5 to 7 minutes. Remove the pan from the oven and reduce the oven temperature to 325°F.

3. While the crust bakes, in a 12-inch nonstick skillet over medium-high, combine the pumpkin and sugar. Cook, stirring frequently, until the mixture is thickened, dark and leaves a film on the pan, about 10 minutes. Transfer to a 2-cup liquid measuring cup (the yield should be 1½ cups).

4. Add the bourbon to the skillet, return to medium-high heat and stir, scraping up any browned bits; add to the pumpkin mixture.

5. In a food processor, combine the pumpkin mixture and crème fraîche; process until smooth. Scrape down the bowl, add the eggs and salt, then process until smooth, about 1 minute. Pour the filling into the warm crust, smoothing the top. Bake on the baking sheet on the middle rack until the edges start to puff and crack and the center sets, 30 to 35 minutes.

6. Cool in the pan on a wire rack for at least 30 minutes. Remove the outer metal ring to serve warm or at room temperature.

HONEY-ORANGE WHIPPED CREAM

Start to finish: **5 minutes**
Makes **about 3 cups**

Don't use creamed, thick or crystallized honey for this recipe. For the cream and honey to properly mix, a thin, pourable honey is needed.

1½ cups heavy cream

3 tablespoons honey

½ teaspoon grated orange zest

In the bowl of a stand mixer, combine all ingredients. Using the whisk attachment, mix on low until frothy, about 30 seconds. Scrape the bowl with a spatula to make sure the honey is incorporated. Mix on medium-high and whip until soft peaks form, 2 to 3 minutes.

Lemon Tart

Start to finish: **1 hour 40 minutes** (25 minutes active), plus cooling
Servings: 8

1 recipe single-crust pie dough
(p. 226)

99 grams (½ cup) white sugar

1 tablespoon grated lemon zest

1 teaspoon grated orange zest

⅛ teaspoon kosher salt

2 large eggs, plus 2 large egg yolks

6 tablespoons heavy cream

5 tablespoons lemon juice
(1 to 2 lemons)

3 tablespoons orange juice

We love the fresh, bright flavor of lemon tarts, but the classic tarte au citron is acidic enough to strip the enamel off your teeth. We wanted to tame the tartness of lemon without relying on heaps of sugar. Pairing lemon with sweeter, mellower orange worked great. Using both the juice and the zest of both citruses provided complex, well-rounded flavor. Rubbing the zest into the sugar helped release the aromatic, flavorful oils. Using a combination of whole eggs and yolks gave us the best texture. The richness of the yolks and the cream also helped balance the lemon.

Don't eat this tart warm. The flavor and texture are best when chilled, or at least at room temperature.

1. Heat the oven to 375°F with racks in the middle and lowest positions. On a well-floured counter, roll the dough into a 12-inch circle. Wrap the dough loosely around the rolling pin and transfer to a 9-inch tart pan with a removable bottom. Ease the dough into the pan, then trim the edges flush with the rim. Freeze for 15 minutes.

2. Line the chilled tart shell with heavy-duty foil and fill with enough pie weights to come three-quarters up, then place it on a rimmed baking sheet. Bake on the oven's lowest rack until the edges are light golden brown, 25 to 30 minutes, rotating the pan halfway through. Remove the foil and weights, then bake until the bottom of the crust just begins to color, another 5 to 7 minutes. Remove the pan from the oven and reduce the oven temperature to 325°F.

3. In a bowl, combine the sugar, both zests and the salt. Rub together with your fingers until fragrant and the mixture begins to clump. Add the eggs and yolks and whisk until pale and slightly thickened, about 1 minute. Whisk in the cream and both juices. Skim the foam off the top.

4. Pour the filling into the warm tart shell and bake on the baking sheet on the middle rack until set, 20 to 25 minutes. Cool in the pan on a wire rack until room temperature, at least 1 hour. Remove the outer metal ring and serve, or chill completely before serving.

Rye-on-Rye **Sticky Toffee Pudding**

Start to finish: 1½ hours (30 minutes active), plus cooling
Servings: 10

For the cake:

8 ounces pitted dates (about 1½ cups)

1 cup brewed coffee

142 grams (1 cup) all-purpose flour, plus more for pan

117 grams (¾ cup) rye flour

1 teaspoon baking powder

1 teaspoon kosher salt

½ teaspoon baking soda

198 grams (1 cup packed) dark brown sugar

4 large eggs

2 teaspoons vanilla extract

1 teaspoon ground allspice

12 tablespoons (1½ sticks) salted butter, melted and cooled slightly, plus more for pan

For the toffee sauce:

198 grams (1 cup packed) dark brown sugar

⅔ cup light corn syrup

2 teaspoons finely grated orange zest

⅛ teaspoon kosher salt

6 tablespoons rye whiskey

8 tablespoons (1 stick) salted butter, cut into 8 pieces and chilled

To update Britain's sticky toffee pudding—a steamed, too-often bland dessert hidden under a gluey, cloying syrup—we worked backward, starting with the sauce. Instead of the traditional cream, we gave the toffee glaze a transatlantic twist by spiking it with rye whiskey. The whiskey's spice and heat cut through the sweetness of the dark brown sugar and corn syrup; orange zest added brightness. For the cake itself, we wanted to mirror the flavor of the rye, so we used a blend of rye and all-purpose flours. Dates that are steeped in coffee, then pureed, gave body and an earthiness that boosted the rye flavor. Together, the nutty rye and bitter coffee balanced the cake's sweetness. To up the dessert's elegance, we made it in a Bundt pan. Covering the pan with foil kept the cake rich and moist. This mimicked the gentle heat of steaming in a water bath (bain marie), but was far less fussy.

Don't chop the dates. Their texture was unpleasant in the finished dish. The food processor is the best bet. And be sure to check your dates for pits.

FOR THE CAKE:

1. Heat the oven to 325°F with a rack in the middle position. Lightly coat a 12-cup nonstick Bundt pan with butter and flour. In a medium saucepan over medium-high, bring the dates and coffee to a boil. Remove from the heat and let sit for 15 minutes. In a large bowl, whisk together both flours, the baking powder, salt and baking soda.

2. Transfer the coffee-date mixture to a food processor, add the sugar and process until smooth, about 1 minute. Add the eggs, vanilla and allspice. Then, with the processor running, add the butter. Pour the date mixture over the flour mixture and whisk gently until combined. Transfer to the prepared pan, cover tightly with foil and bake until firm and a toothpick inserted at the center comes out clean, 55 to 65 minutes. Remove the foil and cool in the pan on a rack for 15 minutes.

FOR THE SAUCE:

3. While the cake cools, in a medium saucepan over medium-high, combine the sugar, corn syrup, orange zest and salt. Bring to a boil, then cook until the mixture hits 240°F, 2 to 3 minutes. Reduce heat to low and add the whiskey, 2 tablespoons at a time, allowing the bubbling to subside before adding more. Whisk in the butter 2 tablespoons at a time until melted and smooth.

4. Invert the cake onto a serving platter. Brush the top and sides generously with the warm toffee sauce. Slice and serve drizzled with additional sauce. The sauced, cooled cake can be wrapped tightly in plastic wrap and kept at room temperature for up to 3 days. Cooled sauce can be refrigerated for up to 1 week. To reheat, wrap the cake in foil and place in a 300°F oven until warmed. Microwave the sauce until bubbling.

Lemon-Buttermilk Pound Cake

Start to finish: 1½ hours (30 minutes active) / Servings: 8

13 tablespoons (1½ sticks plus 1 tablespoon) salted butter, room temperature, divided

433 grams (2 cups plus 3 tablespoons) white sugar, plus extra, divided

312 grams (2¾ cups) cake flour

½ teaspoon baking soda

½ teaspoon kosher salt

¾ cup buttermilk

2 tablespoons grated lemon zest, plus 3 tablespoons lemon juice (about 2 lemons)

5 large eggs, separated

Pound cake historically has had a propensity to density. So thick was the batter of equal parts butter, sugar, flour and eggs that 18th-century cookbook author Hannah Glasse recommended beating it for an hour. But despite all that flogging, and even with modern techniques, the cakes remained resolutely heavy. We figured there was a better way. For our pound cake, we separated the eggs, a trick we learned from pastry chef Kathryn King of Atlanta's Aria restaurant. She makes a lemon-buttermilk pound cake she got from her grandmother that is lofty and light. Gently whipping the egg whites, a trick lifted from sponge cakes, built lightness into the cake. King also adds baking soda, unusual in a pound cake, as well as buttermilk and lemon juice, which contribute a slightly tart flavor and add acid. We made minor tweaks, whisking the dry ingredients instead of sifting them and using a stand mixer to whip the whites, combine lemon zest and sugar, and beat the batter. King, like Violet bakery's Claire Ptak, emphasizes under-whipping the whites. Likewise, we took a gentler hand when creaming the butter and sugar. At Aria, the cake is sliced, buttered, toasted and served with fresh fruit and whipped cream. It's also delicious plain with just a spoonful of tangy whipped cream.

Don't overbeat the whites. They should appear smooth and glossy, with gentle peaks that curl back on themselves. And don't wait until the end of the baking time to check the cake for doneness; pans cook at different rates due to color and composition.

1. Heat the oven to 325°F with a rack in the middle position. Rub 1 tablespoon of the butter evenly over a Bundt pan, then use a pastry brush to ensure it gets into all corners. Sprinkle in a bit of sugar, then turn the pan to evenly coat all surfaces.

2. In a bowl, whisk together the flour, baking soda and salt. In a liquid measuring cup, combine the buttermilk and lemon juice; set aside.

3. In a stand mixer with a whisk attachment, whip the egg whites on medium-high until light and foamy, about 1 minute. With the mixer running, slowly sprinkle in 3 tablespoons of the sugar and continue to whip until the whites are thick and glossy and hold soft peaks, about 1 minute. Transfer the whites to a bowl and set aside, then add the remaining 2 cups of sugar and the lemon zest to the stand mixer's bowl.

4. Using the paddle attachment, mix the sugar and zest on low until the sugar appears moistened and begins to clump, about 1 minute. Add the remaining 12 tablespoons of butter and mix on medium-low until the mixture is cohesive, then increase the mixer to medium-high and beat until pale and fluffy, about 3 minutes. Reduce the mixer to low and add the yolks, one at a time, mixing until incorporated.

5. Add a third of the flour mixture, then mix on low. Add half of the buttermilk mixture, then mix again. Repeat the process of adding and mixing, ending with the final third of flour. Fold ⅓ of the whipped egg whites into the batter until combined, then gently fold in the remaining whites until barely combined. Transfer the batter to the prepared pan and smooth the top.

6. Bake until the cake is golden brown and bounces back when gently pressed, 50 to 60 minutes, rotating the pan halfway through baking. Cool the cake in the pan on a wire rack for 10 minutes, then remove from the pan and cool completely.

Pistachio-Cardamom Cake

Start to finish: 1 hour 10 minutes (15 minutes active), plus cooling
Makes one 9-inch loaf

198 grams (1 cup) white sugar

2 teaspoons grated orange zest, plus
¼ cup orange juice (about 1 orange)

185 grams (1⅓ cups) shelled, unsalted
pistachios, toasted and cooled

142 grams (1 cup) all-purpose flour,
plus more for pan

2 teaspoons baking powder

1½ teaspoons ground cardamom

1 teaspoon kosher salt

4 large eggs

½ cup plus 2 tablespoons plain
whole-milk Greek-style yogurt

¼ cup olive oil, plus more for pan

2 teaspoons vanilla extract

85 grams (¾ cup) powdered sugar

Baking a cake can be daunting. Enter the loaf cake, as easy as a quick bread but with more polish. Rose Bakery in Paris, created by Briton Rose Carrarini and her French husband, Jean-Charles, has elevated the style to an art form, producing tempting loaf cakes in all manner of flavors. We were particularly taken by a green-tinged, nut-topped pistachio cake. For our version, we paired toasted pistachios with cardamom and ground orange zest, giving it a distinctly Middle Eastern flavor. Combining ground nuts with rich Greek-style yogurt, olive oil and plenty of eggs ensured a moist, appealingly coarse crumb. We got the best results from grinding the nuts until they were nearly as fine as flour, but still had some texture. If you can't find unsalted pistachios, reduce the salt in the recipe by half. Cooling the cake was essential to maintain the thick consistency of the glaze.

Don't skip toasting the pistachios. The differences in flavor and texture were significant between raw and toasted. Toast the nuts at 300°F until they're quite fragrant and begin to darken, 10 to 15 minutes.

1. Heat the oven to 325°F with a rack in the middle position. Lightly coat a 9-by-5-inch loaf pan with olive oil and flour. In a food processor, combine the white sugar and orange zest; process until the sugar is damp and fragrant, 5 to 10 seconds. Transfer to a large bowl.

2. Add the pistachios to the processor and pulse until coarse, 8 to 10 pulses. Set aside 2 tablespoons of the nuts for topping. Add the flour, baking powder, cardamom and salt to the processor with the nuts. Process until the nuts are finely ground, about 45 seconds.

3. To the sugar mixture, whisk in the eggs, ½ cup of the yogurt, the oil, orange juice and vanilla. Add the nut-flour mixture and fold until mixed. Transfer the batter to the prepared pan, and smooth the top. Bake until golden brown, firm to the touch and a toothpick inserted at the center comes out with moist crumbs, 50 to 55 minutes. Cool in the pan on a wire rack for 15 minutes. Remove from the pan and let cool completely, about 2 hours.

4. In a small bowl, whisk the remaining 2 tablespoons of yogurt with the powdered sugar until thick and smooth. Spread over the top of the cake. Sprinkle with the reserved nuts. Let set for 10 minutes before serving.

Tangerine-Almond Cake
with Bay-Infused Syrup

Start to finish: **1 hour 10 minutes** (20 minutes active), plus cooling
Servings: **8**

For the cake:

223 grams (2¼ cups) blanched almond flour

95 grams (⅔ cup) all-purpose flour

½ teaspoon baking powder

211 grams (1 cup plus 1 tablespoon) white sugar

1½ tablespoons finely grated tangerine zest (4 to 5 tangerines)

2 teaspoons finely grated lemon zest (1 to 2 lemons)

¾ teaspoon kosher salt

12 tablespoons (1½ sticks) salted butter, room temperature, plus more for pan

4 large eggs, room temperature

3 tablespoons sliced almonds

For the syrup:

66 grams (⅓ cup) white sugar

3 tablespoons tangerine juice

2 tablespoons lemon juice

3 small bay leaves

Syrup-soaked cakes are largely foreign to U.S. bakers, though they're common throughout eastern Mediterranean countries. Easy to make, the cakes also keep well because of the hygroscopic (water retaining) nature of the syrup. Our tangerine-almond cake has a moist, pleasantly dense texture thanks in part to almond meal. (Use blanched almond flour; unblanched almond meal makes for a drier and less appealing cake.) We infuse our citrus syrup with bay leaves, adding an herbal note. We loved the unique flavor of tangerines in this cake, but if you can't find them, substitute orange zest and juice. If you don't have an 8-inch round cake pan, use a 9-inch pan and reduce the baking time to about 45 minutes.

Don't invert the cake without the buttered parchment. The cake's exterior is tacky and will easily stick to other surfaces, peeling off the crust and the almonds.

1. Heat the oven to 325°F with a rack in the middle position. Butter the bottom and sides of an 8-inch round cake pan. Line the bottom with kitchen parchment, then butter the parchment. In a medium bowl, whisk together the almond flour, all-purpose flour and baking powder.

2. In the bowl of a stand mixer with a paddle attachment, mix the sugar, both zests and the salt on low until the sugar appears moistened and clumps, about 1 minute. Add the butter and mix on medium-low until the mixture is cohesive. Increase the mixer to medium-high and beat until pale and fluffy, about 3 minutes. Reduce the mixer to low and add the eggs, one at a time, scraping down the bowl after each addition.

3. Add the dry ingredients and mix on low just until combined, 10 to 15 seconds. Use a silicone spatula to fold the batter until no streaks of flour remain. The batter will be very thick. Scrape the batter into the prepared pan. Spread into an even layer, then sprinkle the almonds on top. Bake until the cake is golden brown and the center feels firm when lightly pressed, about 55 minutes, rotating the pan halfway through.

4. Meanwhile, make the syrup. In a small saucepan over medium, combine all ingredients. Bring to a simmer, stirring until the sugar dissolves. Remove from heat and let the syrup steep until needed.

5. When the cake is done, return the syrup to a simmer over medium. Use a toothpick or skewer to poke holes all over the cake's surface. Brush all of the hot syrup evenly onto the hot cake. Cool the cake in the pan until barely warm to the touch, about 30 minutes.

6. Lightly butter a sheet of kitchen parchment, then place it on the cake, buttered side down. Invert a large plate on top of the parchment, then invert the plate and cake pan together. Lift off the pan and remove the parchment round. Re-invert the cake onto a serving platter and let cool completely.

Ricotta-Semolina **Cheesecake**

Start to finish: 1 hour (20 minutes active), plus cooling and chilling
Servings: 10

149 grams (¾ cup) white sugar, divided

2 teaspoons grated lemon zest, plus 1 tablespoon lemon juice

16-ounce container (2 cups) whole-milk ricotta

8-ounce container (1 cup) mascarpone

43 grams (¼ cup) semolina flour, plus more for the pan

4 large eggs, separated

2 tablespoons dry Marsala wine

¾ teaspoon kosher salt

This is a delicate dessert that mimics the texture of a New York–style cheesecake without the heft. It takes inspiration from a style of cake prepared in Germany and Italy. Instead of cream cheese, whole-milk ricotta kept it light; our favorite supermarket brand is Calabro. Mascarpone added plenty of flavor and a rich, creamy texture. Whipped egg whites also helped keep things light, and semolina flour gave structure to the cheese mixture and created a "crust" on the exterior. Lemon zest and juice brightened the flavors, and Marsala added an Italian touch while also cutting through the richness. If you don't have Marsala, dry sherry is a good substitute. A citrus curd or fruit compote made a great topping for this barely sweet cheesecake. Or try our flavorful fruit compotes (p. 293).

Don't be surprised if the cake cracks as it cools. The whipped egg whites give it a light, fluffy texture, but also make it delicate enough that cracks are inevitable.

1. Heat the oven to 350°F with a rack in the middle position. Coat the bottom and sides of a 9-inch springform pan with cooking spray, then dust evenly with semolina, tapping out the excess.

2. In a food processor, combine ½ cup of the sugar and the lemon zest. Process until moist and fragrant, about 15 seconds. Add the ricotta and mascarpone and process until smooth, about 30 seconds, scraping the sides as needed. Add the semolina, egg yolks, Marsala, lemon juice and salt, then process until combined, about 10 seconds. Transfer to a large bowl.

3. In a stand mixer with a whisk attachment, whip the egg whites on medium-high until light and foamy about 1 minute. With the mixer running, slowly add the remaining ¼ cup of sugar and continue to whip until the whites hold soft peaks, 1 to 2 minutes. Add a third of the egg whites to the cheese mixture and fold until combined. Add the remaining whites and fold until just incorporated. Transfer to the prepared pan, spreading in an even layer and tapping on the counter to release air bubbles.

4. Bake until the top is lightly browned and the cake is just set but still jiggles when shaken, 40 to 45 minutes. Let cool completely in the pan on a wire rack, about 2 hours. Cover and refrigerate for at least 2 hours. Run a knife around the inside of the pan and remove the pan sides before slicing.

Steamed Chocolate Cake

Start to finish: **35 minutes (10 minutes active)**, plus cooling
Servings: 8

142 grams (1 cup) all-purpose flour

29 grams (⅓ cup) natural cocoa powder

1 teaspoon baking soda

½ teaspoon kosher salt

198 grams (1 cup packed) light brown sugar

2 large eggs

½ cup water

1 teaspoon instant espresso powder

½ cup sour cream

6 tablespoons salted butter, melted

1½ teaspoons vanilla extract

Steaming is a basic technique of Asian cooking, and it's not just for savory dishes. Steamed cakes are common in Asia, where stovetop cooking dominates. This method is at home in the Western kitchen, too. After all, Boston brown bread and British Christmas pudding both are steamed. One bonus of steaming is you don't have to wait for the oven to heat up. More importantly, the moist heat keeps the cake from drying out. We used a foil coil set into a Dutch oven to elevate the cake above the water that steams it. Brown sugar and espresso powder gave the cake complexity, while sour cream added richness and a welcome tang. We liked the cake dusted with powdered sugar or topped with whipped cream. If your Dutch oven has a self-basting lid with dimples or spikes on the underside, lay a sheet of parchment or foil over the top of the pot before setting the lid in place to prevent water from dripping onto the cake.

Don't open the Dutch oven too often while steaming, but do ensure that the water is at a very gentle simmer. You should see steam emerging from the pot. If the heat is too high, the water will boil away before the cake is cooked.

1. Cut an 18-inch length of foil and gently scrunch together to form a snake about 1 inch thick. Shape into a circle and set into the bottom of a large Dutch oven. Add enough water to reach three-quarters up the coil. Oil the bottom and sides of a 9-inch round cake pan, line it with kitchen parchment, then oil the parchment. Place the prepared pan on top of the foil coil.

2. Sift the flour, cocoa powder and baking soda into a medium bowl, then whisk in the salt. In a large bowl, whisk the sugar and eggs until slightly lightened, about 30 seconds. Whisk in the water, espresso powder, sour cream, butter and vanilla. Add the flour mixture and stir until nearly combined.

3. Pour the batter into the prepared pan. Cover the pot and heat on high until the water boils. Reduce heat to low and steam, covered, until the cake is just firm to the touch at the center, about 20 to 25 minutes.

4. Turn off the heat and remove the lid. Let the cake sit in the Dutch oven until the pan is cool enough to handle. Transfer the pan to a wire rack, then run a paring knife around the edges to remove the cake.

Staples, Sauces and Seasonings

11

Harissa

Start to finish: **15 minutes**
Makes **about 1½ cups**

4 dried New Mexico chilies, stemmed, seeded and torn into rough pieces

½ cup grapeseed or other neutral oil

6 large garlic cloves

1 teaspoon caraway seeds

1 teaspoon cumin seeds

1 cup drained roasted red peppers, patted dry

½ cup drained oil-packed sun-dried tomatoes

1 tablespoon white balsamic vinegar

Kosher salt

Cayenne pepper

Our version of harissa, the spicy condiment that originated in North Africa, adds delicious punch to dips, soups, sauces and vinaigrettes. New Mexico chilies did the best job of matching harder-to-find North African chilies, bringing balanced heat. For more fire, a bit of cayenne can be added. Plenty of recipes call for either sun-dried tomatoes or roasted red peppers; we found a combination of both gave our harissa the sweet, ketchup-like profile Americans love and helped make it more of an all-purpose sauce, rather than simply a hot sauce. Frying the chilies, whole spices and garlic together in oil was easier and works better than the traditional method of toasting in a dry skillet. And while most recipes call for rehydrating the dried chilies, we found the hot oil softened them adequately, giving the harissa a pleasant, slightly coarse texture. Adding garlic to the mix mellowed its bite, and leaving the cloves whole ensured they wouldn't burn (and meant less prep work). We favored white balsamic vinegar for its mild acidity and slight sweetness. Lemon juice or white wine vinegar sweetened with a pinch of sugar is a good substitute.

In a small saucepan over medium, combine the chilies, oil, garlic, caraway and cumin. Cook, stirring often, until the garlic is light golden brown and the chilies are fragrant, about 5 minutes. Carefully transfer the mixture to a food processor and add the red peppers, tomatoes, vinegar and ¾ teaspoon of salt. Process until smooth, about 3 minutes, scraping the bowl once or twice. Season with salt and cayenne. Serve immediately or refrigerate in an airtight container for up to 3 weeks.

HARISSA HISTORY

Harissa (pronounced ha-REE-sah) may well be one of the original hot sauces, and it has enjoyed a bit of piggyback popularity as Sriracha and other spicy condiments have attracted near cultish followings. Chilies didn't land in Africa until the mid-16th century via conquerors, colonialists and traders returning from Central America. The easy-to-grow ingredient found a warm reception in arid African climates, adding an affordable kick to previously bland grain-based diets. Tunisia is credited with the birth of harissa, but it is popular across the region. Tunisians have a stronger predilection for spice than their neighbors, so their harissa emphasizes heat over nuance. In Morocco, where the cuisine is more complex, tomato paste, rose water and preserved lemon might play into the condiment's flavor. Our recipe is honest to its origins but suited to the foods and flavors of the American palate. We use our harissa sauce in all kinds of ways, including adding some kick to roasted potatoes (p. 87).

GREEK YOGURT-HARISSA DIP

Start to finish: **5 minutes**
Makes **about 2 cups**

This works well as an appetizer with crudités and crackers or as a sandwich spread with cold cuts, leftover chicken or grilled lamb.

2 cups plain whole-milk Greek-style yogurt

3 tablespoons harissa

2 tablespoons chopped fresh parsley, mint or a combination

1 teaspoon white sugar

Kosher salt and ground black pepper

In a bowl, stir together the yogurt, harissa, herbs and sugar. Season with salt and pepper.

HARISSA-CILANTRO VINAIGRETTE

Start to finish: **5 minutes**
Makes **about ½ cup**

This dressing pairs well with assertive greens or can be drizzled over roasted beets, cauliflower or broccoli. It's also a terrific sauce for salmon.

2 tablespoons lemon juice

1 tablespoon harissa

1 tablespoon water

2 teaspoons honey

Kosher salt

5 tablespoons extra-virgin olive oil

Ground black pepper

2 tablespoons chopped fresh cilantro

In a bowl, whisk together the lemon juice, harissa, water, honey and ¼ teaspoon of salt. Add the oil and whisk until emulsified. Season with additional salt and pepper, then stir in the cilantro.

SPICY HARISSA DIPPING SAUCE

Start to finish: **5 minutes**
Makes **1 cup**

Use this sauce anytime you'd reach for ketchup.

¾ cup mayonnaise

2 tablespoons harissa

2 tablespoons ketchup

Hot sauce

In a bowl, stir together the mayonnaise, harissa and ketchup. Season with hot sauce, to taste.

Honey-Chili Sauce

Start to finish: **5 minutes**
Makes **about ¾ cup**

½ cup honey

3 tablespoons unseasoned rice vinegar

1 tablespoon chili-garlic sauce

You can pay big money for spicy honey these days, or you can make your own. Our version skews Asian by spiking mild honey with chili-garlic sauce, and it takes honey to some unexpected places. Any mild honey, such as clover, will work. It's great drizzled over sweet potatoes, grilled or roasted vegetables, corn on the cob, or chicken or pork. And don't stop there. Consider a drizzle over pepperoni pizza, or on a soppresatta and mozzarella sandwich. Or use it to jazz up a grilled cheese.

In a small bowl, stir together all ingredients.

Tamarind Dipping Sauce

Start to finish: 20 minutes
Makes about 2 cups

2 lemon grass stalks, trimmed, bottom 8 inches chopped

1 large shallot, chopped

3 tablespoons grapeseed or other neutral oil

1 serrano chili, stemmed and chopped

1 tablespoon tomato paste

1 tablespoon finely grated fresh ginger

2½ cups water

2 ounces tamarind pulp, seeds removed

5 tablespoons packed light brown sugar

¼ cup fish sauce

1 tablespoon soy sauce

3 tablespoons lime juice (1 to 2 limes)

Ground black pepper

We developed this sauce to go alongside our Chiang Mai chicken, but it's also great with sticky Asian spareribs, stirred into Asian soups, drizzled over steamed or sticky rice, as a base for steaming mussels, or tossed with sliced cucumber and torn mint leaves for a quick salad. And it's good with grilled meats, poultry and fish, especially salmon. Tamarind is a brown pod containing seeds and a sticky, sour pulp. Tamarind pulp is most commonly available as blocks and will keep for several weeks in the refrigerator. A blender gave the sauce its smooth consistency. For a milder flavor, remove the seeds and ribs from the chili. If you can find palm sugar, it would be an authentic substitute for the brown sugar.

1. In a medium saucepan over medium, combine the lemon grass, shallot, oil and chili. Cook, stirring, until just beginning to brown, 3 to 5 minutes. Add the tomato paste and ginger and cook, stirring constantly, until fragrant, about 30 seconds. Add the water, tamarind and sugar. Bring to a boil, then reduce heat to medium-low and simmer until the tamarind has softened, about 15 minutes. Off heat, stir in the fish sauce and soy sauce.

2. Let the mixture cool slightly, then transfer to a blender. Blend until smooth, about 1 minute. Strain through a fine mesh strainer, pressing on the solids; discard the solids. Stir in the lime juice, then taste and season with pepper. Use immediately or refrigerate for up to 2 weeks.

Slow-Roasted Tomatoes

Start to finish: 3½ hours (15 minutes active)
Makes about 32 halves

¼ cup white balsamic vinegar

¼ cup tomato paste

2 teaspoons kosher salt

1 teaspoon ground black pepper

4 pounds plum tomatoes
(about 16 medium), halved
lengthwise

¼ cup extra-virgin olive oil

We love what a burst of bright tomato flavor can do for a recipe. But supermarket tomatoes are a disappointment, especially during winter. So we looked for a way to improve year-round tomatoes and found it by way of a slow roast to concentrate flavor. We began by coating halved plum tomatoes with a mix of tomato paste and vinegar, then roasting them on kitchen parchment–lined baking sheets along with garlic. We tried several variations of vinegar, including white and regular balsamic; we found white balsamic worked best. Mixing olive oil into the coating mixture made the vinegar and tomatoes burn and stick to the parchment. Drizzling the olive oil over the tomatoes separately worked better. Medium plum tomatoes, roughly 4 ounces each, were ideal. If your tomatoes are smaller, start checking them after three hours in the oven.

1. **Heat the oven to 325°F** with a rack in the middle position. Line a rimmed baking sheet with kitchen parchment. In a large bowl, whisk together the vinegar, tomato paste, salt and pepper. Add the tomatoes and toss to coat. Arrange the tomatoes cut side up on the prepared baking sheet. Drizzle evenly with the oil.

2. **Roast until the tomatoes** are shriveled, caramelized and lightly charred at the edges, about 3½ hours, rotating the pan halfway through. Serve immediately, or let cool, transfer to a lidded container and refrigerate for up to 1 week.

SLOW ROAST FOR FAST FLAVOR

A jar of slow-roasted tomatoes can launch a host of meals and accent a variety of dishes. Use them as a relish for sandwiches, add them to soups or stews, toss them with pasta, serve them over grilled polenta, or spoon them over grilled or fried fish. Chop a few and toss with herbs like basil, parsley and thyme for a quick relish. For a quick version of fagioli all'uccelletto (beans braised in tomato sauce), toss a handful of chopped slow-roasted tomatoes with a drained can of white beans, chopped sage, a pinch of red pepper flakes and a few tablespoons of olive oil. Heat until bubbling and creamy; serve with crusty bread.

Homemade Chipotles in Adobo Sauce

Start to finish: 45 minutes (5 minutes active)
Makes 16 chipotles with sauce

20 dried morita chipotle chilies
(about 1¼ ounces), stems removed

3 cups water

1 medium yellow onion,
roughly chopped

6 garlic cloves

⅓ cup cider vinegar

¼ cup ketchup

¼ cup packed brown sugar

1 teaspoon ground cumin

1 teaspoon ground coriander

1 teaspoon kosher salt

½ teaspoon dried thyme

Canned chipotles in adobo are a great pantry staple. The chilies (or even just a spoonful of the sauce) are an easy way to add moderate heat and deep, smoky flavor to sauces, soups, meats and sandwiches. They are made by drying and smoking jalapeno peppers, then packing them in a rich sauce made from tomatoes and even more chilies. We love homemade even more; the texture of the chilies is firmer and the sauce is thicker and more robustly flavored. Be sure to use dried morita chipotles, which are shiny and dark. They are smaller, sweeter and smokier than tan-colored meco chipotles, which tend to be leathery and nutty.

In a medium saucepan, combine the chipotles and water. Bring to a boil, then simmer for 20 minutes. Remove all but 4 of the chilies from the pan and set aside. In a blender, combine the cooking water and the remaining 4 chipotles. Add the remaining ingredients. Blend until mostly smooth, then return to the pan. Add the reserved chilies, then simmer, stirring occasionally, until thickened, about 20 minutes. Cool, then refrigerate. The chipotles keep for up to 1 month.

TURN UP THE HEAT

Chipotle peppers—actually smoked and dried jalapenos—can contribute deep, smoky-sweet flavor and body to a host of different dishes. We like them chopped and stirred into a pot of braised pinto or black beans, or pureed into a can or two of black beans for quick refried beans. They are terrific mixed into mayonnaise for an instant sauce. Or add to a basic tomato sauce with a handful of cilantro and a pinch each of cumin and cinnamon for a simple enchilada sauce. This sauce can also be used to smother a burrito, known as burrito ahogado or "drowned burrito." Smear some of the sauce into a grilled cheese or add a spoonful to mac and cheese (and garnish with toasted pepitas). A chopped chili or two can add welcome spiciness to a basic meat stew.

Cilantro-Jalapeno Adobo Sauce

Start to finish: 20 minutes
Makes about 1 cup

4 large jalapeno chilies

6 large garlic cloves, unpeeled

5 cups (about 4 ounces) lightly packed
fresh cilantro leaves and tender stems

6 tablespoons extra-virgin olive oil

1 tablespoon lime juice, plus more
as needed

¾ teaspoon kosher salt

½ teaspoon sugar

Spanish for marinade, adobo can be many things, but it began as a blend of olive oil, vinegar and spices that was slathered over meat and other foods to keep them from spoiling. We wanted a sauce that could go with just about anything and were inspired by a Mexican-style adobo from Rick Bayless, who blends together garlic, serrano chilies, cilantro, parsley and oil. We wanted to cut back on the oil and heat, so we chose jalapeno peppers over serrano chilies; the latter can vary widely in heat level from dud to scud. We dropped the parsley and went all in on cilantro; its fresh, clean flavor was even bolder when it didn't need to compete with another herb. Our sauce packs moderate heat; if you prefer a milder version, replace two of the jalapenos with one large Anaheim or poblano chili. Since it's blended with oil, the herb sauce can be refrigerated for up to three weeks.

Don't forget to wash and dry your herbs. Cilantro can be quite sandy. A salad spinner is the easiest way to wash and dry it.

1. **Heat the broiler** with an oven rack 6 inches from the element. Arrange the jalapenos and garlic on a rimmed baking sheet and broil, turning as necessary, until the chilies are evenly blistered and the garlic skins are spotted brown, 8 to 10 minutes. If the garlic blackens too quickly, remove it first. Cover with foil and let sit until cool enough to handle, about 10 minutes. Peel, stem and seed the chilies and peel the garlic, trimming away any scorched bits.

2. **In a food processor,** combine the chilies, garlic and all remaining ingredients. Process until smooth, 1 to 2 minutes, scraping the bowl as needed. Taste and adjust salt and lime juice as desired.

A SAUCE FOR ALL SEASONS

Cilantro-jalapeno adobo sauce adds an easy punch of spicy, fresh flavor to numerous dishes, including:

Quesadillas: Smear a thin layer of adobo on tortillas before filling and toasting.

Rice: Fold adobo into a pot of cooked rice (about 1 tablespoon per cup of rice), then season with plenty of lime juice. Serve with grilled meats or alongside stewed beans.

Beans: Stir into cooked pinto or black beans, either whole or refried. Or puree with canned beans to make a spread for tortas or quesadillas.

Meats: Use the adobo as a dipping sauce for roasted or grilled beef or a rich pork shoulder.

Fish: Thin with additional olive oil, then spoon over seared scallops or roasted salmon or halibut; garnish with lime wedges.

Sweet potatoes: Thin the sauce with Greek-style yogurt and drizzle over roasted sweet potato wedges or use as a dipping sauce.

Sandwiches: Stir together equal parts adobo and mayonnaise, then use as a sandwich spread, particularly with turkey, chicken or on a BLT.

Vinaigrettes: Add a spoonful to any neutral-flavored vinaigrette (use citrus juice, rice vinegar or white balsamic vinegar for the acid).

Eggs: Fold into barely set scrambled eggs, drizzle over fried eggs or add to egg salad.

Hummus: Swirl a spoonful into the top hummus. This works equally well with baba ghanoush.

Polenta: Spoon a tablespoon or two over polenta topped with toasted pumpkin seeds, crumbled queso fresco and avocado.

Pickled Vegetables (*Escabeche*)

Start to finish: 45 minutes (30 minutes active), plus cooling
Makes about 4 cups

1 large red onion (¾ pound), halved and thinly sliced lengthwise

½ pound carrots, peeled, halved lengthwise and thinly sliced on a bias

2 jalapeno chilies, thinly sliced crosswise

5 teaspoons kosher salt

1 cup distilled white vinegar

1 cup water

½ cup white sugar

½ teaspoon black peppercorns

½ teaspoon coriander seeds

¼ teaspoon red pepper flakes (optional)

6 allspice berries

1 bay leaf

Escabeche translates as marinade, or pickle, and refers to a variety of pickled dishes popular in Spanish and Latin American cooking. Here, we pickle vegetables for a piquant side dish. Salting the vegetables before pickling them enhanced their crispness and intensified their final flavor. That's because salting removes water, allowing them to better absorb the brine. Once cooled, the pickled vegetables can be eaten immediately, but their flavor improves with time. We left the whole spices in the brine to infuse even more during storage.

Don't slice the onions crosswise. We preferred the texture and appearance of onions sliced from pole to pole. And the thinner the slices the better; aim for about ⅛-inch thickness.

1. **In a bowl,** toss together the onions, carrots, jalapenos and salt. Let sit for 30 to 60 minutes. Transfer the vegetables to a colander and rinse well, then set aside to drain.

2. **Meanwhile,** in a medium saucepan over high, combine the vinegar, water, sugar, peppercorns, coriander, pepper flakes, if using, allspice and bay leaf. Bring to a boil, then reduce to medium and simmer for 5 minutes.

3. **Transfer the vegetables** to a canning jar or heatproof, lidded container. Pour the hot brine over them, ensuring they are fully submerged. Cool to room temperature, about 2 hours, then cover and refrigerate for up to 1 month.

HOW TO SERVE ESCABECHE

- On burgers, sandwiches, wraps, tacos and nachos

- With pulled pork, chili, brisket and grilled fish, poultry or steaks

- Chopped into slaws and potato, tuna, egg or chicken salads

- In a grilled cheese sandwich, and on green or grain salads

- As a condiment for charcuterie platters, smoked fish and baked potatoes

- As a garnish for crostini or bruschetta

GET INTO A PICKLE

The pickling brine for our escabeche can be used:

- To poach fish or boneless chicken breasts (use equal parts water and brine)

- In place of citrus juice in salsa or ceviche

- In vinaigrettes, store-bought barbecue sauces and bloody mary cocktails

- To deglaze a pan

- To braise chicken or pork (use pickling brine for 20 percent of the liquid)

- To brighten the flavor of cooked beans (stir in brine immediately after cooking)

- To glaze vegetables (combine brine, butter and a sweetener, such as maple syrup, honey or sugar)

Other uses for pickling brine:

MUSTARD VINAIGRETTE

Start to finish: **5 minutes**
Makes **about 1 cup**

To vary this recipe, add minced garlic, shallot or fresh thyme and/or a squeeze of honey.

1 tablespoon Dijon mustard

3 tablespoons pickling brine

¾ cup extra-virgin olive oil

Kosher salt and ground black pepper

In a bowl, whisk together the mustard and brine until smooth. Continue to whisk and add the oil slowly until the dressing is emulsified, about 15 seconds. Season with salt and pepper.

SPICY PEANUT SAUCE

Start to finish: **10 minutes**
Makes **about 1 cup**

This recipe works equally well with creamy or chunky peanut butter.

½ cup natural peanut butter

¼ cup pickling brine

1 tablespoon soy sauce

1 tablespoon white sugar

1 garlic clove, minced

½ teaspoon red pepper flakes

2 tablespoons water, plus more as needed

In a blender, combine all ingredients. Blend until smooth, adding water 1 tablespoon at a time to achieve desired consistency.

VINEGAR-BASED BARBECUE SAUCE

Start to finish: **10 minutes**
Makes **about 1⅓ cups**

1 cup pickling brine

¼ cup ketchup

2 tablespoons packed brown sugar

1 tablespoon red pepper flakes

1 teaspoon ground black pepper

Kosher salt

In a medium bowl, whisk together all ingredients except the salt. Season to taste.

Central Mexican **Guacamole**

Start to finish: **10 minutes** / Servings: 4

4 tablespoons finely chopped
fresh cilantro, divided

1 to 2 serrano chilies, stemmed
and finely chopped

2 tablespoons finely chopped
white onion

Kosher salt

3 ripe avocados, halved and pitted

1 pint (10 ounces) grape tomatoes,
finely chopped

Many guacamole recipes are a muddle of flavors. We prefer the simplicity of Central Mexican guacamole, which is seasoned with just three things—serrano chilies, white onion and cilantro. No garlic. No lime juice. Whether you use a mortar and pestle or a mixing bowl and the back of a fork, the onions, chilies and cilantro get mashed to a paste that permeates the avocados. Though acid is needed to balance the fat of the avocados and slow down oxidation (that ugly browning), lime juice can overpower guacamole. In Central Mexico, tomato provides the acid. Chopped fresh tomatoes offer a gentler acidity and flavor that—unlike limes—complement rather than compete with the other ingredients. Guacamole hinges on the ripeness of the avocados; they should be soft but slightly firm.

Don't discard the seeds from the chilies. This recipe relies on them for a pleasant heat.

In a bowl, combine 2 tablespoons of the cilantro, the chilies, onion and ½ teaspoon salt. Mash with the bottom of a dry measuring cup until a rough paste forms, about 1 minute. Scoop the avocado flesh into the bowl and coarsely mash with a potato masher or fork. Stir in half of the tomatoes until combined. Taste and season with salt. Transfer to a serving bowl and sprinkle with the remaining cilantro and tomatoes.

Jalapeno-Mint Sauce

Start to finish: **5 minutes**
Makes **about 1¼ cups**

---

1 cup lightly packed fresh mint leaves

⅔ cup extra-virgin olive oil

3 medium jalapeno chilies, stemmed, seeded and roughly chopped

2 tablespoons lime juice

1 tablespoon honey

2 teaspoons finely grated fresh ginger

1 garlic clove, smashed

¾ teaspoon kosher salt, plus more as needed

This light, bright sauce takes moments to prepare and pairs particularly well with grilled or roasted fish, especially meaty swordfish, halibut and salmon. We also like it as a sauce alongside grilled vegetables and roasted cauliflower. Or use it as a sauce for tacos or lettuce wraps, or as a dressing for room-temperature pasta salads. Three-inch jalapenos—ribs and seeds removed—worked best for balanced heat. If you prefer a spicier sauce, incorporate a few seeds.

Don't let this sauce sit for more than an hour or two; it's best served soon after it is made. If it begins to separate, stir to recombine.

In a food processor, combine all ingredients. Process until smooth, about 1 minute, scraping the bowl as necessary. Taste and season with salt. Serve immediately.

Pickled Chilies (*Nam Prik*)

Start to finish: **35 minutes** (5 minutes active)
Makes **1 cup**

4 jalapeno chilies, stemmed, seeded (if desired) and thinly sliced crosswise

¼ cup fish sauce

¼ cup lime juice (1 to 2 limes)

1 teaspoon white sugar

These jalapeno chilies pickled in fish sauce, lime juice and a little sugar are a milder variation of the often fiery Thai dressing called nam prik. The chilies, and their sauce, add a balanced hit of heat, sweet and acid. We find them a delicious way to add bright flavor to our Thai fried rice (p. 94), or any Thai or Vietnamese dish. Whisk in a little peanut oil for a quick salad, vegetable or slaw dressing. Add a spoonful to stews, or even scrambled eggs or roasted or sautéed vegetables.

In a bowl, stir together all ingredients. Refrigerate for at least 30 minutes or up to 1 week.

Spicy Garlic-and-Herb Oil

Start to finish: **10 minutes**
Makes **about 1 cup**

2 cups lightly packed fresh
flat-leaf parsley leaves

½ cup plus 2 tablespoons
extra-virgin olive oil

½ cup coarsely chopped
fresh chives

¼ cup coarsely chopped fresh dill

1 tablespoon red pepper flakes

1 large garlic clove, smashed

1 teaspoon kosher salt

½ teaspoon ground black pepper

This herb-rich oil is great brushed on to warm piadine (p. 191). It also can be served as a dip for bread. If you like, substitute fresh oregano, marjoram or mint for the dill. Other uses: Drizzle over pasta, polenta and fried eggs, or use as a base for vinaigrettes with lemon juice or white balsamic vinegar.

In a food processor, combine all ingredients and process until smooth, about 20 seconds, scraping the bowl as needed.

Spiced Yogurt Dressing

Start to finish: **5 minutes**
Makes **about 1½ cups**

1 cup plain whole-milk
Greek-style yogurt

2 teaspoons ground coriander

¾ teaspoon ground cumin

½ teaspoon ground turmeric

½ teaspoon kosher salt

¼ teaspoon ground black pepper

⅛ to ¼ teaspoon cayenne pepper

⅛ teaspoon finely grated garlic

3 tablespoons extra-virgin olive oil

3½ teaspoons red wine vinegar

1 teaspoon honey

Water, as needed

Our spiced yogurt dressing was inspired by Madhur Jaffrey, the Delhi-born actress, cookbook author and television chef who has spent decades exploring the food of her homeland and beyond. We loved the yogurt dressing in her book, "Vegetarian India." The warm spices in this thick dressing work with everything from simple salads of romaine or spinach to poached salmon, herbed chickpeas and roasted vegetables, such as beets, cauliflower and broccoli. Use it to dress farro or barley salads, as a dipping sauce for whole artichokes, over warm or room-temperature potatoes or with grilled or roasted lamb. For a thinner consistency, add water, a tablespoon at a time, whisking until smooth after each addition. Because it is made without herbs or much garlic, it refrigerates well for up to five days.

Don't overdo the garlic. More than ⅛ teaspoon of finely grated raw garlic—use a wand-style grater—easily overpowered the dressing.

In a medium bowl, whisk together the yogurt, coriander, cumin, turmeric, salt, pepper, cayenne and garlic. Add the oil, vinegar and honey, then whisk until smooth. Add water, 1 tablespoon at a time, to reach desired consistency.

Sweet-and-Sour Mint Dressing (*Sekanjabin*)

Start to finish: **10 minutes active, plus 1 hour cooling**
Makes **about ½ cup**

½ cup plus 2 tablespoons cider vinegar, divided

½ cup clover honey

½ teaspoon kosher salt

1 ounce fresh mint leaves and stems

French vinaigrette may be the dressing we know best, but step out of Europe and the choices multiply. In many cultures, sauces—not just vinegar and oil—dress vegetables, grains or greens. The range of acids and fats expands, as does the potential for sweeteners and wild cards such as tamarind paste, miso or a bold splash of fish, soy or oyster sauce. We were introduced to one of the simplest, most appealing dressings by Yasmin Khan, author of "The Saffron Tales." The Iranian dressing sekanjabin is an ancient blend of cider vinegar, honey or sugar, and mint concentrated into a syrup to use straight as a dressing or diluted in a drink. We preferred unfiltered cider vinegars. And we loved the dressing on cold roasted vegetables.

Don't use a distinctively flavored honey, such as orange blossom or buckwheat. The flavor will overpower the delicate mint.

In a small saucepan over medium, combine ½ cup of the vinegar, the honey and salt. Simmer until large bubbles appear and the mixture reduces to about ½ cup, about 7 minutes. Off the heat, add the mint, pushing it into the syrup. Let cool to room temperature. Strain into a bowl, pressing the solids. Stir in the remaining 2 tablespoons of vinegar. Cool. Refrigerate for up to 1 month.

Three ways to use sekanjabin:

BROILED EGGPLANT WITH CHILIES AND CILANTRO

Start to finish: 20 minutes
(10 minutes active)
Servings: 4

2 pounds eggplant, cut crosswise into 1-inch slices

½ cup olive oil

Kosher salt and ground black pepper

½ cup chopped fresh cilantro

2 tablespoons chili-garlic sauce

2 tablespoons sweet-and-sour mint dressing

Heat the broiler and set an oven rack 6 inches from it. Line a rimmed baking sheet with foil. Arrange the eggplant on the foil and brush both sides with the olive oil. Season with salt and pepper. Broil until well browned, about 10 minutes. Flip each slice and broil again until well browned, another 5 to 10 minutes. Let cool. In a large bowl, combine the cilantro, chili-garlic sauce and dressing. Cut each eggplant slice into 6 pieces and toss with the dressing.

ROASTED BROCCOLI RAAB WITH FENNEL AND CHILI FLAKES

Start to finish: 30 minutes
(10 minutes active)
Servings: 4

1 pound broccoli raab, ends trimmed, well dried

½ cup olive oil

1 tablespoon ground fennel

1 teaspoon kosher salt

1 teaspoon ground black pepper

1 teaspoon red pepper flakes

2 tablespoons sweet-and-sour mint dressing

Heat the oven to 500°F with an oven rack in the middle position. Line a rimmed baking sheet with foil. In a large bowl, toss the broccoli raab with the oil, fennel, salt, black pepper and red pepper flakes. Transfer to the baking sheet, reserving the bowl. Roast, stirring halfway through, until just beginning to brown, 12 to 15 minutes. Let cool. Return to the bowl and toss with the dressing.

ROASTED CAULIFLOWER WITH CURRY AND MINT

Start to finish: 45 minutes
(10 minutes active)
Servings: 4

½ cup olive oil

1 teaspoon curry powder

1 teaspoon ground cumin

1 teaspoon kosher salt

½ teaspoon ground black pepper

2 medium heads cauliflower (about 4 pounds total), cored and cut into 2-inch pieces

3 tablespoons minced fresh mint

2 tablespoons sweet-and-sour mint dressing

Heat the oven to 475°F with an rack in the middle position. Line a rimmed baking sheet with foil. In a large bowl, combine the oil, curry powder, cumin, salt and pepper. Add the cauliflower and toss. Transfer to the prepared baking sheet, reserving the bowl. Arrange the pieces cut side down. Roast until well browned, about 30 minutes. Let cool. In the reserved bowl, combine the mint with the dressing. Add the cauliflower and toss to coat.

Fig-Olive **Tapenade**

Start to finish: **20 minutes**
Makes **about 2 cups**

---

5 ounces (1 cup) dried black mission figs, stemmed

1 cup Kalamata olives, pitted, rinsed and patted dry

½ cup oil-cured olives, pitted

¼ cup capers, rinsed and squeezed dry

2 anchovy fillets, patted dry

1 teaspoon minced fresh rosemary

½ teaspoon grated orange zest

½ teaspoon red pepper flakes

¼ cup extra-virgin olive oil

A paste made of figs and olives may sound like an oddball pairing, but the two work well together. The sweetness of the figs mitigates the brine and bitterness of the olives. A combination of Kalamata and more pungent oil-cured olives provided the best balance of flavor and creamy texture. To easily pit the olives, whack them with the side of a chef's knife to flatten, then simply use your fingers to pull out the pits. Soaking the figs made up for any difference in moisture content and ensured they ground easily to a smooth paste. We love this tapenade smeared on crostini, either alone or with fresh cheese or caramelized onions, as a dip for crudités, tossed with steamed vegetables or potatoes, as a topping for beef, chicken or fish, combined with olive oil and vinegar for a quick vinaigrette, or stirred into pasta.

Don't forget to check your olives for pits, even if they're labeled "pitted." We prefer to buy olives with pits and prep them ourselves, but pitted olives will work.

1. In a small saucepan, bring 1 cup water to a boil. Add the figs, remove from the heat, then cover and let sit for 15 minutes. Drain the figs, reserving the soaking liquid. In a food processor, combine the figs, both olives, capers, anchovies, rosemary, zest, pepper flakes and 2 tablespoons of the fig soaking liquid. Process until a smooth paste forms, 1 to 2 minutes, scraping the bowl halfway through.

2. With the processor running, add the oil in a steady stream and process until incorporated, about 30 seconds. Transfer to a bowl or lidded container and let sit for 1 hour before serving. Tapenade can be refrigerated for up to 3 weeks.

Whipped **Feta**

Start to finish: **15 minutes**
Makes **about 1½ cups**

8 ounces feta cheese

2 tablespoons lemon juice

1 garlic clove, peeled and smashed

3 ounces cream cheese, room temperature

⅓ cup extra-virgin olive oil

½ teaspoon smoked paprika

½ teaspoon red pepper flakes

¼ teaspoon ground black pepper

2 tablespoons chopped fresh mint leaves, plus more to garnish

2 tablespoons chopped mild Peppadew peppers

This easy, whipped feta cheese spread is based on the traditional Greek dip, htipiti (pronounced h'tee-pee-tee). There are many variations, some as simple as feta, red pepper flakes and extra-virgin olive oil, others with herbs and roasted red peppers. We shifted to Peppadew peppers, which added a sweet-tart kick to balance the creaminess of the cheese. A brief soak in water removed some of the salt from the cheese and made it easier to control the dish's seasoning. Raw garlic tasted harsh and bitter; infusing lemon juice with a smashed clove provided gentler flavor. Processing the feta and cream cheese before adding the remaining ingredients was the key to a light, whipped texture. To increase the heat, use cayenne pepper or hot Peppadews, or add more red pepper flakes. The whipped feta can be refrigerated for up to a week. This makes the perfect dip for crudités or pita points, or use as garnish on pasta or grilled meats and vegetables. It's terrific as a sandwich spread, too, especially when topped with sautéed greens—spinach, kale or chard—and a fried egg. Try serving it alongside lamb chops or even slices of seared steak.

Don't use pre-crumbled feta. It can be dry and chalky. Look for block feta packed in brine, ideally made with sheep's or goat's milk.

1. In a medium bowl, cover the feta with fresh tap water and let sit for 10 minutes. In a small bowl, combine the lemon juice and garlic and let sit for 10 minutes. Discard the garlic clove. Drain the feta and pat dry, then crumble.

2. In a food processor, combine the feta and cream cheese. Process until smooth, about 30 seconds. Add the oil, lemon juice, paprika, pepper flakes and black pepper. Process until well mixed, about 30 seconds. Scrape the bowl, add the mint and Peppadews, then pulse until combined.

3. Taste and season with pepper flakes and black pepper. Refrigerate for at least 30 minutes before serving. Garnish with mint.

Miso-Ginger Dressing

Start to finish: **10 minutes**
Makes **about 1 cup**

⅓ cup walnuts

⅓ cup white miso

1 teaspoon grated lemon zest,
plus ¼ cup lemon juice
(1 to 2 lemons)

¼ cup water

1-ounce piece fresh ginger,
peeled and thinly sliced

1 teaspoon Dijon mustard

1 teaspoon honey

½ teaspoon ground white pepper

½ cup grapeseed or other
neutral oil

Miso and ginger are mainstays of the Asian pantry. Here, we combine them with items common to the Western pantry—Dijon mustard and honey—to create a zesty dressing. The creamy texture and mild, sweet-salty flavor of white miso, also called shiro miso, worked best. Walnuts gave the dressing richness and body. If the dressing becomes too thick after being refrigerated, gradually whisk in water to thin it. Because of its creamy, thick texture, this dressing goes well with heartier salad greens, as well as vegetables, grains, beans, chicken and fish.

Don't toast the walnuts. They provide texture, but their flavor should be subtle. Toasting them makes them too assertive.

In a blender, combine all ingredients except the oil. Blend until the walnuts are finely ground and the dressing is smooth, about 1 minute. Add the oil and blend until emulsified, about 30 seconds.

USE THIS DRESSING:

• On a chopped salad of romaine, cucumbers, cherry tomatoes, radishes, red onion and mint

• On a radicchio, endive and arugula salad with roasted beets and toasted chopped walnuts

• Tossed with or drizzled over blanched vegetables, especially green beans, asparagus, broccoli, cauliflower and carrots

• As a sauce for poached whitefish or salmon

• As a dressing for cabbage slaws— thinly sliced red, white or napa cabbage with grated carrots, sliced scallions, diced jalapeno and herbs, such as fresh parsley, cilantro, basil or mint

• As dressing for a shredded chicken salad with blanched sugar snap peas, thinly sliced red pepper and celery and fresh herbs

• As dressing for a rice salad with diced celery, cucumber, toasted chopped almonds, raisins, sliced scallions and chopped parsley or mint

• Drizzled on grilled vegetables, especially eggplant, zucchini, yellow squash, asparagus and onions

Green Goddess Tofu Dressing

Start to finish: 5 minutes, plus chilling
Makes about 1½ cups

2 tablespoons white balsamic vinegar

1 small garlic clove, smashed

8 ounces drained silken tofu (1 cup)

¾ cup lightly packed fresh flat-leaf parsley leaves

⅓ cup coarsely chopped fresh chives

¼ cup grapeseed or other neutral oil

2 tablespoons chopped fresh tarragon

1½ teaspoons grated lemon zest

1 anchovy fillet

½ teaspoon kosher salt

¼ teaspoon ground black pepper

Green goddess salad dressing is one of those enchantingly retro recipes most of us have heard of even if we haven't actually tried it. The original recipe went heavy on the mayonnaise and later versions included sour cream and even avocado. We took the dressing to a lighter place with silken tofu, which provided a creamy base. From there we piled on the herbs. We liked parsley's clean, herbaceous flavor combined with the mellow onion note of chives and tarragon's distinctive licorice flavor. Lemon zest added a hit of citrus, but the juice was too sharp. Instead, we opted for sweet-tart white balsamic vinegar. We preferred the more neutral flavor of shelf-stable tofu—found in the Asian foods aisle—over its refrigerated counterpart. While the dressing can be served right away, we preferred to let the flavors meld for at least an hour. It keeps for up to four days refrigerated.

Don't use dried tarragon. If fresh tarragon isn't available, substitute 3 tablespoons of chopped fresh dill or basil.

In a blender, combine all ingredients. Blend until smooth and uniformly pale green, 1 to 2 minutes. Transfer to a jar and refrigerate for at least 1 hour.

- Rice salad with chopped toasted almonds, diced celery and peas

- Chopped chicken salad with bacon, avocado and tomatoes

- Shredded chicken salad with spinach, sliced cucumbers, grated carrots and sliced red cabbage

- Fusilli pasta salad with grilled zucchini, summer squash, olives and cherry tomatoes

- Broiled or grilled fish

- Shrimp or seafood salad with diced celery, red pepper and lemon zest on frisee

- Romaine and watercress salad with chopped hard-cooked eggs and avocado

Fruit **Chutney**

Start to finish: **25 minutes, plus cooling**
Makes **about 2½ cups**

---

1 large red onion, diced
(about 1½ cups)

2 tablespoons salted butter

1 tablespoon grapeseed
or other neutral oil

Kosher salt

2 teaspoons coriander seeds,
crushed

1 teaspoon yellow mustard
seeds, crushed

2 Granny Smith apples,
peeled, cored and diced

¼ cup white sugar

⅓ cup dried apricots, diced

⅓ cup dried cherries,
coarsely chopped

⅓ cup dried currants

⅓ cup cider vinegar

⅓ cup water

In India, chutney, or chatni, refers to a variety of sauces made from numerous ingredients. Elsewhere in the world, it is translated mostly as a sweet-savory jam-like condiment. In our version—which was inspired by a chutney by London baker Claire Ptak—red onion lent a slight, pleasant bite. A combination of salted butter and neutral oil worked best for sauteing. Sulfured and unsulfured dried apricots fared equally well in this recipe. The cooled chutney can be refrigerated for up to two weeks. Our favorite way to use this chutney was in a gooey grilled cheese (see sidebar), but it also is great as a topping for grilled pork chops, in a turkey sandwich or simply as a component on a cheese board.

Don't grind the mustard and coriander seeds. Crush them with a mortar and pestle, or use the side of a wide chef's knife to crush them against the cutting board.

In a medium saucepan over medium, combine the onion, butter, oil and ⅛ teaspoon salt. Cook, stirring occasionally, until the onion is softened, 9 to 11 minutes. Add the coriander and mustard seeds and cook for 1 minute. Stir in the apples, sugar and ¼ teaspoon salt. Cook until the sugar is dissolved, about 1 minute. Add the apricots, cherries, currants, vinegar and water, then stir to combine. Bring to a simmer and cook until the chutney is thickened but the apples still hold their shape, 10 to 12 minutes. Remove from the heat and cool.

GRILLED CHEESE
WITH FRUIT CHUTNEY

Start to finish: **10 minutes**
Makes **1 sandwich**

Homemade chutney is the highlight
of this sandwich, but if you use store-
bought, look for Stonewall Kitchen
Apple Cranberry Chutney or
another high-quality variety with a
thick texture. This recipe is easily
doubled using a 12-inch skillet.

3 to 4 tablespoons chutney

Two ½-inch-thick slices
sourdough or seeded rye bread

2 to 3 ounces Gruyere, Comte, Gouda
or raclette cheese, thinly sliced

1 tablespoon salted butter,
softened

Kosher salt

1. Evenly spread the chutney over
1 slice of bread, then top with the
cheese in an even layer, followed
by the second slice of bread. Spread
half the butter over the top of the
sandwich, then sprinkle with a
pinch of salt.

2. Heat a 10-inch stainless steel or
cast-iron skillet over medium-high
for 2 minutes. Reduce heat to low
and add the sandwich, buttered
side down. Spread the remaining
butter over the top of the sandwich,
then cover the pan and cook until
the bottom is golden brown, 3 to
5 minutes.

3. Flip the sandwich and cook,
covered, until the second side is
golden brown and the cheese is
melted, 2 to 3 minutes. If the bread
toasts faster than the cheese
melts, remove from the heat and
let sit, covered, for 1 to 2 minutes,
or until the cheese is fully melted.

Fruit Compotes

Compote is French for "mixture" and generally refers to fruit that's been slowly stewed in syrup long enough to soften, but not lose its shape. Unlike preserves and conserves, it's usually made fresh for consumption with a particular meal. Just what that meal should be is up to you. Our fruit compotes play well with yogurt, oatmeal and granola in the morning, but also can help elevate a bowl of ice cream or slice of pound cake later in the afternoon. These compotes are perfect served over cakes—we particularly like the blueberry-lavender with our lemon-buttermilk pound cake (p. 238) and ricotta cheesecake (p. 245).

SPICED APRICOT COMPOTE

Start to finish: 15 minutes, plus cooling
Makes about 2 cups

We liked the texture and tartness pomegranate seeds gave this compote, but they can be omitted. Both sulfured and unsulfured apricots worked.

12 ounces dried apricots (about 2 cups), roughly chopped

1¼ cups water

2 tablespoons packed brown sugar

Two 3½-inch cinnamon sticks

2 star anise pods

Two 3-inch strips lemon zest, plus ½ teaspoon lemon juice

Pinch of kosher salt

⅓ cup pomegranate seeds

In a medium saucepan over medium-high, combine the apricots, water, sugar, cinnamon, star anise, lemon zest and salt, then bring to a boil. Reduce to medium-low and simmer, stirring occasionally, until the apricots are plump and softened, and the liquid is thick and syrupy, 10 to 12 minutes. Off heat, stir in the lemon juice and pomegranate seeds. Discard the cinnamon sticks, star anise and zest. Cool to room temperature.

BLUEBERRY-LAVENDER COMPOTE

Start to finish: 10 minutes, plus cooling
Makes about 2 cups

Frozen blueberries can be substituted for fresh, but be sure to thaw and drain them first.

15 ounces blueberries (about 3 cups)

¼ cup white sugar

Two 2-inch strips lemon zest, plus ¼ teaspoon lemon juice

¼ teaspoon dried lavender

Pinch of kosher salt

In a medium saucepan, use a potato masher or fork to mash half of the berries. Stir in the sugar, lemon zest, lavender and salt. Bring to a boil over medium-high, stirring frequently. Add the remaining blueberries and return to a boil. Reduce heat to medium-low and simmer, stirring occasionally, until the juices thicken and most of the berries have popped, 6 to 8 minutes. Off heat, stir in the lemon juice. Discard the zest. Cool to room temperature.

APPLE-PEAR COMPOTE

Start to finish: 25 minutes, plus cooling
Makes about 2 cups

Gala, Golden Delicious, Cortland or Jonagold apples all worked well; Bartlett and Anjou pears were our favorite. Calvados or apple brandy also was delicious in place of the bourbon. To make it easier to fish out the cloves at the end, stick them through the lemon zest before adding them to the pan.

2 apples (12 to 16 ounces), peeled, cored and cut into ½-inch chunks

2 firm, ripe pears (12 to 16 ounces), peeled, cored and cut into ½-inch chunks

½ cup bourbon

½ cup packed light brown sugar

Two 3-inch strips lemon zest, plus 1 teaspoon lemon juice

5 whole cloves

Pinch of kosher salt

In a medium saucepan over medium-high, combine all ingredients but the lemon juice, then bring to a boil. Reduce to medium-low, cover and cook, stirring occasionally, until the fruit is soft but still intact, about 15 minutes. Uncover, increase heat to medium-high and cook until the liquid is thick and syrupy, 5 to 7 minutes. Off heat, stir in the lemon juice. Discard the zest and cloves. Cool to room temperature.

Index

milk
    buttermilk, pound cake with, 238–39
    goat, 117
    See also coconut milk
mint, 7
    cauliflower with, 280
    napa coleslaw with, 60–61
    sauce with jalapeno and, 270–71
    sweet-and-sour dressing with, 278–79
mirin, 13, 144
miso, 14
    dressing of ginger and, 286–87
    and shiitake soup, 38–39
    soba noodles with, 120–21
mojo sauce, pork shoulder with, 156–57
molasses, pomegranate, 4, 130
mushrooms, bistro, 113
    See also shiitake mushrooms
mussels with chorizo and tomatoes, 182–83, 259
mustard, vinaigrette with Dijon, 266
mustard seeds, 9
    avocado salad with pickled, 54–55
    fruit chutney with, 290

N

nabemono (hot pot), 39
nam prik (pickled chilies), 272–73
Napoleon Bonaparte, 228
noodles
    Asian, 18
    buckwheat, 120
    Chinese chili-and-scallion, 114–15
    cinnamon and beef soup with, 42–43
    soba, with asparagus, miso butter, and egg, 120–21
    udon, 18, 42, 115
    See also pastas
nutmeg, 9

O

oats, cookies with rolled, 216–17
oil, 2–3
    browning sesame seeds in, 115
    coconut, 3, 47
    garlic-and-herb, 274–75
    grapeseed, 3
    mixing cheese with, 117
olive, 3, 22–23
    peanut, 3
    sesame, 3
    sizzling greens in, 72–73
olive oil, 3
    extra-virgin, 22
    fluffy scrambled eggs with, 22–23
olives, tapenade with, 282–83
omelet, Persian herb, 26–27
onions
    slicing, 264
    tabbouleh with shallots, 56–57
    See also scallions
orange, 4
    caramel oranges, 93, 222–23
    lemon tart with, 235
    pork caramelized with, 176–77
    whipped cream with, 233
oregano, 7
Ottolenghi, Yotam, 57, 99, 207
oven temperature, 28, 154, 198
Oxaal, Stephen, 55

P

pain d'épices (spice bread), 200–201
pajeon (Korean scallion pancakes), 34–35
palm sugar, 17, 256
panade technique, 137
pancakes, Korean scallion, 34–35
pancetta, Thai fried rice with, 94

paprika, 9
parchment paper
    inverting cake on, 242
    roasting pork in, 156–57
    roasting tomatoes on, 259
    steaming food in, 158, 167
parsley, salad with lemon and, 168–69
pastas, 18
    cooking tips for, 57, 120, 125
    gemelli, with chevre, arugula, and walnuts, 116–17
    Peruvian pesto, 118–19
    spaghetti, with lemon, anchovies, and capers, 124–25
    Trapani pesto, 122–23
    whole-wheat, with yogurt and tahini, 126–27
    See also noodles
peanut sauce, spicy, 266
pears, spiced compote with, 293
pepitas, salmon salad with, 108–9
Peppadew peppers, 14
    skirt steak salad with, 110–11
    whipped feta with, 284–85
pepparkakor (gingersnaps), 212–13
pepper, 7
    Aleppo, 7, 168
    black, 7
    red, flaked, 9, 70, 115, 280
    white, 10
peppercorns
    roast beef with, 154–55
    Sichuan, 10
peppers. *See* chili(es); chipotles; jalapenos; Peppadew peppers
pernil asado (Cuban-style pork shoulder), 156
pesto
    Peruvian, 118–19
    Trapani, 122–23

green beans, 82–83

stock. *See* broth

strawberries, macerated, with lime, 198, 199

stuffing, herbed, 148–49

sugar, 17

    browning, 222

    palm, 17, 256

    See also brown sugar

sumac, 10

    tabbouleh with, 56–57

sweeteners, 17

    See also honey; sugar

sweet potatoes

    adobo sauce for, 263

    gratin of, 78–79

Swiss chard, hot oil–flashed, 72–73

syrup, cake with bay-infused, 242–43

T

tabbouleh, Lebanese-style, 56–57

tagine, chicken, 184–85

tagliata (Italian sliced steak), 110–11

tahini, 3–4

    brownies with, 206–7

    cauliflower with, 84–85

    hummus with, 140–41

    pasta with, 126–27

    stirring, 140, 207

tallarines verdes (Peruvian pesto), 118–19

tamari, 14

    Japanese fried chicken with, 150

tamarind, 14, 15

    dipping sauce with, 256–57

tangerine, almond cake with, 242–43

tangzhong technique for pastry, 226

tapenade, fig-olive, 282–83

tarragon, green goddess tofu dressing with, 288–89

tarts

    brown sugar, 228–29

    chocolate, 230–31

    dough for, 226–27

    lemon, 234–35

    pumpkin, 232–33

Thai cooking, x, xv–xvi, 94

Thiam, Pierre, xvi

thyme, oven-poached salmon with, 164–65

toffee sauce, rye-on-rye sticky pudding with, 236–37

tofu

    green goddess dressing with, 288–89

    miso-shiitake soup with, 39

    pork and kimchi stew with, 40–41

tomatillos, Mexican chicken soup with, 48–49

tomatoes

    beans with pickled, 130–31

    Chinese stir-fried eggs with, 32–33

    guacamole with, 268–69

    Indian rice with, 93, 100–101

    slow-roasted, 182–83, 258–59

    Trapani pesto, 122–23

toppings

    piadine, 192–93

    spiced beef, 141

tortillas

    for shrimp in chipotle sauce, 162–63

    for spatchcocked roast chicken, 178

turkey, brown ale, 146–47

V

vanilla bean, sweet potato gratin with, 78–79

vegetables

    Chinese cleavers for, 74–75

    crisping with salt, 65

grating, 67

    pickled, 264–67

verjus, 4

vermouth, 13

    cracked potatoes with, 76–77

    oven-poached salmon with, 164–65

Vietnamese cooking, ix

vinaigrettes

    adobo sauce for, 263

    harissa-cilantro, 252

    marjoram, 54–55

    mustard, 266

    shallot-sherry, 63

    See also dressings

vinegar, 4–5

    balsamic, 4, 66

    cider, 4

    pickling brine with, 264–67

    rice, 4

    sherry, 4, 63

Vongerichten, Jean-Georges, 167

W

walnuts

    gemelli pasta with, 116–17

    miso-ginger dressing with, 286–87

water

    coconut, 171

    cooking pasta in, 120, 123, 125

    rose, 214

    soaking beans in, 130

    substituting other liquid for, 93

Watson, Quealy, 60

Welsh rarebit, 112–13

wheat, cracked, 18

wine, 10, 13

    cheesecake with Marsala, 245

    See also sherry

Y

yam neua (Thai beef salad), 160–61

yogurt

    Greek vs. traditional, 127, 137, 194

    harissa dip with, 252

    multigrain soda bread with, 194

    sauce of lime and, 136–37

    spiced dressing with, 276–77

    whole-wheat pasta with, 126–27

yosenabe (hot pot), 39

Z

za'atar (seasoning), 14, 17, 168

ACKNOWLEDGMENTS

Milk Street is a real place with, oddly enough, real people. It's a small crew, but I want to thank everyone who has made our first book a reality. We can hold Milk Street in our hands, an idea that finally has come to life. Thanks to all but, in particular, I want to acknowledge J.M. Hirsch, our tireless editorial director, Matthew Card, food editor, and Michelle Locke, staff writer, for leading the charge on conceiving, developing and editing all of this. Jennifer Baldino Cox, our art director, and the entire design team who deftly captured the look and feel of Milk Street, including Brianna Coleman, Connie Miller, Gary Tooth, Christine Tobin, Catrine Kelty, Channing Johnson, Ben Schaefer, Kristin Teig, Joyelle West, Michael Piazza, Heidi Murphy, Catherine Smart, Monica Mariano, Molly Shuster, and Sally Staub. Our team of production cooks and recipe developers kept the bar high, throwing out recipes that did not make the cut and improving those that did. Our team includes Rebeccah Marsters, Erin Ross, Diane Unger, Elizabeth Germain, Bianca Borges, Erika Bruce, Alison Ladman, Dawn Yanagihara, Laura Russell, Jeanne Maguire and Yvonne Ruperti. Finally, Deborah Broide, Milk Street director of media relations, has done a spectacular job of introducing our young Milk Street to the world.

We also have a couple of folks to thank who work outside of 177 Milk Street. Michael Szczerban, editor, and everyone at Little, Brown and Company have been superb and inspired partners in this project. Yes, top-notch book editors still exist! And my long-standing book agent, David Black, has been instrumental in bringing this project to life both with his knowledge of publishing and bourbon. Thank you, David!

Additional thanks for exacting editorial help from Jenn Ladd, Holly Ramer and Deborah Weiss Geline. Finally, a sincere thank you to my business partner and wife, Melissa, who manages our media department, from television to radio to social media. Melissa has nurtured the Milk Street brand from the beginning so that we ended up where we thought we were going in the first place! Thanks.

And, last but not least, to all of you who have supported the Milk Street project. Everyone has a seat at the Milk Street table, so pull up a chair and dig in!

Christopher Kimball

CLEAN

DO NOT TOUCH / DO NOT TOUCH / DO NOT TOUCH / DO N

Christopher Kimball is founder of *Christopher Kimball's Milk Street*, a food media company dedicated to learning and sharing bold, easy cooking from around the world. It produces the bimonthly *Christopher Kimball's Milk Street Magazine*, as well as *Christopher Kimball's Milk Street Radio*, a weekly public radio show and podcast heard on over 300 stations nationwide. Kimball is host of *Christopher Kimball's Milk Street Television*, which airs on public television. He founded *Cook's Magazine* in 1980 and served as publisher and editorial director through 1989. He re-launched it as *Cook's Illustrated* in 1993 and founded *Cook's Country* magazine in 2004. Through 2016, Kimball was host and executive producer of *America's Test Kitchen* and *Cook's Country*, the two highest-rated cooking shows on television. He also hosted *America's Test Kitchen* radio on public radio. Kimball is the author of several books including, most recently, *Fannie's Last Supper*.

Christopher Kimball's Milk Street is located at 177 Milk Street in downtown Boston and is home to our editorial offices and cooking school. It also is where we record *Christopher Kimball's Milk Street* television and radio shows. *Christopher Kimball's Milk Street* is changing how we cook by searching the world for bold, simple recipes and techniques. Adapted and tested for home cooks everywhere, these lessons are the backbone of what we call the *new* home cooking. For more information, go to www.177milkstreet.com